Hands-on Azure Boards

Configuring and Customizing Process Workflows in Azure DevOps Services

Chaminda Chandrasekara
Pushpa Herath

Hands-on Azure Boards: Configuring and Customizing Process Workflows in Azure DevOps Services

Chaminda Chandrasekara
Dedigamuwa, Sri Lanka

Pushpa Herath
Hanguranketha, Sri Lanka

ISBN-13 (pbk): 978-1-4842-5045-7
https://doi.org/10.1007/978-1-4842-5046-4

ISBN-13 (electronic): 978-1-4842-5046-4

Managing Director, Apress Media LLC: Welmoed Spahr
Acquisitions Editor: Smriti Srivastava
Development Editor: Siddhi Chavan
Coordinating Editor: Shrikant Vishwakarma

Cover designed by eStudioCalamar

Cover image designed by Freepik (www.freepik.com)

Distributed to the book trade worldwide by Springer Science+Business Media New York, 233 Spring Street, 6th Floor, New York, NY 10013. Phone 1-800-SPRINGER, fax (201) 348-4505, e-mail orders-ny@springer-sbm.com, or visit www.springeronline.com. Apress Media, LLC is a California LLC and the sole member (owner) is Springer Science + Business Media Finance Inc (SSBM Finance Inc). SSBM Finance Inc is a **Delaware** corporation.

For information on translations, please e-mail rights@apress.com, or visit www.apress.com/rights-permissions.

Apress titles may be purchased in bulk for academic, corporate, or promotional use. eBook versions and licenses are also available for most titles. For more information, reference our Print and eBook Bulk Sales web page at www.apress.com/bulk-sales.

Any source code or other supplementary material referenced by the author in this book is available to readers on GitHub via the book's product page, located at www.apress.com/978-1-4842-5045-7. For more detailed information, please visit www.apress.com/source-code.

Printed on acid-free paper

Let this book be a beginning point of thousands of future Azure Boards teams to run their software projects effectively and efficiently.

Table of Contents

About the Authors

Chaminda Chandrasekara is a Microsoft Most Valuable Professional (MVP) for Visual Studio ALM and Scrum Alliance Certified ScrumMaster. He focuses on the continuous improvement of the software development lifecycle. He works as the Lead DevOps Engineer at Xameriners, Singapore. Chaminda is an active Microsoft Community Contributor (MCC) who has been recognized for his contributions in Microsoft forums, TechNet galleries, wikis, and Stack Overflow, and he contributes extensions to Azure DevOps Server and Services (formerly VSTS/TFS) in the Microsoft Visual Studio Marketplace. He also contributes to other open source projects on GitHub. Chaminda has published three books with Apress, and he blogs at `https://chamindac.blogspot.com/`.

Pushpa Herath is a DevOps engineer at Datavail Lanka (Pvt) Ltd. She is an author, blogger, and speaker at public technical events and has many years of experience administering, configuring, and coaching Azure DevOps and test automation engineering. Pushpa blogs about technology at `https://devopsadventure.blogspot.com/`. Pushpa has experience with Microsoft tools (C#, Azure DevOps, SQL Server, Azure Platform Services) and other DevOps tools (Octopus, Jira, Jenkins). She is also the coauthor of *Hands-On Functional Test Automation*, published by Apress.

About the Technical Reviewer

Mittal Mehta has 15 years of IT experience and currently works as a configuration manager. He has worked in the TFS, C#, Navision, build-release, Azure DevOps, automation, and configuration areas for the past eight years using Microsoft technologies.

Acknowledgments

We are thankful for all the mentors who have encouraged and helped us during our careers and who have provided us with so many opportunities to gain the maturity and the courage we needed to write this book.

We would also like to thank our friends and colleagues who have helped and encouraged us in so many ways.

Last, but in no way least, we owe a huge debt to our families, not only because they have put up with late-night typing, research, and our permanent air of distraction, but also because they have had the grace to read what we have written. Our heartfelt gratitude is offered to them for helping us make this dream come true.

Introduction

Technology is evolving faster than ever before, and modern software is expanding into each and every industry and sector in society. Most businesses and people's day-to-day lives are closely intertwined with technology and software. To come up with innovative solutions for the software needs of modern industry, it is vital for software firms to continuously improve their software delivery processes.

The continuous improvement of software delivery processes requires the work being carried out to be tracked, effectively providing traceability and visibility. Predictability plays a key role in the success of this work and is essential for identifying trends or work patterns in teams, risks, and bottlenecks, and for addressing them in a timely manner with proper capacity, risk management, and skill planning.

Azure Boards comes with Kanban boards, backlogs, team dashboards, and custom reporting to help you turn an idea into a working piece of software. Comprehensive traceability is available with flexible work item tracking, allowing you to plan your work in iterations/sprints, and Azure Boards allows you to track your work from idea to the completion of implmenting the idea. Azure Boards—in combination with Azure repos, pipelines, artifacts, and tests—offers visibility and traceability in every step of the software delivery process.

As the first book in the Hands-on Azure DevOps series, *Hands-on Azure Boards* covers the capabilities of Azure Boards comprehensively. We describe the features of the built-in templates that you can use to run your software delivery teams with Agile, Scrum, or CMMI processes. We give hands-on lessons for configuring Azure Boards to behave in the way you want and to emit the information you need, including when customizing and building your own process workflows. These lessons will give you a broader and in-depth understanding of the tool. Advanced topics include administering and setting up a command-line interface, using a REST API for custom reporting or any other needs, setting up security and permissions, and setting up and managing small to large teams. *Hands-on Azure Boards* is the book that project managers/Scrum masters, team members, and anyone involved in the software delivery process can use as a day-to-day reference manual to improve the way they work. You can use it to convert your software delivery process to a real implementation using the Azure Boards capabilities that are available in the Azure DevOps on-premises servers and services.

CHAPTER 1

Getting Started with Azure Boards

The objective of this chapter is to get you started with Azure Boards in Azure DevOps. You'll start by creating a new Azure DevOps organization. You'll learn about different process templates and get a good overall understanding of Azure Boards in this chapter before diving into more details in the coming chapters.

Lesson 1-1. Creating an Azure DevOps Organization

This lesson explains how to create a new Azure DevOps organization.

Prerequisites: You need to have a Microsoft account (`https://account.microsoft.com/account`).

Go ahead and create a new Azure DevOps project by following these steps:

1. Go to `dev.azure.com`. If you have a Microsoft account, you can log in by clicking "Sign in to Azure DevOps." Otherwise, you can use the "Start free" option. See Figure 1-1.

© Chaminda Chandrasekara and Pushpa Herath 2019
C. Chandrasekara and P. Herath, *Hands-on Azure Boards*, https://doi.org/10.1007/978-1-4842-5046-4_1

Figure 1-1. *Azure DevOps login page*

2. After logging in to Azure DevOps or going through start free process, you can create a new DevOps organization. Click new organization after logging in.

3. Give the new organization a name and select the organization region from the drop-down. The region defines the primary Azure region for the Azure DevOps organization being created. However, your data is replicated to other Azure data centers to assure high availability. You can see that the organization name is sldevop in this example. After entering the relevant details, click the Continue button to create an organization. See Figure 1-2.

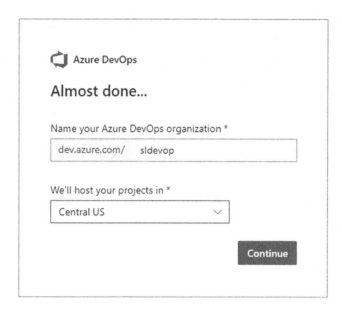

Figure 1-2. *Naming the organization*

This will take about a minute, and then you will be redirected to the start page of the new Azure DevOps organization.

In this lesson, you created a new Azure DevOps organization to be used in the rest of the lessons in the book.

Lesson 1-2. Creating a Public/Private Agile Project

In this lesson, we will discuss how to create private and public projects with Agile process templates. When you create a new DevOps project, you can create the project as a public project or a private project. If the project is private, only authorized people can access the project. If you create a public project, anyone with a Microsoft account can access the project, which is really useful when you are working on open source projects.

Prerequisites: You need to have an Azure DevOps organization.

Let's create a private project with Agile as the process template and Git as the version control system.

1. Go to dev.azure.com and log in with your Microsoft account credentials.

2. In the Organizations section, select the organization you created in the previous lesson.

3

3. When you access a newly created organization, you will get the project creation page as the start page by default. If there are projects available in an organization, you will see the Create Project button in the top-right corner of the Azure DevOps start page.

4. Enter the project name, select Private, set Git as the version control system, and set Agile as the work item process. Then click "Create project" to create the project. See Figure 1-3.

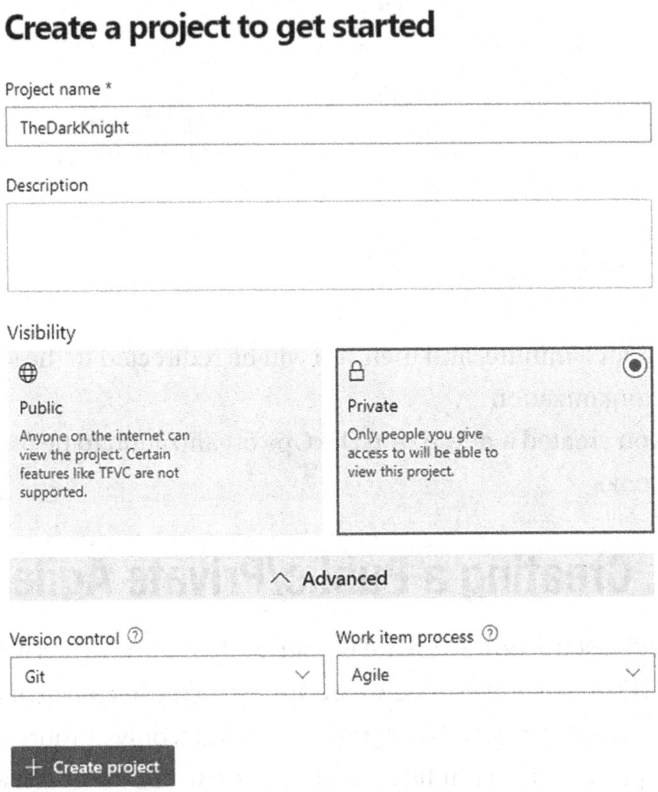

Create a project to get started

Project name *

TheDarkKnight   ✓

Description

Visibility

⊕	🔒 ⦿
Public	**Private**
Anyone on the internet can view the project. Certain features like TFVC are not supported.	Only people you give access to will be able to view this project.

∧ Advanced

Version control ⑦   Work item process ⑦

Git   ∨   Agile   ∨

+ Create project

***Figure 1-3.** Creating a new DevOps project*

Now you have created a new DevOps project with the Agile process template.

Azure DevOps provide four process templates. Those are Basic, Agile, CMMI, and Scrum. You can select the preferred process template from the "Work item process" drop-down list when creating a new project.

This lesson explained how to create a new Azure DevOps project with Git as the version control system and Agile as the process template. Furthermore, you learned it is possible to create projects with Basic, CMMI, and Scrum process models. Let's learn more about these project templates in the next lesson.

Lesson 1-3. Comparing Project Templates

Azure DevOps facilitates four main process models: Basic, Scrum, Agile, and CMMI. You can discover the differences between these process models by referring to the comparative explanation in this lesson.

Work Item Types

Before understanding what a process model is, we have to define work items in Azure DevOps. A *work item* is any type of work you do as a team member or as a team. A *work item type* (WIT) in Azure DevOps comes with fields and a specific workflow to enable you to track the work being carried out by the team. Feature, User Story/Requirement/Product Backlog Item, Bug, Task, Test Case, and so on, are some of the default available work item types. You can even introduce your own work item types and alter the behavior of the existing default work item types.

Process Templates

With this understanding, let's look at the available process templates in Azure DevOps.

1. **Basic**: Most light-weight process models provide three work item types as default work items: Epic, Issue, and Task. A team that wants to get started simply and model the process as they continue to work with Azure DevOps can choose this template.

2. **Scrum**: This template is best suited for the teams that follow Scrum as their process model. Bugs are tracked along with product backlog items by default in the Scrum template, and you can configure Boards to track bugs in the same level as task work item level. Tasks in this process template track only the remaining work.

3. **Agile**: Teams that are using Agile methodologies including Scrum can use this process model. By default, bugs are tracked with the task level in the Agile template, but you can configure them to be tracked with the user stories level.

4. **CMMI**: Teams following the capability maturity model and using a more formal process to track change requirements can use this template to track their work. Requirements, change requests, reviews, and risks can be tracked, enabling the teams to follow and adhere to the CMMI process standards.

Figure 1-4 shows a process template overview comparing each process model.

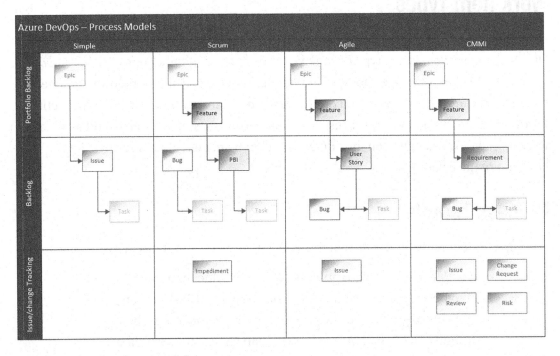

Figure 1-4. *Process model overview*

In the Agile and CMMI process models, you can configure the Bug work item to be tracked along with the user story/requirement level, similar to the Scrum template's default Bug work item's tracking behavior. In the Scrum process, you can set bugs to be on the same level as tasks. These configurations will be discussed in later chapters when you learn how to configure Azure Boards in hands-on lessons.

There are a common set of work item types shared in all process templates. For managing tests, there are the following work item types: Test Plan, Test Suite, Test Case Shared Steps and Shared Parameters. Feedback Request and Feedback Review are used to manage feedback on the project. Code Review Request and Code Review Response are two work item types that support managing code reviews. All these different types of work items will be discussed in relevant areas of this book.

Work Item State Flows

Work items in each process model contain a state field representing the current state of the work item. The Basic template contains the simplest state workflow out of the four process templates available. Figure 1-5 shows the states in each template by default. You can introduce your own states and modify templates with inherited templates; this will be discussed in Chapter 5 of this book.

Workflow States			
Basic	Scrum	Agile	CMMI
• To Do • Doing • Done	• New • Approved • Committed • Done • Removed	• New • Active • Resolved • Closed • Removed	• Proposed • Active • Resolved • Closed

Figure 1-5. Work item states

The work item states are categorized into state categories in Azure DevOps. Each process template contains the Proposed, In Progress, and Completed state categories. The Removed state category is used in the Scrum and Agile templates. The Resolved state category is used in the Agile and CMMI templates. Figure 1-6 shows state categories used in each template and the states assigned to them by default. You can see the Resolved state used in both the Resolved category and the In Progress category in Agile and CMMI. This is because in the context of a bug, the Resolved state is used in the Resolved state category in both templates. However, User Story/Requirement in both templates has the Resolved state under the In Progress category.

Workflow States			
Basic	Scrum	Agile	CMMI
• **Proposed** To Do • **In Progress** Doing • **Completed** Done	• **Proposed** New Approved • **In Progress** Committed • **Completed** Done • **Removed** Removed	• **Proposed** New • **In Progress** Active Resolved • **Resolved** Resolved • **Completed** Closed • **Removed** Removed	• **Proposed** Proposed • **In Progress** Active Resolved • **Resolved** Resolved • **Completed** Closed

State Categories

Figure 1-6. *State categories*

In addition to the workflow states when transitioning between the work item states, you can select a reason for state transition. Implementation Started is one such reason when you move a work item from the New to Active state. These reasons are further explaining the state transition. You'll learn more about the state transitions in each work item type in later chapters of this book. Figure 1-7 shows default transitions of the User Story work item in the Agile template.

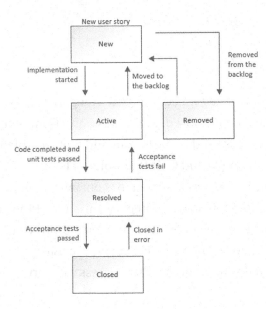

Figure 1-7. *User Story default transitions*

In this lesson, we identified the key differences between the process templates in Azure DevOps. This information will be useful when you are choosing the right template for your team.

Lesson 1-4. Navigating Azure Boards

You can navigate through almost all the main pages in Azure DevOps with the left-side menu. This lesson will give you a brief understanding of the available features in the Overview and Boards sections.

Hover your mouse over the Overview menu item in the left-side menu. Then you will see Summary, Dashboard, and Wiki in the model pane. We'll now identify the features in each area.

Summary Page

You can get to the Azure DevOps Summary page by going to the left menu of an Azure DevOps project, selecting the Overview menu, and selecting the Summary submenu item. See Figure 1-8.

Figure 1-8. *Summary submenu item*

On the Summary page, you will find five sections. See Figure 1-9.

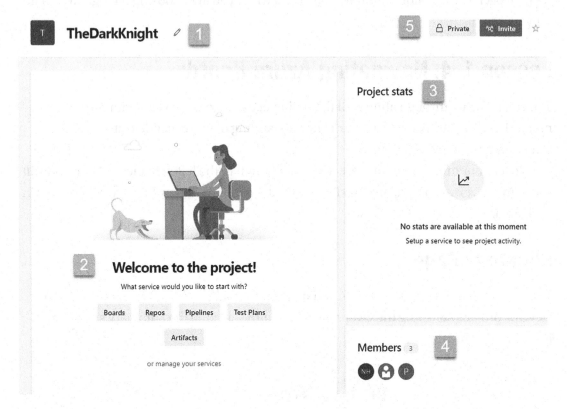

Figure 1-9. *Summary page*

1. ***Edit project name***: Click the pencil icon next to the project name. See Figure 1-10. After clicking the pencil icon, you will navigate to the project's edit page.

Figure 1-10. *Project's edit pencil icon*

On the project's edit page, you will find the sections shown in Figure 1-11.

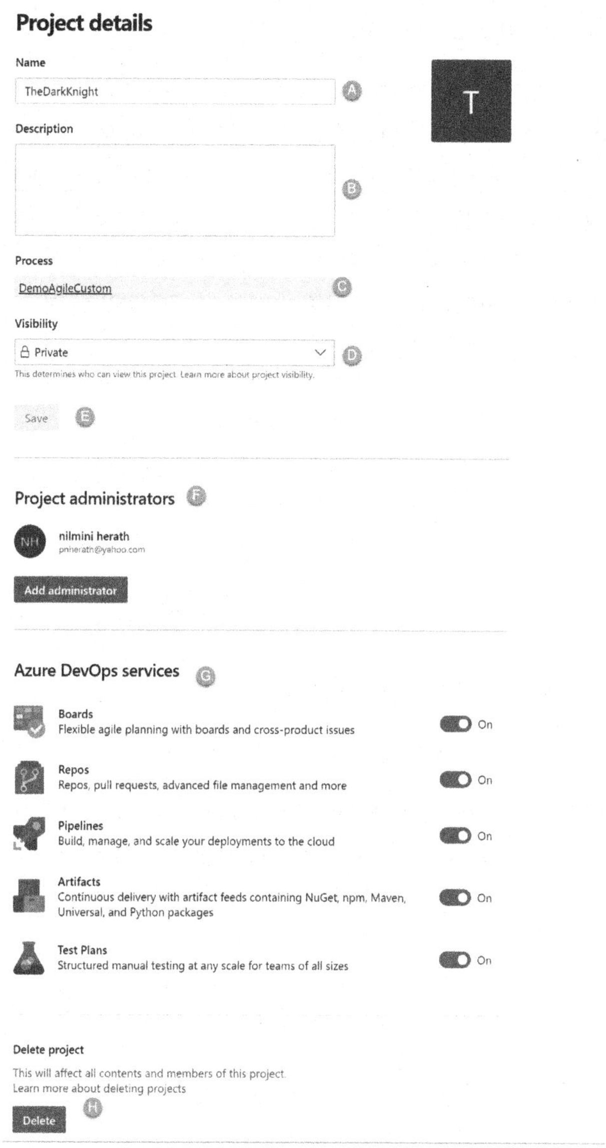

Figure 1-11. *Project properties edit page*

A. Edit the project name.

B. Add or edit the project description.

C. View the process template.

    D.   Change the project visibility options to private or public.

    E.   Save the changes.

    F.   Add project administrators.

    G.   Remove services from the project by clicking the button in front of each service. After clicking the button, the Remove Service pop-up will appear. As an example, if you click the On button in front of Boards, a pop-up will open that has a Remove Boards button on it. See Figure 1-12. After clicking the Remove Boards button, the Boards service will be removed from the project.

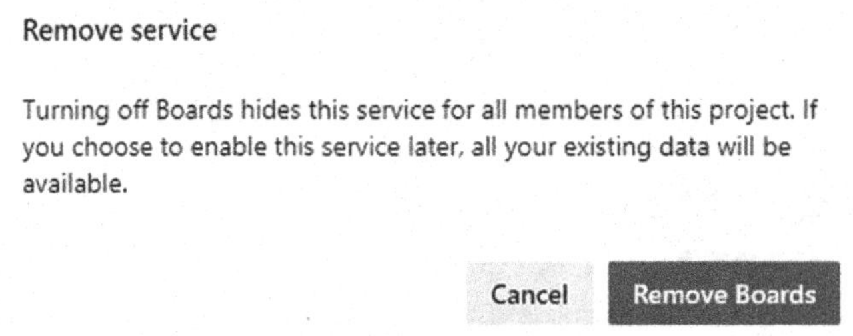

> **Remove service**
>
> Turning off Boards hides this service for all members of this project. If you choose to enable this service later, all your existing data will be available.
>
> Cancel   **Remove Boards**

Figure 1-12. *Remove service pop-up for Boards service*

    H.   Delete the project by clicking the Delete button.

2.   **Project welcome message section**: You can see a welcome message and buttons to navigate through the project. This area has buttons to navigate to boards, repos, pipelines, test plans, and artifacts. Also, there is a link to navigate to the service management area of a project's edit page. See Figure 1-13.

Welcome to the project!

What service would you like to start with?

Boards   Repos   Pipelines   Test Plans

Artifacts

or manage your services

Figure 1-13. *Project welcome message section*

3. **Project Status section**: This area displays project progress charts. You will explore this in later chapters and in the other books in the series.

4. **Members**: The names of all the project members are displayed here. See Figure 1-14. It is possible to view more information about each member by clicking the name of the member.

Members 1

Figure 1-14. *Names of project members*

5. **Add new members**: This section has two buttons. The gray button indicates the current project type. This can be either private or public. The second button is the Invite button. See Figure 1-15.

Figure 1-15. *Current project type and Invite button*

After clicking the Invite button, the left model pane will open. You can add and search for names of team members. Then click the Add button to add members to the dashboard. See Figure 1-16.

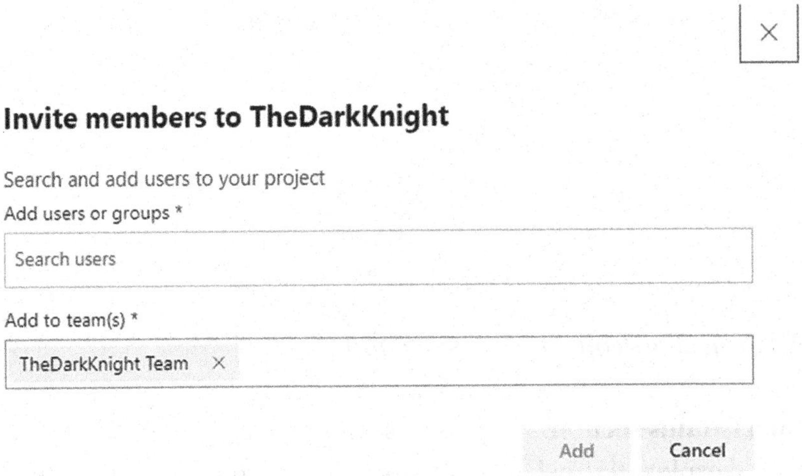

Figure 1-16. *Inviting members to the project*

Dashboards

Dashboards help you visualize the progress of the project. Azure DevOps provides a facility to create multiple dashboards. You can add default widgets and additional widgets from the marketplace to visualize the project progress in these dashboards. Let's look at Figure 1-17 to understand the options in the dashboards.

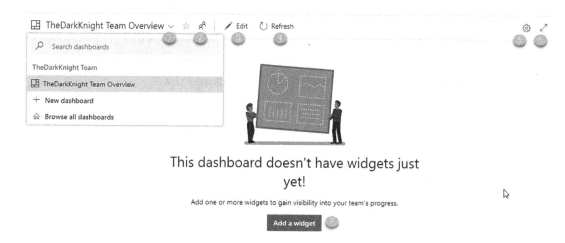

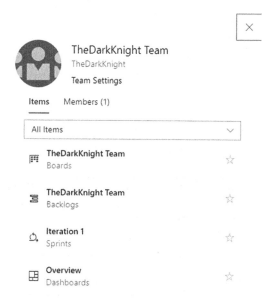

Figure 1-17. *Azure DevOps dashboard*

1. Add new dashboards, navigate between dashboards, search dashboards, and browse all dashboards options that are available.

2. The team profile settings in the right-side model pane will open when you click this icon. In the team settings section, you can see the names of the project members and navigate through the project. There is a capability to navigate to boards, backlogs, sprints, and dashboards. See Figure 1-18.

Figure 1-18. *Team settings*

3. By clicking the edit button, it is possible to add, edit, move, or resize the dashboard widgets. Azure DevOps provides a facility to add marketplace widgets, as well as charts generated using the project queries, to the team dashboard. See Figure 1-19.

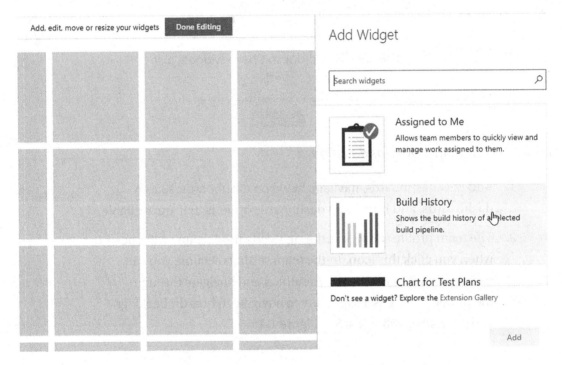

Figure 1-19. Adding widgets

4. You can refresh the dashboard by clicking this refresh icon.

5. After click this cogwheel icon dashboard setting, the window opens. You can change dashboard settings through the pop-up.

6. Change the page view to full-screen mode.

7. In fresh projects, you will find this button. This will help you to navigate to the widget management area mentioned in Figure 1-19.

Wiki

Azure DevOps has a wiki section that provides a facility to create your own documentation. There are two options for creating a wiki. See Figure 1-20. This lesson explains how to create your own wiki. We'll discuss how to publish code as a wiki option in a future book (Azure Repos) of this book series. Publishing code as a wiki is a mechanism that allows you to create a wiki by referring to .md files in the repository folder.

Get everyone on the same page

Create wiki pages to help your team members collaborate.

Create Wiki   Publish code as Wiki   ⊙

Figure 1-20. *Adding a wiki page*

After clicking the Create Wiki button, you will be navigated to the wiki's edit page. See Figure 1-21.

Figure 1-21. *Wiki's edit page*

1. The wiki has three header options. You can click the down arrow and then select the headers.

2. Add bold text to the wiki.

3. Add italic text to the wiki.

4. Add a link to the wiki.

5. Add code to the wiki.

6. Add a bulleted list to the wiki.

7. Add a numbered list to the wiki.

8. Add a task list to the wiki.

9. Add a table to the wiki.

10. Mention work items in the wiki.

11. Insert files to the wiki.

12. Add HTML to the wiki.

13. After clicking more options, you will be able to see other available features of the wiki.

    The options are as follows:

    - Insert table of contents

    - Insert videos

    - Insert Yaml tags

    - Insert formulas

    - Insert team members

    - Insert query results

14. You can select "Edit only view," "Preview only view," or "Edit and preview view."

15. Save the wiki.

16. You can add a new page from the section display after clicking the side pane named Pages.

So far, you have navigated through the submenu items under Overview. The next section will navigate you through the Boards menu. You can find work items, boards, backlogs, sprints, and queries as submenu items of Boards.

Work Items

You can find the Work Items submenu item under Boards of the Azure DevOps project. See Figure 1-22.

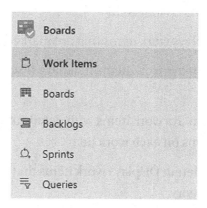

Figure 1-22. *Work Items submenu item in the side menu*

Let's identify the features available under Work Items. See Figure 1-23.

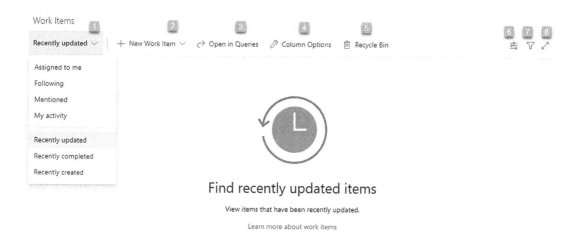

Figure 1-23. *Work Items page*

1. You can filter work items using the filters available in this drop-down. The following are the filtering options:

    - **Recently updated**: Displays recently updated work items

    - **Assigned to me**: Displays work items assigned to the specified team member who is logged in

    - **Following**: Displays work items that are marked as Following

    - **Mentioned**: Displays work items that have discussions with the mentioned tag

    - **My activity**: Displays work items with details of activities the member performs on each work item

    - **Recently completed**: Displays work items that belong to the Completed category

    - **Recently created**: Displays work items created recently

2. You can add new work items from this section. When you click the down arrow, you can see work item types in the drop-down. This drop-down has list of work items available in the current process template. In an Agile process, you can see the following work items:

    - Bug

    - Epic

    - Feature

    - Issue

    - Task

    - Test Case

    - User Story

3. You can navigate to queries by clicking this button.

4. After clicking the column options button, the left-side model pane will open. You can add or remove columns from here. Furthermore, you can change the column order. See Figure 1-24.

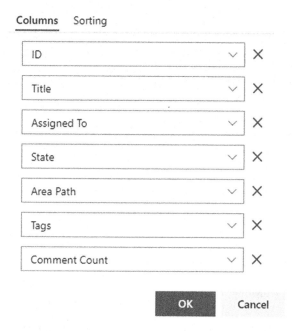

Figure 1-24. *Column options pane*

5. You can delete work items, and the recycle bin will contain the deleted items.

6. You can see the view option. This allows you to turn on the button to view completed work items.

7. This allows you to view filters. You will find the following filter options available:

- **Filter by keyword**: Filters work items by keywords

- **Types**: Filters work items by work item type

- **Assigned to**: Filters work items by assigned user

- **State**: Filters work items by states

- **Area**: Filters work items by area

- **Tags**: Filters items by tags

8. You can change the screen size from here. This allows you to move to full-screen mode.

Boards

You can see the work items in board view here. By default you can see four columns in the board that represent each stage of the work item lifecycle in the Agile process. Let's identify features on the Boards page. See Figure 1-25.

Figure 1-25. *Boards page*

1. In front of the team name you can see the down arrow to open a drop-down. From this drop-down you can select the teams available in the project and search teams. See Figure 1-26.

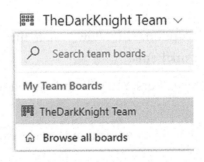

Figure 1-26. *Teams drop-down*

2. You can navigate to a backlog view of the work items by clicking this icon.

3. You can open the team settings window by clicking this icon.

4. The velocity chart provides you with the team's velocity in each sprint, based on the size of backlog items that were completed during a given sprint. For each sprint, a bar is shown in the chart. We will discuss this more in Chapter 6.

5. The cumulative flow chart provides an area graph of the number of work items in each state in a specific time period. We will further discuss this in Chapter 6.

6. You can select different work item types from this drop-down to filter work items on the board. By default you will find the User Story and Feature types only.

7. You can use this view option to turn on the live updates option. If you enable live updates, changes happening to work items elsewhere will be automatically updated in your board.

8. You can add filters to filter work items on the board. The following are the available filter options:

    -   **Filter by keyword**: Filters using keywords such as part of a work item name

    -   **Type**: Filters by work item type such as Feature

    -   **Assigned to**: Filters the values by giving a team member name

    -   **Tags**: Filters values with tag values

    -   **Iteration**: Filters values belonging to a selected iteration

    -   **Area**: Filters values belonging to each team

    -   **Parent work item**: Filters using a parent work item type

9. You can move to the settings page by clicking this icon.

10. You can move to full-screen mode of the page with this button.

11. You can hide the new column with this arrow.

12. You can hide the closed column with this arrow.

13. You can add a new work item.

14. You can filter the values in the first column only.

Backlogs

The backlog provides you with the list of backlog items. You can start by adding work items to the backlog. By default, the product backlog level is selected as the backlog level. You can change to portfolio backlog levels using the drop-down in the top right of the Backlogs page. See Figure 1-27.

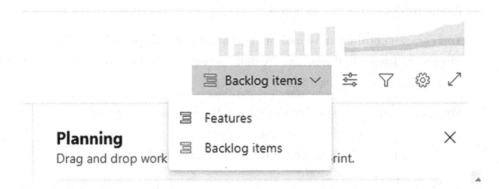

Figure 1-27. *Backlog levels*

The backlog allows you to select a few options to enable different views. See Figure 1-28.

Figure 1-28. *Viewing options for the backlog*

1. This allows you to show the parent hierarchy of the backlog items. When this is on, Forecasting cannot be switched on.

2. Forecasting allows you to forecast how many iterations it would take to deliver the backlog item depending on the work item size and the velocity of the team. We will discuss this in later chapters of this book.

3. This setting defines whether to show the In Progress state backlog items in the backlog view.

4. This setting shows the parent portfolio backlog in the side pane.

5. This setting shows iterations in the side pane. This is easier when planning iterations because you can drag items from the backlog to the iterations.

6. You can turn off the side pane.

Filter supports filtering work items by a few useful fields or by keyword search, which searches the title of backlog items. See Figure 1-29.

Figure 1-29. *Filter backlog*

Several other useful options are available on the backlog page. Let's take a quick look at them. See Figure 1-30.

Figure 1-30. *Options in the backlog page*

1. You can add new work items to the backlog.

2. This allows you to select different teams. We will discuss multiple teams in same team project in Chapter 7 of this book.

3. Add the current team to the favorites list.

4. View the Team Settings pane, which pops up on the right side.

5. Switch to the Boards view.

6. Open column options in the side pane of the Backlog view. You can add/remove columns or reorder them by dragging and dropping.

7. Create a query for a backlog.

8. E-mail selected work items from the backlog.

9. Switch backlog view levels.

10. The velocity chart provides you with the team's velocity in each sprint, based on the size of backlog items that were completed during a given sprint. For each sprint, a bar is shown in the chart. We will discuss this in Chapter 6.

11. The cumulative flow chart provides an area graph of the number of work items in each state over a specific time period. We will discuss this in Chapter 6.

12. These are the view options that we discussed earlier.

13. These are the filters we discussed earlier.

14. Settings of boards. We will discuss this in Chapter 4.

15. Expand the backlog view to full-screen.

Sprints

The Sprints page allows you to view the previous, current, and future sprints. Let's take a quick look at the options available in the Sprints page. See Figure 1-31.

Figure 1-31. *Sprints page options*

1. This shows the task board view where stories/ (Product Backlog Items) PBIs/bugs of the sprint/iteration will be shown with the child tasks.

2. This is the backlog view for the sprint/iteration work items.

3. This is the capacity for team members. You can define Activity as the daily capacity of team members and set the days for the individuals or for the team. See Figure 1-32.

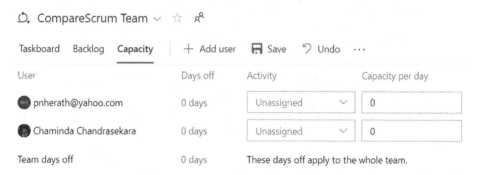

Figure 1-32. *Team capacity*

4. You can switch teams when there are multiple teams in the project.

5. You can add the team to the favorites list.

6. Open the team settings side pane.

7. Add new work items to the sprint/iteration. If bugs are set to use at the User Story/PBI/Requirement level, you can add bugs to the sprint as well. See Figure 1-33. We will discuss configuring the bug behavior in Chapter 3.

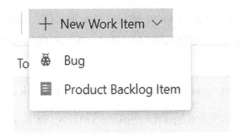

Figure 1-33. *Adding an item to the sprint backlog*

8. You can select the sprint/iteration to view.

9. This is a shortcut for setting dates for the iteration.

10. The view options (see Figure 1-34) for the Sprints page in the task board view allows you to group tasks by assigned person or by the parent backlog item. The group by options are not available in the Sprints backlog view. The side pane provides two view options. "Work details" shows the capacity versus effort requirements when the capacity for the team is defined and tasks are added with remaining work. We will discuss details about capacity and remaining work in Chapter 2. The Planning option will show current and future sprints, allowing you to drag and drop work items for planning purposes.

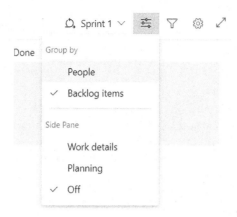

Figure 1-34. *View options on the Sprints page*

11. Filter allows you to filter and search work items.

12. This opens the settings for the team in the context of the task board view or sprint backlog. We will discuss these settings in Chapter 4.

13. This allows you to expand to full-screen mode.

14. This is the burndown chart for the sprint. We will discuss this in Chapter 6.

15. This is the backlog work item card in the task board view.

16. This allows you to add child tasks for a given backlog item.

Queries

Queries are useful for you to view and visualize your work items. You can write simple and complex queries in Azure DevOps. We will discuss queries in depth in Chapter 6. Let's just take a quick look at what is available on the Queries page for now. See Figure 1-35.

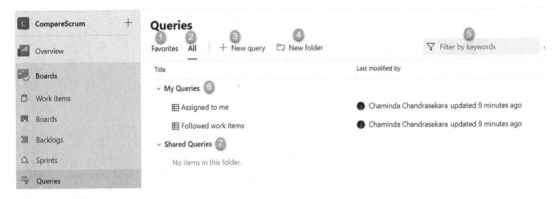

Figure 1-35. *Queries page*

1. Favorites displays queries marked as your favorites or team favorites.

2. This lists all queries.

3. You can start creating a new query.

4. You can create folders to group queries under My Queries or Shared Queries.

5. You can filter queries.

6. The My Queries ones are the only queries available to you.

7. The Shared Queries ones are available to all the members of the team to view.

The My Queries list has a few options in the context menu of each query. See Figure 1-36.

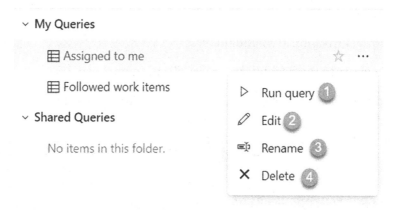

Figure 1-36. *My Queries menu*

1. Run the query.

2. Edit the query in the query editor. We will discuss queries in detail in Chapter 6.

3. Rename the query.

4. Delete the query.

In the Shared Queries area, a few additional menu options are available. See Figure 1-37.

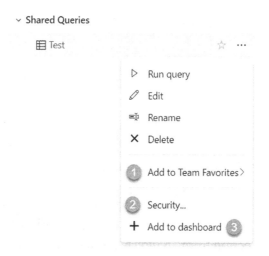

Figure 1-37. *Shared Queries menu*

1. Add the query to the team's favorites.

2. Set up security for the shared query.

3. Add a query to the dashboard for visualization purpose.

In this lesson, we gave you an overview of Azure Boards and its interface.

Lesson 1-5. Customizing Organization Settings

There are couple of organization-level settings in Azure DevOps that allow you to set up the behavior of the Azure DevOps organization. Let's look at the available options in this lesson.

You can navigate to an organization's settings page by clicking "Organization settings" in the Azure DevOps organization home page. See Figure 1-38.

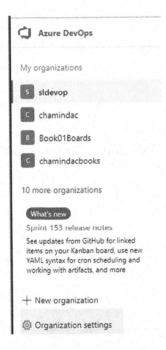

Figure 1-38. *Getting to the organization settings*

On the Overview tab you can change the organization name if required. However, this should be done with caution as the URL of the organization gets changed with the name change. A redirection from an old URL will not happen, and users have to manually start using the new URL. This option is there to change the URL from `https://orgname.visualstudio.com` to `https://dev.azure.com/orgname`. By default, any new organization uses the new URL pattern. The privacy policy URL can be set to your organization's data protection and privacy policy documentation URL. Time zone selection for the organization can be updated on the Overview page. The ownership of the organization can be transferred to another user who has access to the organization from the Overview tab. See Figure 1-39. If the organization is no longer required, you can delete the organization as well from the Overview page.

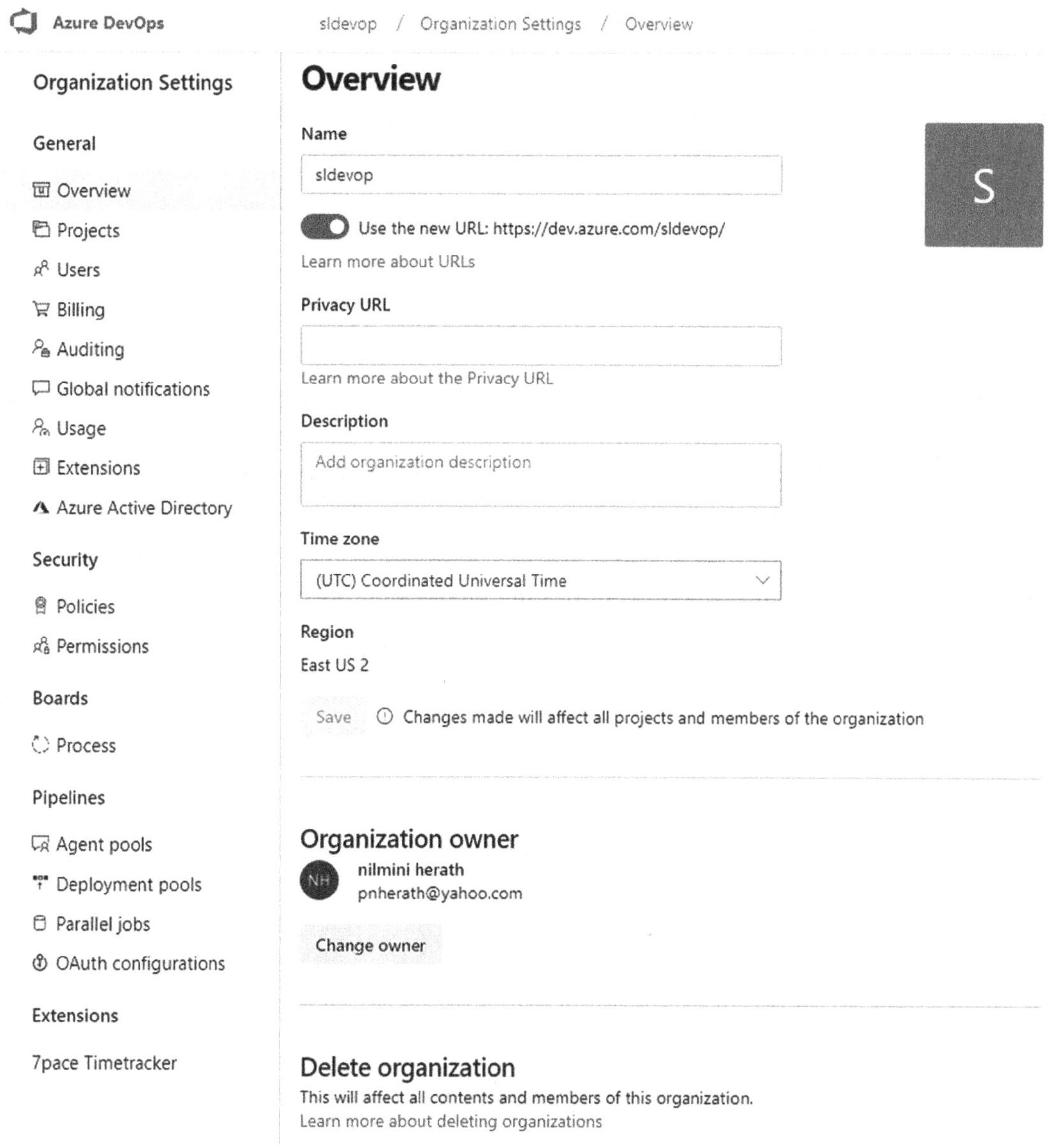

Figure 1-39. *Overview tab on Organization Settings page*

The Projects tab lists all the available team projects in the organization. You can rename a team project or delete a team project. Clicking New Project will allow you to create a new team project. See Figure 1-40.

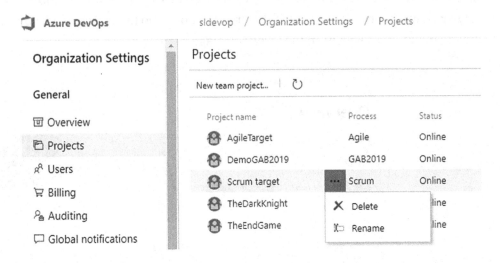

Figure 1-40. *Projects tab*

The Users tab will be described in Chapter 8 with security options.

The Billing tab lets you set up billing by connecting the Azure DevOps organization with an Azure subscription. See Figure 1-41. When the billing is set up, you are able to add paid extensions to Azure DevOps from the marketplace. We will discuss extensions in Chapter 10. The default available trial extension for test plans can be activated for a 30-day trial from this billing page.

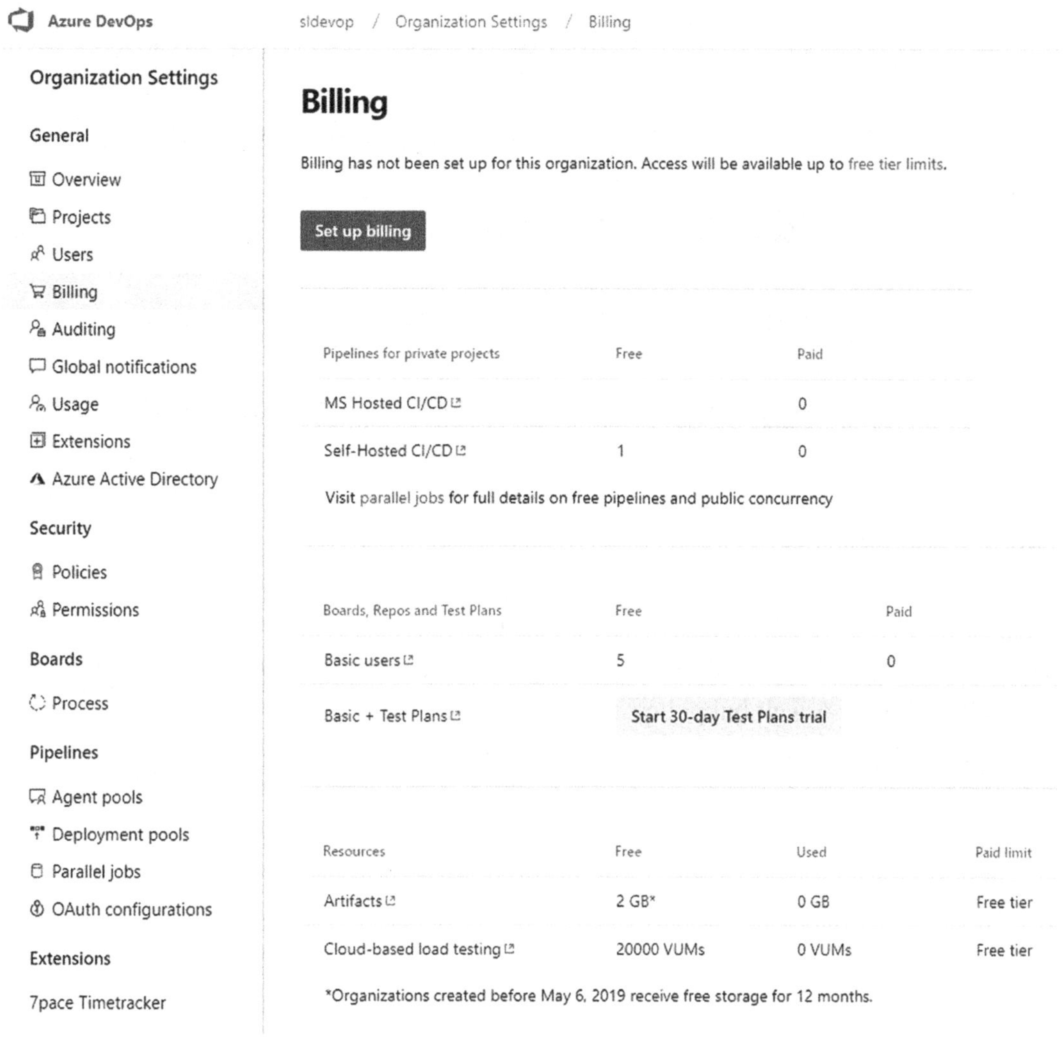

Figure 1-41. *Billing for Azure DevOps*

The Auditing tab allows you to view the admin actions audit in the organization. The log can be filtered by a date range and can be downloaded in CSV and JSON formats. See Figure 1-42.

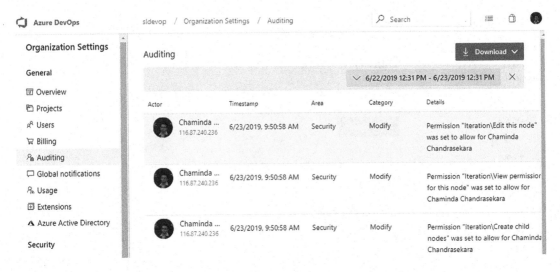

Figure 1-42. *Auditing*

Global notifications let you disable organization-level notification subscriptions made by default. With the settings on this page, you can enable delivering notifications to member e-mails as a global policy. See Figure 1-43. This can be overridden at the project level. We will discuss notifications in detail in Chapter 4.

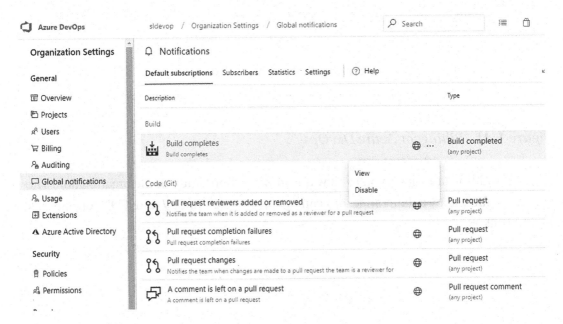

Figure 1-43. *Global notifications*

The Usage tab will show the usage of Azure DevOps with several filter capabilities. You can filter for time period, user, and so on, to view usage details. See Figure 1-44.

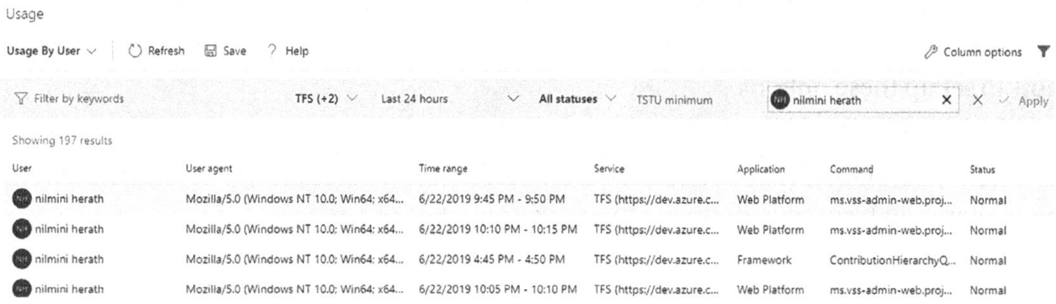

Figure 1-44. Usage

We will discuss the Extensions tab in Chapter 10. The Azure Active Directory tab lets you associate an Azure DevOps organization with your company's Azure Active Directory. If your organization has been created with an organization user, then it will be automatically linked with the organization's Azure Active Directory. However, you can associate an Azure DevOps organization that is created with a Microsoft account to a company Azure Active Directory. Before associating, you need to transfer the ownership of the Azure DevOps organization to a user from the company who has access to the Azure Active Directory of the company. For further information on how to do this, you can refer to http://chamindac.blogspot.com/2019/05/join-personal-azure-devops-organization.html.

We will discuss security policies and permissions at the Azure DevOps organization level in Chapter 8 of this book. Other organization settings will be covered in the relevant books of the series. For example, agent pools will be covered in the *Hands-on Azure Pipelines* book.

In this lesson, we discussed a few organization-level settings that are useful to set up the behavior of the Azure DevOps organization.

Lesson 1-6. Previewing Features and Themes

The Azure DevOps services often get released with preview features. You can enable such features for yourself or can enable some of these features for your organization. Additionally, you can opt to use the Light or Dark theme in Azure DevOps. Let's look at how to set up these options.

Clicking your profile avatar at the top left of Azure DevOps will show a menu. In this menu you can click "'Preview features" to see any available preview features. The Theme menu item can be used to open the theme settings. See Figure 1-45.

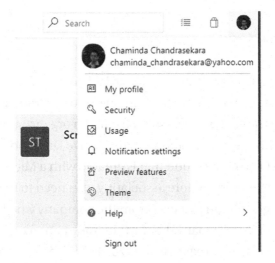

Figure 1-45. *Preview features and themes*

Once you click "Preview features," a pane will open where you can enable or disable preview features for your account or for the organization. See Figure 1-46.

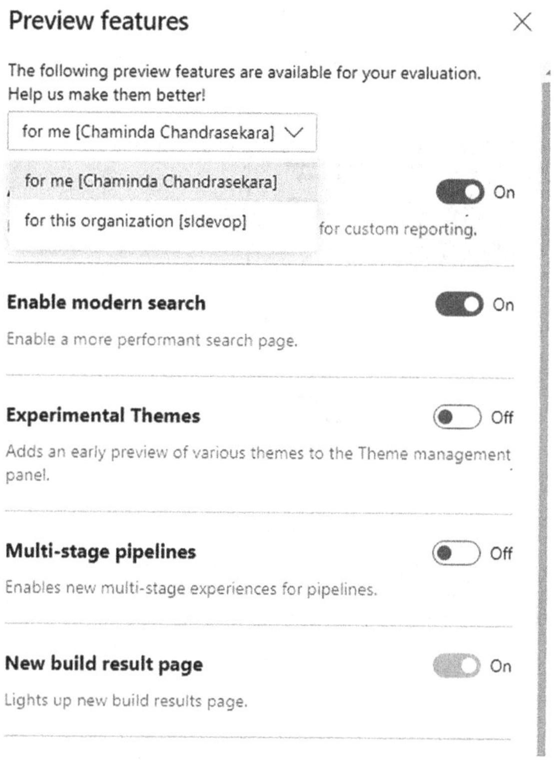

Figure 1-46. *Preview features*

In the theme settings, you can select one of the available themes, and it will be applied to you. See Figure 1-47.

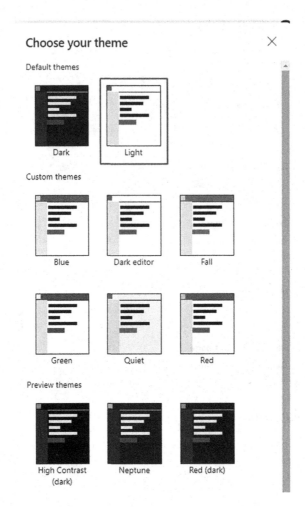

Figure 1-47. *Themes*

In this lesson, you learned how to enable preview features and changed themes based on your preferences.

Summary

In this chapter, you explored how to get started by creating an Azure DevOps organization. We explained how to create team projects with different templates and compared the process models/templates to give you an understanding of the capabilities of Azure Boards in supporting typical software development process models such as Agile, Scrum, and CMMI. In addition, we discussed the Basic process model so as to help your team to get started in the simplest way possible with Azure Boards. Further, we discussed how to customize the organization settings, how to enable and disable preview features, and how to use themes.

We gave you a quick overview of all the areas available in Azure Boards and in the Overview section. You now have an overall understanding of Boards for diving deep into each area in the coming chapters. In the next chapter, we will discuss how to set up a team project in a simple way to get you started with Azure Boards in the context of a small team.

CHAPTER 2

Setting Up a Team Project

The objective of this chapter is to help you create an Azure DevOps project and use Azure Boards to plan and deliver work. The initial preparation involves adding team members, setting up areas and iterations, and planning team capacity. By the end of this chapter, you will have a thorough understanding of the initial setup requirements in a team project of Azure Boards.

Lesson 2-1. Creating a Team

As the starting point, let's look at how to create a new team in a team project. We covered how to set up a new team project in the previous chapter.

Prerequisites: You need to have a Microsoft account and a new Azure DevOps team project in an Azure DevOps organization where you are the administrator.

In an Azure DevOps project, you can create a new team in the Settings section. Go to the project settings and then select Teams in the General section. You will see the "New team" link. Click the link to add a new team. See Figure 2-1. In addition, you will be able to see the existing teams in this Teams section.

© Chaminda Chandrasekara and Pushpa Herath 2019
C. Chandrasekara and P. Herath, *Hands-on Azure Boards*, https://doi.org/10.1007/978-1-4842-5046-4_2

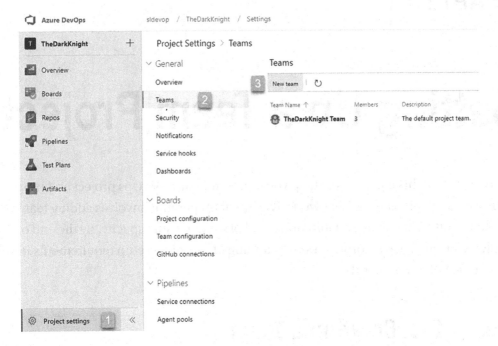

Figure 2-1. *Adding a new team using the project settings*

After clicking the "New team" link, you will see a pop-up menu that allows you to create a new team. Let's identify each section of the pop-up. See Figure 2-2.

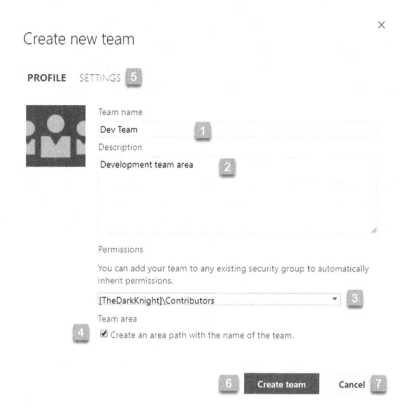

Figure 2-2. *Pop-up for creating a new team*

1. Name the team.

2. Add a description of the team.

3. You can add the team to any existing security groups in this drop-down. Then members of this team will get the same permission as the selected group. See Figure 2-3.

Figure 2-3. *Selecting a security group to add team permissions*

4. If you want to create an area path with the team name, you can select this check box; otherwise, you can create a team without an area path. There may be situations where you need to add a team to an existing area path or to the root area path. So, you can deselect the check box and create a team without an area path but with a team name.

5. You can move to the Settings tab. You can add team administrators in this Settings section. After moving to the Settings tab, you will see the existing team administrators and also an Add link to add new team administrators. See Figure 2-4.

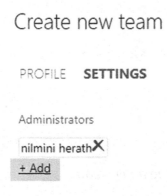

Figure 2-4. *Adding new team administrators*

After doing this, click the Add link, and a new pop-up will open. You can add administrators using this pop-up. You will be able to see the Identities drop-down list. You can select the project members from this drop-down who are going to become administrators of the new team. See Figure 2-5. Also, you can add new users who are not currently known to Azure DevOps services. After entering the sign-in address of a new user, you can click "Check name" to verify the validity of the entered name. After selecting or entering a team member, click "Save changes" to add the selected member as an administrator.

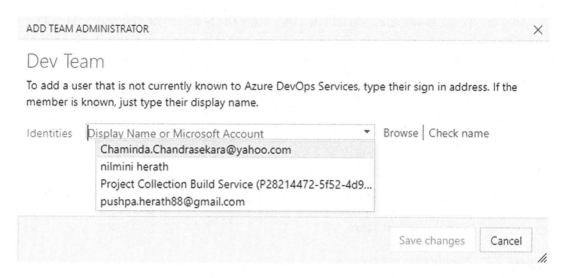

Figure 2-5. *Selecting an existing project member as an administrator*

If you click the Browse link, you can search and select existing project members to be administrators. See Figure 2-6. After selecting the members, you can click the Add button to add the selected members as administrators.

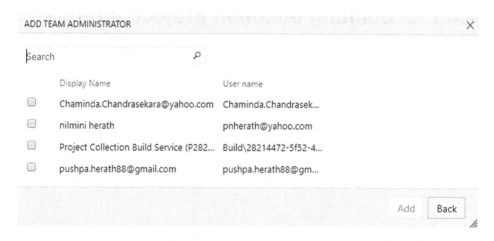

Figure 2-6. *Searching for team members*

6. Click the "Create team" button to create a team.

7. Click the Cancel button to cancel the creation of the team.

After creating a new team, you will be able to see the team in the Teams section of the Project Settings page. See Figure 2-7.

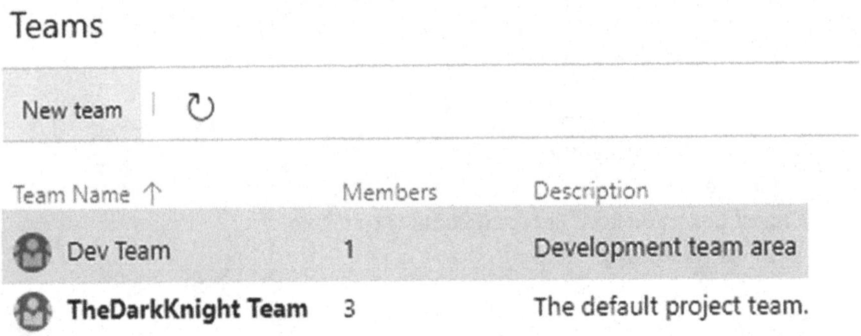

Figure 2-7. *Newly created team*

In this lesson, you learned how to create a new team in an Azure DevOps project. You also understand that you can add multiple teams according to your project requirements.

Lesson 2-2. Defining Common Project Settings

Let's take a look at all the project settings in this lesson, while getting a detailed understanding of the sections not covered already in previous lessons.

Project Settings

To view the project settings, you can click "Project settings" (Figure 2-8) at the bottom left of the team project page. The Project Settings section has multiple areas.

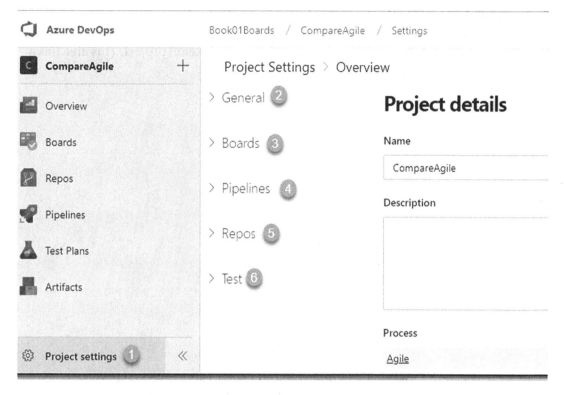

Figure 2-8. *Project Settings*

1. Navigate to the Project Settings section.

2. This area contains general settings.

3. This area contains settings related to Azure Boards.

4. This area contains settings related to Azure pipelines.

5. This area contains settings related to Azure repos.

6. This area contains settings related to testing.

Let's take a look at the General and Boards sections as they are related to Azure Boards. The other sections will be discussed in the next relevant books of the series.

General Project Settings

The General project settings are the common settings for a team project. This area has a few subsections. See Figure 2-9.

Figure 2-9. *General settings*

1. **Overview:** This section contains settings such as the project name and project visibility options to enable or disable Azure DevOps services for the project. We covered this section in detail in Chapter 1.

2. **Teams:** This section contains a list of teams available in the team project. You can create a new team by clicking "New team." Each team has a context menu that allows you to set the team as the default team of the team project or delete the default setting, if it is not the default one anymore. See Figure 2-10.

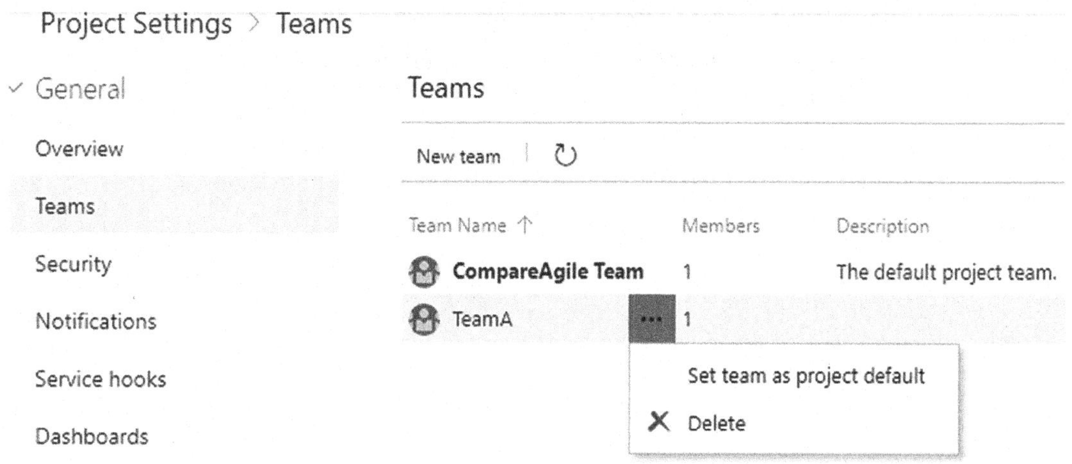

Project Settings > Teams

✓ General

Overview

Teams

Security

Notifications

Service hooks

Dashboards

Teams

───

New team | ↻

───

Team Name ↑   Members   Description

🖧 **CompareAgile Team**   1   The default project team.

🖧 TeamA   ···   1

                    Set team as project default

              ✗ Delete

Figure 2-10. *Teams section*

3. **Security**: The security settings of the team project can be defined
   here. We will further discuss this in Chapter 8.

4. **Notifications**: This section lets you subscribe to notifications
   generated by Azure DevOps based on events that occur on work
   items, builds, and so on. See Figure 2-11.

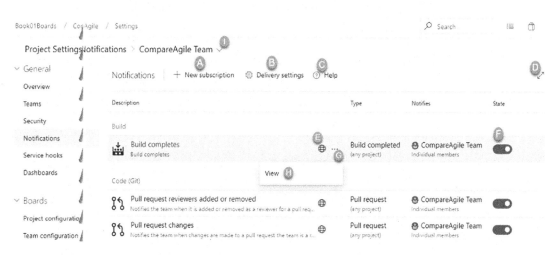

Figure 2-11. *Notifications*

A. Allows you to create a new subscription for a notification/alert. Select the category of the alert and use the available template to set up the notification. See Figure 2-12.

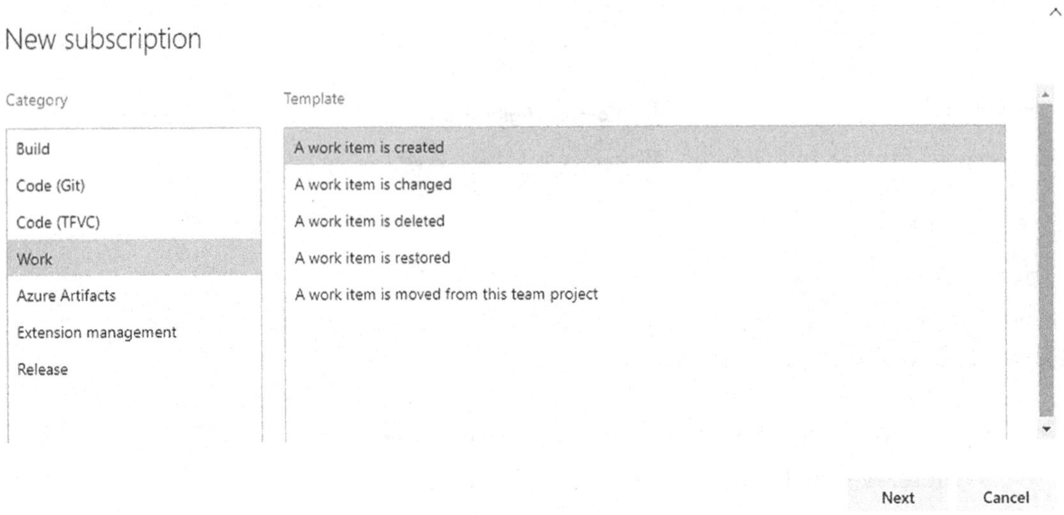

New subscription

Category	Template
Build	A work item is created
Code (Git)	A work item is changed
Code (TFVC)	A work item is deleted
Work	A work item is restored
Azure Artifacts	A work item is moved from this team project
Extension management	
Release	

Next   Cancel

Figure 2-12. *New subscription*

When you click Next, you will be able to add filter criteria for the notification and subscribe. We will discuss subscribing to a notification in Chapter 3.

B. The "Delivery setting" section lets you set the preferences of notification delivery for a given team. You can set up notifications to be delivered to a fixed e-mail address, deliver them to individual team members, or not deliver them at all. See Figure 2-13.

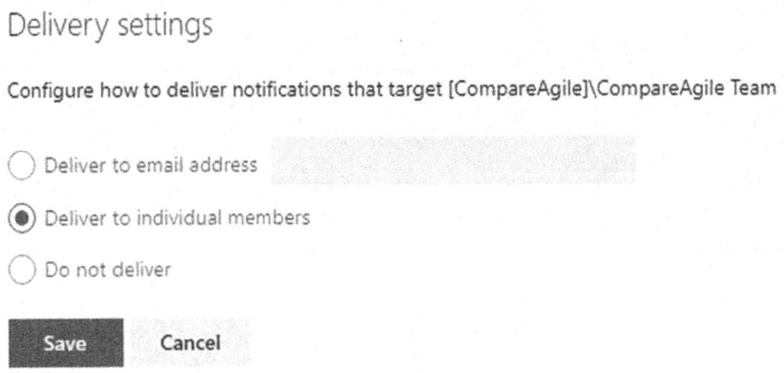

Delivery settings

Configure how to deliver notifications that target [CompareAgile]\CompareAgile Team

◯ Deliver to email address

◉ Deliver to individual members

◯ Do not deliver

Save   Cancel

Figure 2-13. *"Delivery settings" section*

C. Help will take you to the Microsoft documentation on notifications.

D. You can expand the interface to full-screen mode.

E. This shows that a subscription for an alert is a default one. These cannot be edited. However, they can be disabled, as shown in F.

F. You can enable or disable subscriptions.

G. This opens the subscription context menu.

H. You can view the default subscription details. Edit and delete options will be available for the custom subscriptions created.

I. You can select a team for the team project.

5. **Service hooks**: These can be created for many services such as Microsoft Teams to allow you to notify those services based on an event in Azure DevOps. You can get notified at your own web URL as well. For that you can select Web Hooks in the dialog that appears after clicking "Create subscription" in the Service Hooks section. See Figure 2-14.

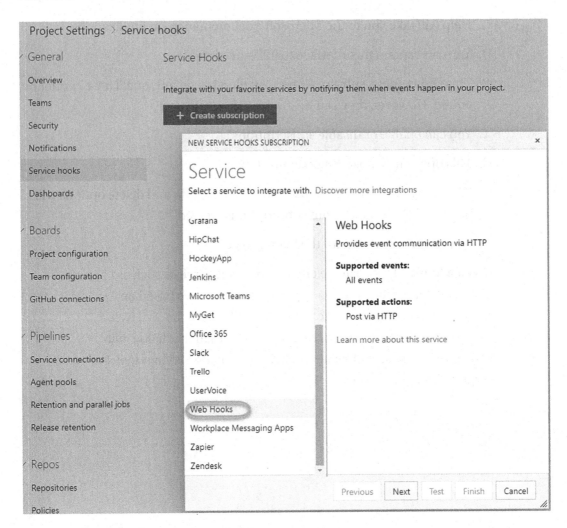

Figure 2-14. *Setting up service hooks*

You can select from the many events available such as work item
created, build completed, and so on. See Figure 2-15.

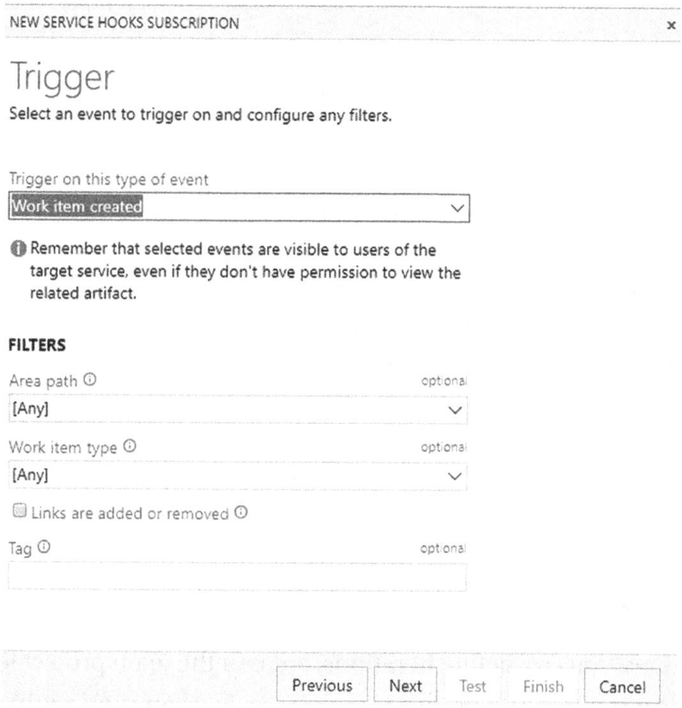

Figure 2-15. *Service hook trigger*

Then you can provide the URL you want to post the event to, and any authentication information as well can be included to authorize posting to the URL. You can also filter the information sent and define the format for a web hook. For more information, refer to `https://docs.microsoft.com/en-us/azure/devops/service-hooks/services/webhooks?view=azure-devops`.

6. ***Dashboard***: This section lets you define the permission for team members to create, edit, and delete dashboards. Only a team administrator or higher-level user such as project admin or collection admin can change these settings. See Figure 2-16.

Figure 2-16. *Dashboard permissions*

Boards Settings

In the Boards settings, you can define iterations, areas at the team project level, and areas and iterations for a given team. In addition, there are a few common settings that can be set in the Boards section. Let's identify the subsections under Boards first. See Figure 2-17.

Figure 2-17. *Boards settings*

1. **Project configuration**: This section allows you to define areas and iterations for the team project. We'll discuss these in detail in the next two lessons of the chapter.

2. **Team configuration**: You are allowed to select team iterations and areas and a few other settings for a selected team here. Let's look at team settings that you can set in this section.

3. **GitHub connections**: This allows you to set up a connection so that you can work with Azure Boards while integrated into GitHub repos. We will discuss this further in Chapter 10.

Team Configuration General Tab

On this tab, you can set general settings by selecting a team in the team project. See Figure 2-18.

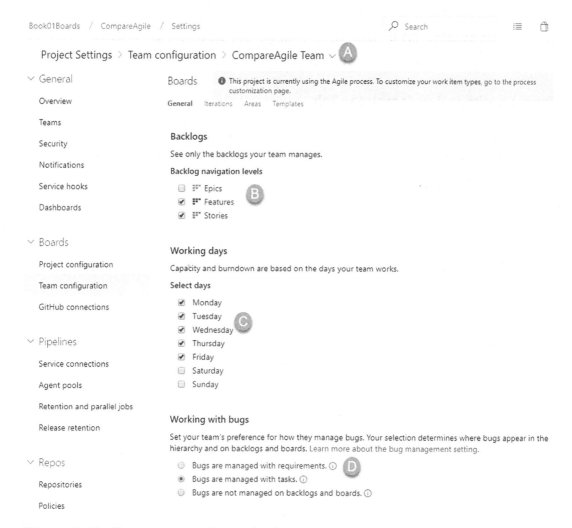

Figure 2-18. *Team settings, General tab*

    A. Select a team.

    B. Select the backlog levels for the team.

    C. Define the workdays for the team.

D. Define how a bug work item should be used in the team. The options are to manage bugs in the same level with requirements/user stories/product backlog items, manage bugs with tasks, or not to show Bug work items in boards. We will discuss this in Chapter 3.

We will skip discussing the Iterations and Areas tabs as we will have separate lessons for them in this chapter.

Team Configuration Templates Tab

The Template tab allows you to create templates for work items in a selected team. Using the Template link, you can create new work items with predefined values as defined in the template. See Figure 2-19.

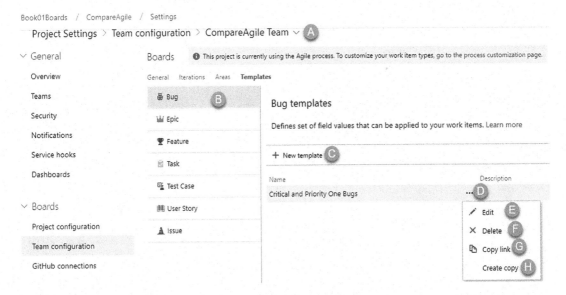

Figure 2-19. *Team settings, Templates*

A. Select the team.

B. Select the work item.

C. Create a new template.

D. This is the context menu of the template.

E. Edit the template.

F. Delete the template.

G. Copy the link to create a work item with the template.

H. Create a copy of the template and open up a new template create dialog with the selected template values.

In the new template create/edit template dialog, you can define a name and description for the template. You can select multiple fields and set values for them for the template in this dialog. Further, you can provide a comment that will be added as a discussion comment when the work item is created via the template-provided link. See Figure 2-20.

Figure 2-20. *Editing the template*

You can copy the link and use it in any browser or application. The link will take you to the relevant work item create page with values from the template filled in automatically. See Figure 2-21.

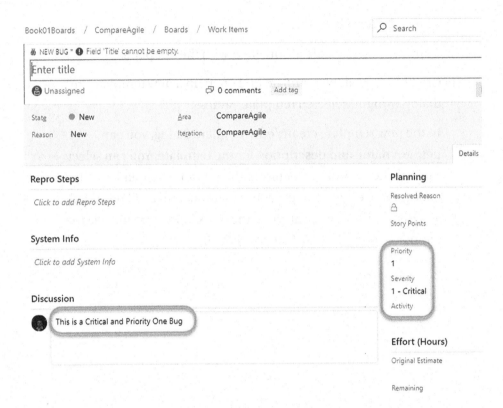

Figure 2-21. *Creating a work item with template*

    4.   We will discuss GitHub connections in Chapter 10.

In this lesson, you looked at the common general and board-related settings. These settings are important to get you started working with Azure Boards.

Lesson 2-3. Setting Up Areas

The area path in Azure DevOps helps you to modularize your work by grouping work items by product, feature, or business area. A new project will have a single root area corresponding to the project name as well as the default team that is created when a new team project is created.

Project Areas

To find the list of area paths available in the project, select "Project settings," select "Project configuration," and then select the Areas tab. You will be able to see all the available area paths of the project. See Figure 2-22.

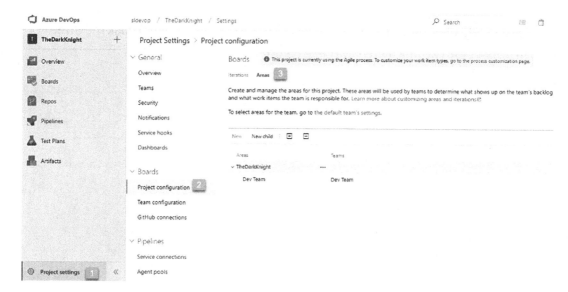

Figure 2-22. *Area path section of project settings*

You will be able to see the root area and all the added areas as child areas. You can add new child areas in this section. See Figure 2-23.

Figure 2-23. *Areas list*

1. When you select the subarea, this link will be enabled. It allows you to add another area in the same level as the selected item.

2. You can add a child item to a selected item.

3. You can expand one level.

4. You can collapse one level.

You can add new items using options in the pane that opens when click the three dots in front of the existing area name. See Figure 2-24.

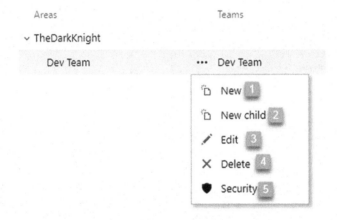

Figure 2-24. *Selected project area context menu*

If you click the three dots in front of the root item, you will be able to see that the "New child" and Security items are the only items enabled. Let's identify each option in the pane.

1. Add a new item to the same level as the selected item. Click New, and a pop-up will open. You can name the new area path, and the default location is the root area. See Figure 2-25.

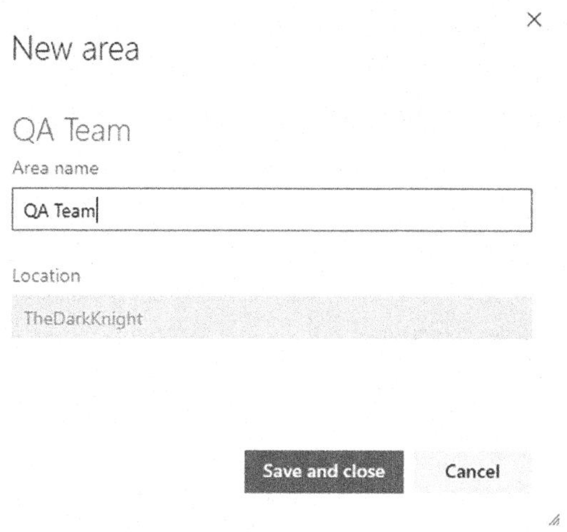

Figure 2-25. *Adding a new area path*

2. Add a new child item to the selected item. After clicking this link, you will be able to see a pop-up similar to Figure 2-25.

3. Click Edit to edit the name of the area path and change the parent item of the area path. After you click Edit, pop-up will open. It allows you to change the area path name and location. See Figure 2-26.

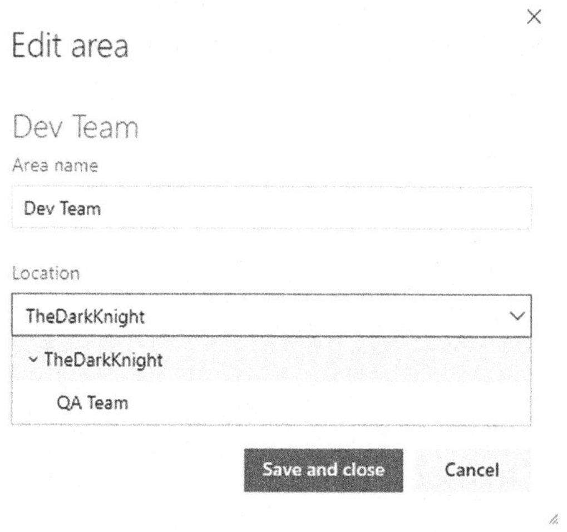

Figure 2-26. *Editing the area name and location*

4. You can delete the area by clicking Delete. If you click Delete, you will see a pop-up message. You can delete an area by clicking the "Delete path" button in the pop-up, and any existing work item will be moved to the reassignment path selected, as shown in Figure 2-27.

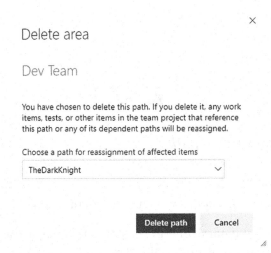

Figure 2-27. *Deleting an area*

5. You can control the permission of a given area using this option. When you click Security in the context menu, a security pop-up will open, which allows you to control the area permissions. See Figure 2-28.

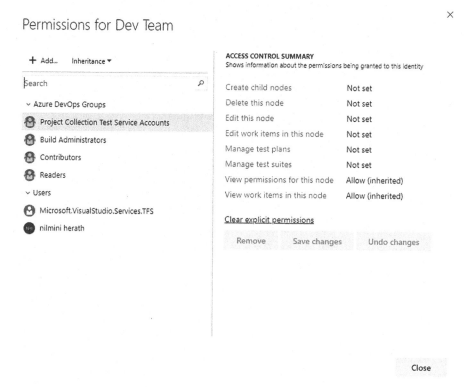

Figure 2-28. *Area security*

Now that you have configured the area path for a project level, let's explore the team-level area path settings.

Team Areas

A team can select a subset of areas defined in the team project. An area can be shared with multiple projects, and it is possible to use separate area paths to isolate the work items of a team from another team in the same team project.

Click Project Settings, expand Boards, and click Team Configurations. Then click the Areas tab to view the team's Area settings. See Figure 2-29.

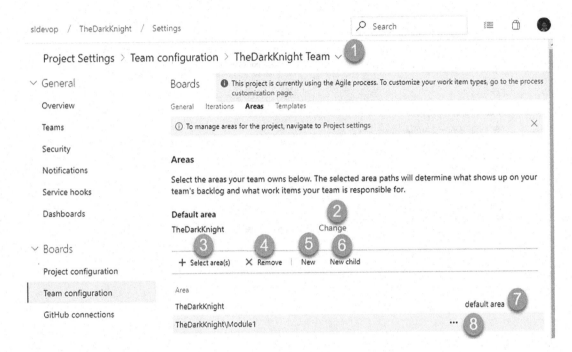

Figure 2-29. *Team areas*

1. You can select a team in the team project.

2. It is possible to change the default area of the team. The default area of the team determines to which area path a newly created work item's Area path field is set, when created in the context of the team.

3. Select the area for the team using the pop-up that opens. It is possible to select multiple areas at once using the +Area button. You can check the Include subareas to make work items belong to the selected areas and all child areas of the selected areas and make them visible to the team. Removing a selected area before saving is possible via the X in the right corner of the selected area path. See Figure 2-30.

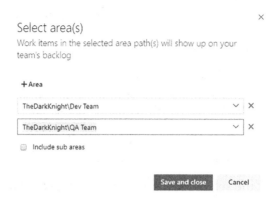

Figure 2-30. *Selecting areas for the team*

4. Remove a selected area.

5. Create a new area at the same level of the selected area. When you add areas from a team, they will be available at the team project level as well.

6. Create a child area for the selected area.

7. The default area of the team is autoselected as a selected area.

8. This loads the context menu of a given selected area. See Figure 2-31.

Figure 2-31. *Selected team area context menu*

A. You can create a new area at the same level of the selected area.

B. You can create a new child area for the selected area.

C. You can edit the selected area.

D. You can remove the selected area from the team.

E. You can open the permissions dialog for the selected area path where you can set permissions.

F. You can set the selected area as the default area for the team.

G. You can include the subareas of the selected area so that the work items of the selected area and all the subareas of the selected area are visible to the team.

In this lesson, you explored the area path configuration at the team project and team levels. This knowledge will help you to group your work items based on business needs.

Lesson 2-4. Setting Up Releases and Iterations

The iteration path allows you to group work items based on timebox intervals, such as sprints or iterations. Similar to the area paths, the iteration paths can be defined at the project level, and teams can use them as shared or as isolated iterations. This lesson will explain how to set up iterations on the project level and use them on the team level.

Team Project Iterations

Let's try to add new iterations to the Azure DevOps project from the team project's Settings page.

Click "Project settings" and then select "Project configuration" in the Boards section. Then you will be able to see the Iterations tab. Select the Iterations tab, and you will see the default set of iterations in the Azure DevOps team project. See Figure 2-32.

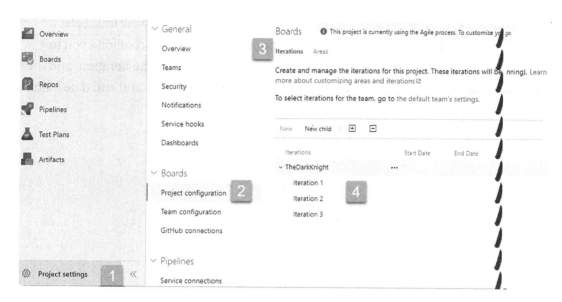

Figure 2-32. *Team project iterations*

You will find an iteration with a name similar to the project name and child iterations of it. It is possible to add new child iterations from here. If you click the root iteration (TheDarkKnight in Figure 2-32), you will see a grayed-out New link. When you click a child item, it becomes clickable. This behavior is because you cannot create the same level of iteration in the root iteration level. You can add a new iteration at the same level using the New link in any child-level iteration. To add a child iteration to any selected iteration, use the "New child" link. See Figure 2-33.

Figure 2-33. *Iteration toolbar*

1. Add a new item to the same level as the selected item.

2. Add a new child item to the selected item.

3. Expand one level.

4. Collapse one level.

Let's add a new iteration at the same level of Iteration 1 with the New link. Select Iteration 1 and click the New link. A pop-up window will appear, which allows you to create a new iteration by giving the iteration name, the start date of the iteration, and the end date of the iteration. See Figure 2-34. You can keep the start date and end date blank and set them later if required.

Figure 2-34. *New iteration*

If you try to add a new child iteration to Iteration 1, you will be able to see the same pop-up. The only difference is that the location will be TheDarkKnight\Iteration1.

Besides using the previously mentioned New and "New child" links, you can add new iterations with the context menu that opens when you click the three dots next to each iteration. See Figure 2-35.

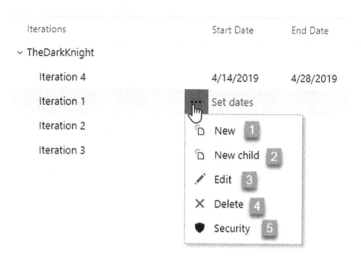

Figure 2-35. *Iteration context menu*

1. Add a new iteration to the same level as the selected iteration.

2. Add a new child iteration to the selected iteration.

3. You can edit the iteration values using this option. After clicking the edit button, a pop-up will appear, and you will be able to edit the iteration name, start date, end date, and location from the pop-up dialog. See Figure 2-36.

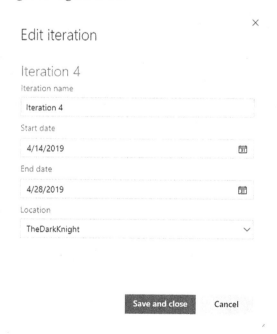

Figure 2-36. *Editing an iteration*

4. Delete the selected iteration with the Delete option. After you click
    Delete, you will see the pop-up where you can select a path to
    reassign the work items if any belong to the deleted iteration. See
    Figure 2-37.

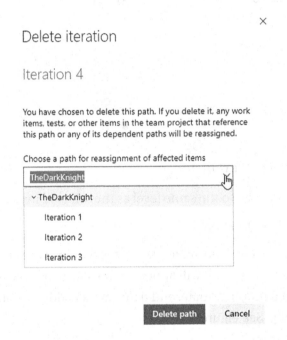

Figure 2-37. *Deleting an iteration*

5. You can control the security of the iteration using this option. After
    clicking this security menu item, a pop-up will appear. You can
    control the iteration permission from this pop-up. See Figure 2-38.

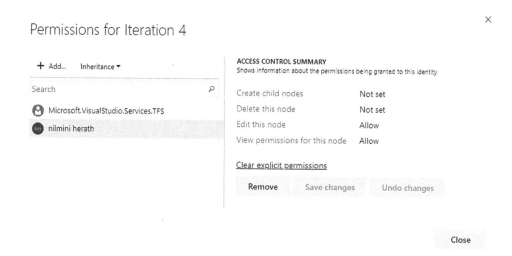

Figure 2-38. *Iteration permission*

So far, you have learned how to add iterations to the Azure DevOps project. Now, you'll learn how to use iterations when you have multiple teams for the project.

Team Iterations

Go to the project settings and then select Teams under General. You will see a list of teams available in the team project. See Figure 2-39.

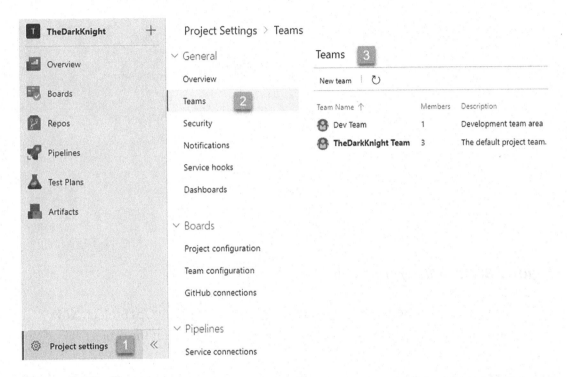

Figure 2-39. Teams

Now click one of the required teams. The team profile will open. Click the "Iterations and areas" link under the "Manage other settings for this team" item. See Figure 2-40. This will navigate you to the team configuration values of the selected team. Click the Iterations tab.

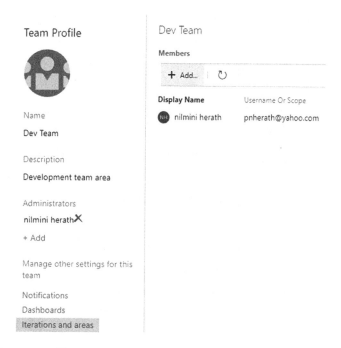

Figure 2-40. *Team profile*

Instead of navigating through that path, you can click "Project settings" and then click "Team configuration" under Boards. Then can click the Iterations tab and select the required team from the drop-down at the top of the page. See Figure 2-41.

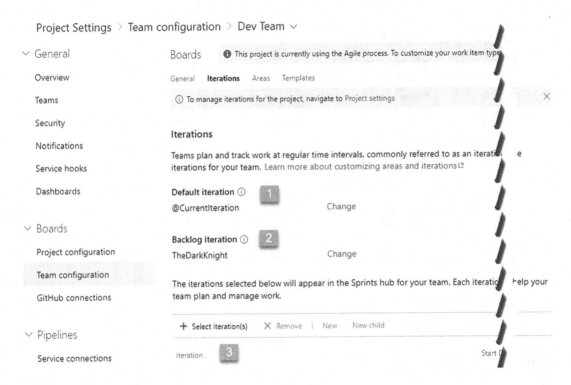

Figure 2-41. *Team iterations*

1. You can find the default iteration of the team here. The default iteration of a team determines the iteration a new work item is getting added to when it is created within the team context. Dev Team in this example has the selected current iteration as the default iteration. That means when you add a new work item, it is getting added to the current iteration.

2. You can change the backlog iteration of the team from here. The backlog iteration determines which work items are shown in the team's backlog and boards. You can change these backlog iteration values by using the Change link. After clicking the Change link, select iterations from the drop-down and click Set to save the selected value or click Cancel to dismiss the changes. See Figure 2-42.

Backlog iteration
TheDarkKnight
Set Cancel
TheDarkKnight
Iteration 4
Iteration 1
Iteration 2
Iteration 3
in the Sprints hu
your
New child

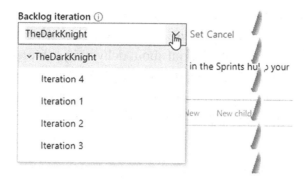

Figure 2-42. *Changing the backlog iteration*

3. You can add the iterations to the team. In Figure 2-43, you can see there is no iteration selected for the team. You can click the "Select iterations" link and add the iterations to the team. See Figure 2-43.

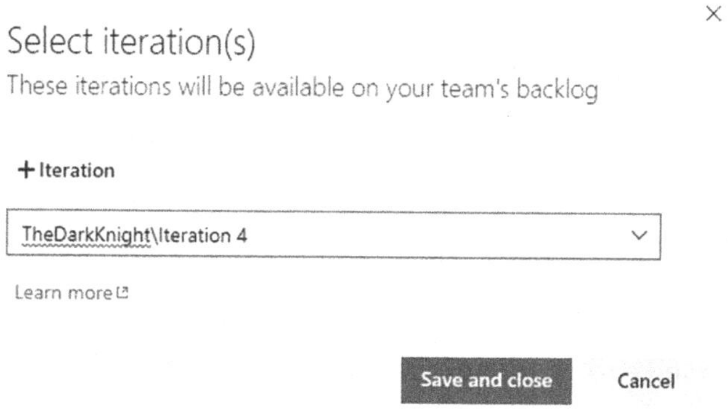

Select iteration(s)
These iterations will be available on your team's backlog
+ Iteration
TheDarkKnight\Iteration 4
Learn more
Save and close
Cancel

Figure 2-43. *Selecting an iteration for the team*

After an iteration is added, the team will be able to work with iterations/sprints. Also, you will see that a context menu is available for a selected iteration, with the same actions that we discussed in the selected iterations of the team project. See Figure 2-44.

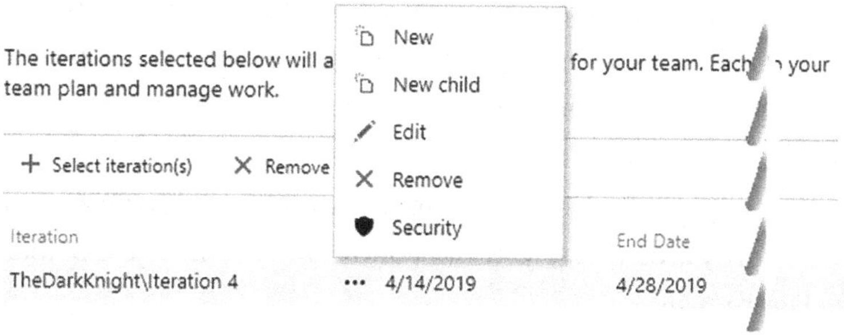

New
New child
Edit
Remove
Security
The iterations selected below will a
team plan and manage work.
for your team. Each
your
+ Select iteration(s)
Remove
Iteration
End Date
TheDarkKnight\Iteration 4
4/14/2019
4/28/2019

Figure 2-44. *Selected iteration context menu*

Since iterations are hierarchical in structure, and you can define timeboxes with practical needs such as grouping multiple iterations into one release iteration. This is against the Agile methodology, which is all about delivering a shippable product in every sprint/iteration. However, in the practical world, even though you might have shippable product each iteration, shipping to the actual client may happen after a couple of iterations. An example setup looks like Figure 2-45.

	Start Date	End Date
New New child ⊞ ⊟		
Iterations	Start Date	End Date
⌄ Account Management Solution	10/16/2017	2/26/2018
⌄ Release 01	10/16/2017	11/28/2017
Rel 01 - Iteration 01	10/16/2017	11/6/2017
Rel 01 - Iteration 02	11/7/2017	11/28/2017
⌄ Release 02	11/29/2017	1/11/2018
Rel 02 - Iteration 01	11/29/2017	12/20/2017
Rel 02 - Iteration 02	12/21/2017	1/11/2018
Release 03	1/12/2018	2/23/2018

Figure 2-45. Release and iterations

In this lesson, you explored how to set up iterations in a team project and use them in a team. As mentioned earlier, iterations can be shared or used in isolation in a given team.

Lesson 2-5. Setting Up Team Members and Permissions

A team should have team members to perform work. This lesson will describe how you add new team members to the team. You can add members individually or as groups.

First let's identify the default groups available in the Azure DevOps team project and the permissions of each group.

Go to the project settings and select Security in the General section. You will be navigated to the Security area where you can control the permissions of team members and groups. See Figure 2-46.

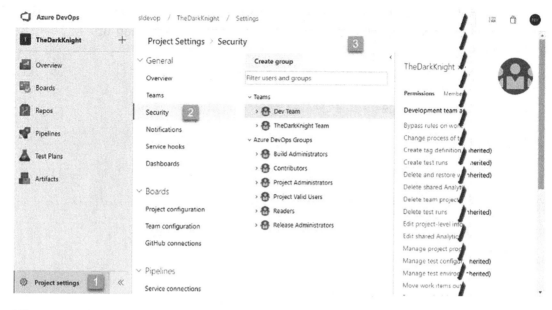

Figure 2-46. *Team project security*

Let's identify the basic capabilities of the security settings in this lesson; you will learn more about security in Chapter 8 of this book. See Figure 2-47.

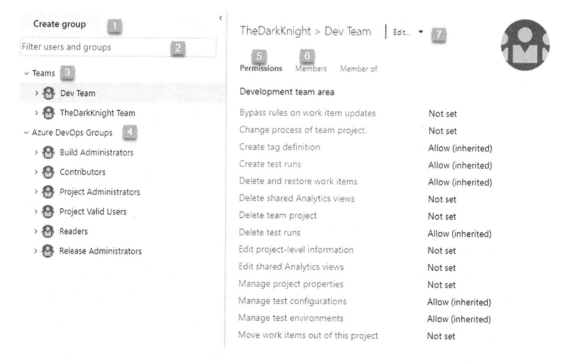

Figure 2-47. *Team project permissions*

1. Create a new group using this link. Clicking this link will open up a dialog. You will be able to add new group details using the pop-up window. See Figure 2-48.

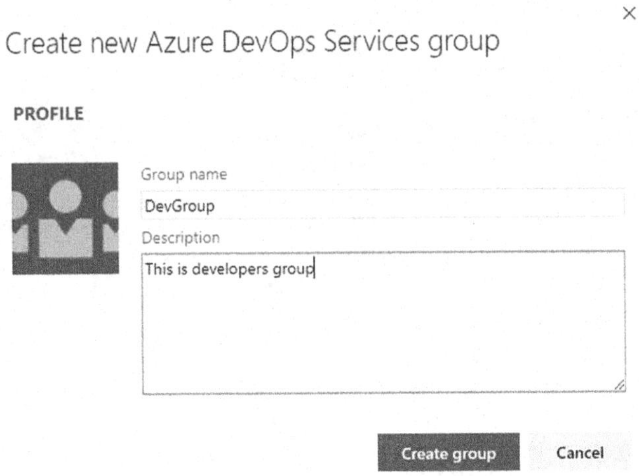

Create new Azure DevOps Services group   ×

PROFILE

Group name

DevGroup

Description

This is developers group

Create group   Cancel

Figure 2-48. *Creating a new security group*

2. You can filter users and groups.

3. You can display all the teams available in the Azure DevOps project.

4. You can display all the groups available in the Azure DevOps project.

5. The Permission tab displays all the permissions of the selected team or group.

6. The Members tab displays the members of the selected team or group.

7. You can edit or delete the selected team or group.

Now you have a basic idea of groups in an Azure DevOps team project; let's move to the team settings of the Azure DevOps project and see how to set permissions there.

Go to the project settings, select Teams, and select the name of a specific team from the team list. You will be navigated to the team profile.

Click the Add button to add new members. See Figure 2-49.

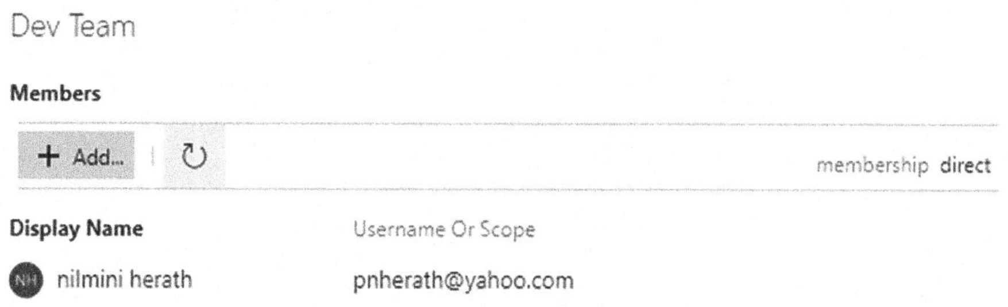

Dev Team

Members

+ Add...   ↻   membership **direct**

Display Name   Username Or Scope

(NH) nilmini herath   pnherath@yahoo.com

Figure 2-49. *Adding a member to a team*

A pop-up will appear that allows you to add new team members. You can add
members by providing sign-in addresses or group aliases. See Figure 2-50.

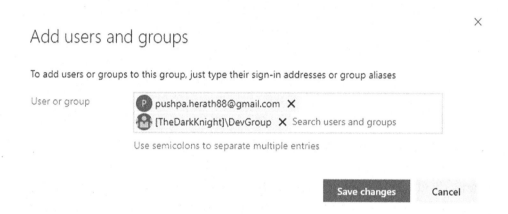

Figure 2-50. *Adding a new member or group*

In addition, you can add team administrators from the team profile. Click the Add
button, and a pop-up will appear. See Figure 2-51.

Figure 2-51. Adding a team administrator

Add an individual member or group as the team administrator using the pop-up.

We discussed team permission settings in this lesson. You learned how to add individual members and groups as team members. Additionally, we discussed how to add administrators to the team.

Lesson 2-6. Defining Team Capacity and Days Off

We defined iterations in a previous lesson. In iterations, you can define the team's capacity in order to allow you to find the available capacity for each activity type within the team. This will enhance the team's ability to commit to completing an iteration and give you an idea of whether the team can meet the commitments made.

Select the Sprints/Iterations menu item from the side menu under Boards. Select the team that you need to define the capacity for from the drop-down. Then move to the Capacity tab. See Figure 2-52.

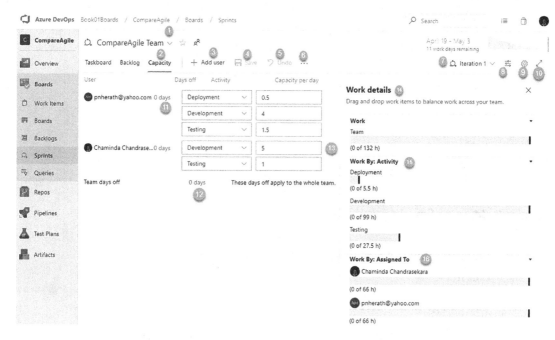

Figure 2-52. *Team capacity*

1. Select the team. Next to this drop-down you can click the star icon to add the team to the favorites list, and you can click the people icon to see the team profile.

2. You can select the Capacity tab here.

3. You can add a team member to the capacity planning.

4. You can save the capacity plan.

5. You can undo a change made to the capacity plan before saving.

6. You can add all the team members and copy the capacity planning of the previous sprint/iteration to the current/future one. See Figure 2-53.

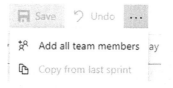

Figure 2-53. *Team capacity context menu*

7. You can select the sprint/iteration.

8. You can show/hide work details in the side pane. See Figure 2-54.

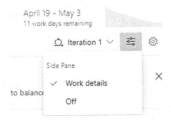

Figure 2-54. *Configuring the side pane*

9. You can open the Settings page, which we will discuss in the next chapters.

10. You can go to full-screen view.

11. You can define individual days off. You can add multiple periods of days off and remove added days off by clicking the X to the right of the days off. See Figure 2-55.

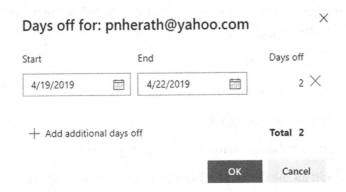

Figure 2-55. *Individual days off*

12. You can define team days off applicable to all members of the team.

13. You can add another activity type from the available list to a given member and set capacity. You can remove the user or one of the activity types for a user as well. See Figure 2-56.

User	Days off	Activity		Capacity per day
pnherath@yahoo.com 0 days		Deployment ⌄		0.5
		Development ⌄		4
		Testing ⌄		1.5 •••
Chaminda Chandrase...0 days		Development ⌄		+ Add an activity
		Testing ⌄		✕ Remove this activity
Team days off	0 days	These days (		✕ Remove this user

Figure 2-56. *Team days off*

14. You can view the work details in the side pane. We will discuss this pane in Chapter 3 where the work estimation is described with work items assigned to a given sprint.

15. You can view the work capacity and assignments by activity.

16. You can view the work capacity and assignment by team member.

In this lesson, you explored how to set up the team capacity for the team members for a given iteration. We will discuss team capacity and work estimations more in the next chapters.

Summary

In this chapter, you explored how to create teams in a team project and use general and Azure Boards–related settings. Further, we discussed how to set up areas, iterations, and team capacity. This will enable you to get started with Azure DevOps Boards and follow the next lessons in this book.

In the next chapter, you will learn about setting up boards and work items and using boards to work with work items.

CHAPTER 3

Working with Backlogs and Boards

Keeping track of the work that your team does is important so you can make process improvements to your team's way of working and increase productivity. The work of your team can be captured as *work items* in Azure DevOps, and you can use various boards and backlogs to organize and plan the work items. In this chapter, we'll cover the options you have in Azure Boards to organize your work hierarchically, to plan the work process using Kanban, and to use iterations to plan for time-based cycles of work. We will also discuss the available features to successfully run your project teams with Agile/Scrum or with traditional processes, including the options you have to handle software bugs discovered during the development and testing processes or in production.

Prerequisites: It is essential that you have worked through the first two chapters of this book so that you have the required basic understanding to successfully follow the lessons in this chapter.

Lesson 3-1. Understanding the Backlog Hierarchy

Azure DevOps allows you to create a hierarchy in the backlog to group work according to business needs. By default, two levels of backlogs are enabled in an Azure DevOps team, as explained in Lesson 2-2. They are the feature for all three templates Agile, Scrum and CMMI and user story for Agile workflows, the product backlog item in Scrum, or the requirement in CMMI. Lesson 2-2 also explains how to enable a top backlog level of Epic. There is another way to enable or disable backlog levels for a team. In a team's backlog or board view, you can open the Settings pop-up by clicking the cogwheel icon just below the cumulative flow diagram, at the top right of the page. In the General section of the Settings pop-up, you can enable or disable the backlog levels to be used in your team on the Backlogs tab. See Figure 3-1. Select the Epics, Features, and Stories levels for this lesson.

© Chaminda Chandrasekara and Pushpa Herath 2019
C. Chandrasekara and P. Herath, *Hands-on Azure Boards*, https://doi.org/10.1007/978-1-4842-5046-4_3

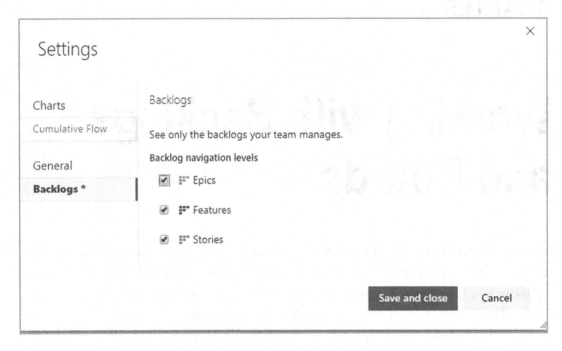

Figure 3-1. *Selecting backlog levels*

To understand the backlog levels, let's look at a common business example such as a banking system. When implementing the banking system, there could be a broad requirement of "A need to have a banking system to manage savings and lending accounts." This requirement could be broken into two levels: "A need for savings account management facility" and "A need to manage leading accounts such as personal and vehicle loans." You could use the Epics level to manage these three requirements with a parent-child hierarchy. (You will learn how to create work items in that manner in Lesson 3-2.)

Then if you take the loans section, there could be several features such as "Capture new customer and loan requirement details," "Review process of loan application and approval," and so on. You can use the Features backlog level to keep the backlog organized into features as child requirements of the Epics level defined previously. (You will learn how to do this in Lesson 3-2 of this chapter.)

To implement each of these features, you might need several stories, and each story may need a couple of tasks to get it implemented. The user stories (Agile)/product backlog items (Scrum)/requirements (CMMI) can be created as child work items of the relevant feature work item. It is even possible to create multiple levels within a work item type. However, keeping the story/PBI/requirement level as a flat level without creating a hierarchy is recommended. One reason for this recommendation is to keep the estimates of size and effort from getting too large in Azure DevOps; you will learn about this in Lesson 3-3. In addition, a story in the Agile process should be an independent testable unit of work, which should not include any dependencies other than the set of tasks needed to implement that story. The tasks should be the child items of a user story work item. See Figure 3-2.

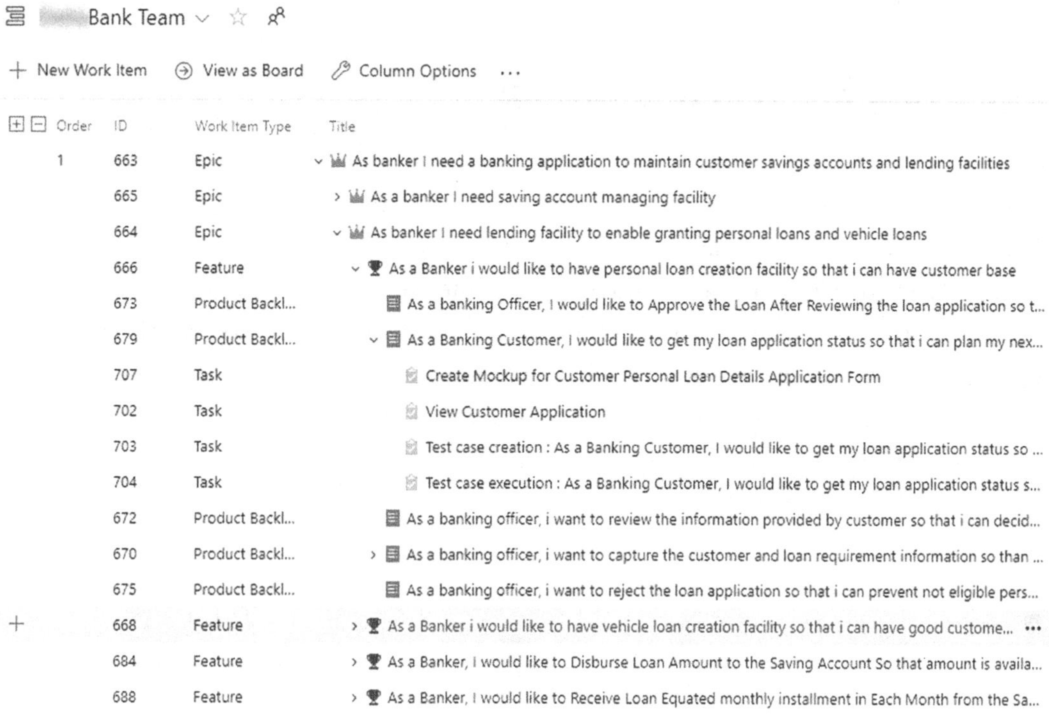

Order	ID	Work Item Type	Title
1	663	Epic	As banker I need a banking application to maintain customer savings accounts and lending facilities
	665	Epic	As a banker I need saving account managing facility
	664	Epic	As banker I need lending facility to enable granting personal loans and vehicle loans
	666	Feature	As a Banker i would like to have personal loan creation facility so that i can have customer base
	673	Product Backl...	As a banking Officer, I would like to Approve the Loan After Reviewing the loan application so t...
	679	Product Backl...	As a Banking Customer, I would like to get my loan application status so that i can plan my nex...
	707	Task	Create Mockup for Customer Personal Loan Details Application Form
	702	Task	View Customer Application
	703	Task	Test case creation : As a Banking Customer, I would like to get my loan application status so ...
	704	Task	Test case execution : As a Banking Customer, I would like to get my loan application status s...
	672	Product Backl...	As a banking officer, i want to review the information provided by customer so that i can decid...
	670	Product Backl...	As a banking officer, i want to capture the customer and loan requirement information so than ...
	675	Product Backl...	As a banking officer, i want to reject the loan application so that i can prevent not eligible pers...
	668	Feature	As a Banker i would like to have vehicle loan creation facility so that i can have good custome...
	684	Feature	As a Banker, I would like to Disburse Loan Amount to the Saving Account So that amount is availa...
	688	Feature	As a Banker, I would like to Receive Loan Equated monthly installment in Each Month from the Sa...

Figure 3-2. *Banking system sample backlog*

We used a banking application as an example in this lesson to explain how to use the backlog hierarchy.

Lesson 3-2. Defining a Backlog

In this lesson, you'll learn how to create a backlog of work and add it to your team project and teams, which will allow you to extend the understanding you have gained in the previous chapter.

Prerequisites: You need to work through Chapters 1 and 2 and have familiarity with the navigation of and various options available in Azure Boards. You also need to have worked through Lesson 3-1. You have a team project created in Azure DevOps with the Agile template for your team, and you have enabled the Epics, Features, and Stories backlog levels.

Organizing Epics in a Hierarchy

You can create a backlog of work items in the Work Items, Boards, or Backlogs page in Azure Boards. Let's use the Backlogs page so you can define your backlog hierarchically. Click Backlogs, and in the "Backlog work item type" selection drop-down, select Epics. Click the New Work Item button in the middle of the page or in the toolbar, and you will be able to provide the title of the first epic. Enter **As banker I need a banking application to maintain customer savings accounts and lending facilities** as the title in the text box, as shown in Figure 3-3, and click the "Add to top" button. Since this is the first work item, adding it to the top, adding it at the selection, and adding it to bottom will all have the same effect.

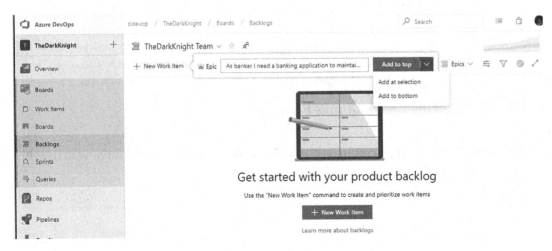

Figure 3-3. Creating the first Epic work item

You can click the title of the first epic to view its details. In the epic form/page, inspect the iteration path and area path set by default. As discussed in Chapter 2, you can set the team preference to Default Iteration and Default Area in the Team Configurations page, which the iteration and area will be set automatically for any work item that is created in the context of the team.

Once the first epic is added, you can add a child Feature work item to it by clicking the + sign next to the epic in the backlog. See Figure 3-4.

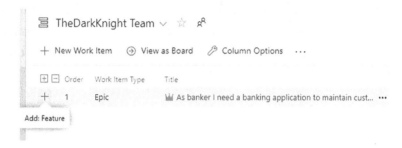

Figure 3-4. *Adding a child Feature work item to the Epic work item*

However, before adding features, you need to add child epics because you are going to use two epic levels parent and child to group the requirements.

Tip   You can add more backlog levels to avoid creating a parent-child relationship within the same work item type. You'll explore how to add more backlog levels while customizing the process templates.

To add another epic level as a child to an existing Epic work item for the first time, you have to use the "Add link" option in the parent's Epic work item form. Open the epic you just created by clicking the title of it. In the work item form, you will see a section named Related Work. Here when you click "Add link," you will be able to link another work item to the current work item, with one of the predefined sets of relationships. Since you have not created the second-level epic yet, click "New item." See Figure 3-5.

Figure 3-5. *Adding a new work item as related work*

Set "Link type" to Child and "Work item type" to Epic. Then enter the title **As a banker I need saving account managing facility** and click OK to create the new child epic under the current Epic work item. See Figure 3-6. Then save and close the work item form to save the child-parent link between the two work items.

Figure 3-6. *Adding a child epic to create two levels of Epic work items*

Before proceeding, let's discuss the available relationships between work items in brief.

- **Child-Parent**: This relationship is used to organize work items in a hierarchy using one-to-many relationships.

- **Affects-Affected By (CMMI only)**: This is used to track the change requests for requirements.

- **Duplicate-Duplicate of**: This allows you to define that a work item is a duplicate of another. It is especially useful when you want to add multiple parent work items to a work item, because the duplicate work item can be linked to a different parent work item (only one parent is allowed for any work item in Azure DevOps).

- **Reference By-References**: This is used to link test cases to shared parameters, enabling a repeat of a test with different data. We will discuss this further in the *Hands-on Azure Test* book in this series.

- **Related**: This is used to identify the relationship between work items in the same level.

- **Successor-Predecessor**: This link is used to identify dependencies between work items. It is especially useful to identify a task that should be completed before starting another task work item.

- **Tested By-Tests**: This is a link between test cases and work items such as user stories, features, or epics.

- **Test Case-Shared Steps**: This is used to share common steps between multiple test cases. We will discuss this further in the *Hands-on Azure Test* book of this series.

Note   For further information on work item link types, refer to `https://docs.microsoft.com/en-us/azure/devops/boards/queries/link-type-reference?view=azure-devops#work-link-types`.

Now that you have added a child epic for the savings account area in banking under the main banking system epic, you should be able to see that a hierarchical backlog is available within the same work item type in the epic backlog view. It is possible to create this type of hierarchy within any backlog level available; however, as previously mentioned, it is advisable to keep the Stories level as a flat level.

To add another epic in the backlog view, click "New Work item" and enter the title **As banker I need lending facility to enable granting personal**. Click "Add to bottom." This will add a new Epic work item, but not as a child work item of the main banking system epic. To add this third epic to the first epic as a child, open the work item form of the first epic and click "Add link" in the Related Work section. Then click Existing Item to open the pop-up for adding a link to an existing work item (see Figure 3-5). You can search for the third epic by typing in part of the title or the ID of the work item and then select the correct one from the list that appears. See Figure 3-7. Then save and close the work item form to save the child-parent link between the two work items.

Figure 3-7. *Adding an existing work item as a child link*

Using either of the previously described procedures, add another child epic with the title "As banker I need lending facility to enable granting vehicle loans" to the banking system's main epic. See Figure 3-8.

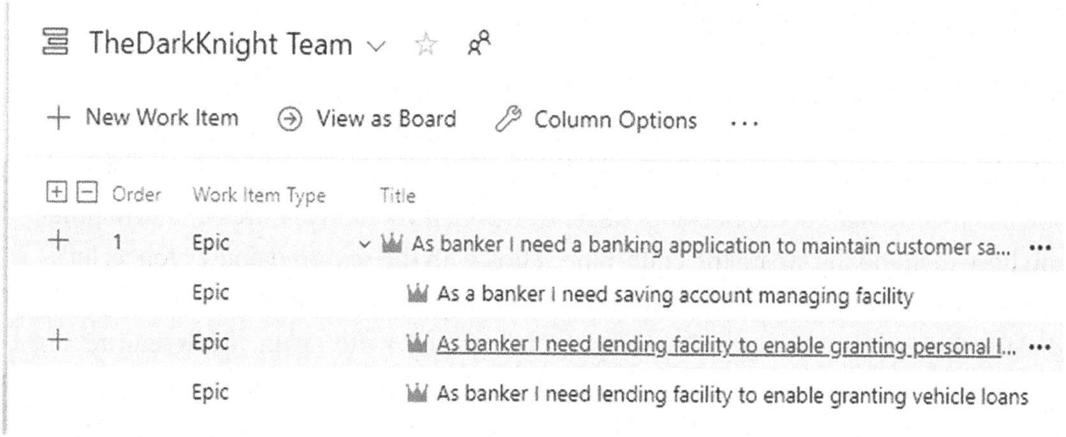

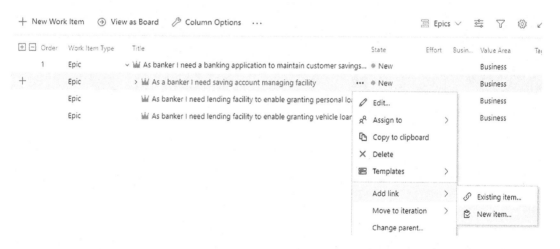

Figure 3-8. *Hierarchical epics*

Instead of opening the work item form and trying to add the link, you can add a link to any work item using a context menu. See Figure 3-9.

Figure 3-9. *Adding a link to a work item via a context menu*

You have created subepics for a sample banking system and grouped them as children under a parent to create a hierarchy under the main banking system epic. You can use the Boards view of the epic as well to add child features to a given epic, which we will discuss in Lesson 3-5.

Adding Features to Epics

Now that you have three major epics as requirements of the sample banking application, let's move on to identify how you can create features under these epics. To create new features, you can switch to the feature backlog view by selecting Features in the drop-down at the top right of the Backlogs page. However, if you add features in this manner, you have to manually create the child-parent link with the required epics. Hence, let's stay in the epic backlog view and add features to each epic from the Epics view by clicking the + sign to the right of each epic. Once you click the + sign, a new feature work item form will open and have a parent link with the relevant epic. See Figure 3-10. Provide a feature with the title "Facilitate customers to open savings accounts" and save the feature.

Figure 3-10. *Adding a child feature to an epic*

Now add a couple more features to the epic such as "Facilitate savings cash deposit over the counter" and "Facilitate savings cash withdrawal over the counter." You could even go ahead and create another child at the Features level under the saving accounts epic such as enabling ATM transactions, or you could add a child feature level, as we discussed earlier.

Adding Stories to Features

Now that you have epics and features of the sample application organized into a hierarchical grouping, let's add user stories to implement each feature. Again, you can move to the user story backlog view using the drop-down in the Backlogs view page to add new user stories. However, it is recommended that you use the feature or epic backlog view and add the required child stories to Feature work items using the + sign right to each feature (see Figure 3-11) or the context menu of each feature. Or you can use feature board view to add child user stories to Feature work items, which we will discuss in Lesson 3-5.

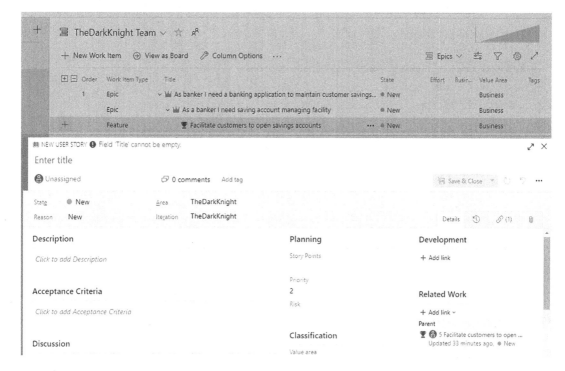

Figure 3-11. *Adding a child user story to a feature*

Add a couple of user stories to the relevant features. For example, you can add "Facilitate customers to open savings accounts" with user stories such as the following:

- "As a banking officer, I need to capture customer details so that a new customer can be added to the bank"

- "As a banking officer, I need to open a savings account for a customer"

- "As a banking officer, I need to perform initial cash deposit for a new savings account so that the account to get activated"

See Figure 3-12.

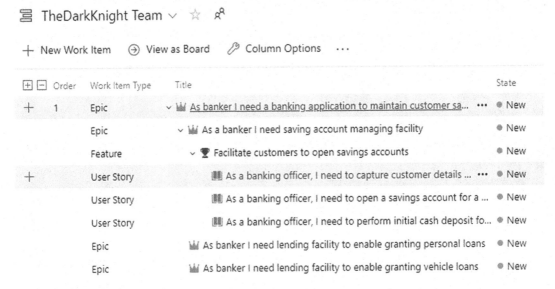

Figure 3-12. *Stories added to a feature*

Add a couple more features and user stories to fully understand how the child-parent relationship can be used to hierarchically organize the backlog.

Adding Tasks to User Stories

To implement user stories/product backlog items/requirements, you can define *tasks*. To add tasks to a given user story, you can use the user story backlog view or even the epic backlog view. In either view, you can click the + sign to the right of the user story (see Figure 3-13) or use the context menu to select "Add link" and then "New item."

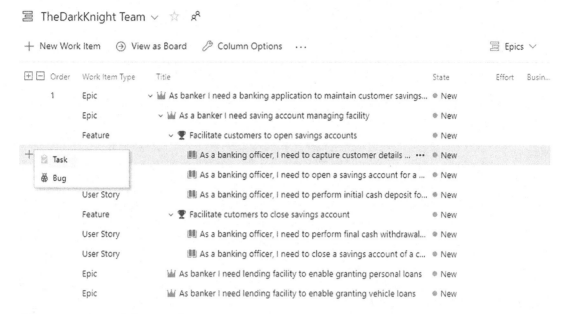

Figure 3-13. *Adding tasks to a user story*

Add a couple of tasks for each user story so you can see how it looks and understand how it works in the backlog view.

Changing the Parent

You can change the parent of any backlog item except the topmost backlog level (as of now the epic is the topmost backlog level) by using that work item's context menu and selecting "Change parent." See Figure 3-14. You can select multiple work items of the same type and change the parent.

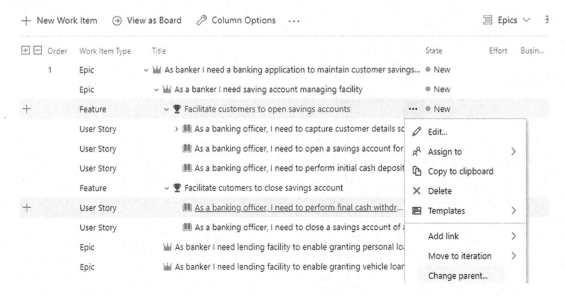

Figure 3-14. *Changing a parent*

A pop-up window will allow you to select immediate top level a work item from backlog items, which you can reparent the work item to. See Figure 3-15.

Figure 3-15. *Changing the parent pop-up*

Additionally, you can use drag and drop in the backlog view to change the parent of a given work item. You can select multiple work items of the same type and change the parent. See Figure 3-16.

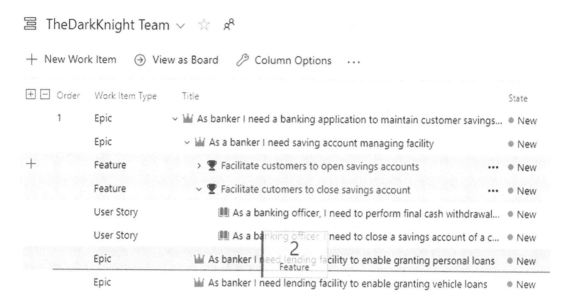

Figure 3-16. *Dragging and dropping to change the parent*

Using the Work Item Context Menu in the Backlog View

You have already used a couple of options in the work item context menu. Let's explore each available menu action to make sure you understand all of them. See Figure 3-17.

Figure 3-17. *Work item context menu in backlog view*

1. Selecting Edit will open a dialog that will allow you to edit work item fields selectively. You can select multiple work items from different types and perform bulk edits on all selected work items using this option. You are allowed to add a note while you make the edit to the fields, which will appear in the history of each work item edited. See Figure 3-18.

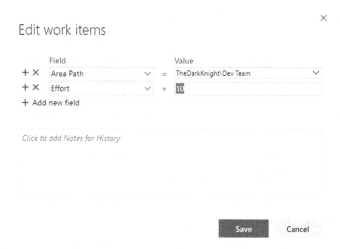

Figure 3-18. *Editing work item fields*

2. "Assign to" will allow you to assign selected work items to a user all at once.

3. "Copy to clipboard" lets you copy the selected work item's visible columns in the backlog view to the clipboard. When you paste in Word, Excel and so on, in addition to the data, you get a link to a temporary query where you can navigate to a query view of the selected work items.

4. Delete allows you to move work items to the Recycle Bin, which can be found via the Work Items page of Azure Boards. A message will pop up to confirm the delete. From the recycle bin you can restore the deleted work items or permanently delete them.

5. Template allows you to capture a template from a single work item; we discussed the usage of templates in Lesson 2-2.

6. "Add link" lets you add the linked work items as we have been discussing throughout this lesson.

7. "Move to iteration" allows you to move selected work items to a given iteration.

8. "Change parent" lets you change the parent work item of selected work items as we have been discussing in this lesson.

9. "Move to position" lets you move work items in the order of the backlog. It's especially useful when you have a longer backlog and when you want to move an item at the bottom to the top or near to the top.

10. "Change type" lets you change the type of work item for selected work items. For example, you might have created a set of items as user stories, but you may want to make them features instead of stories. You can use this option and easily change the work item type without having to re-create each work item.

11. You can move selected work items to a different team project in your Azure DevOps organization. You are able to select the target team project, area path, or iteration path, and you can even change the work item type during the move.

12. You can e-mail selected work items to the required team members. See Figure 3-19.

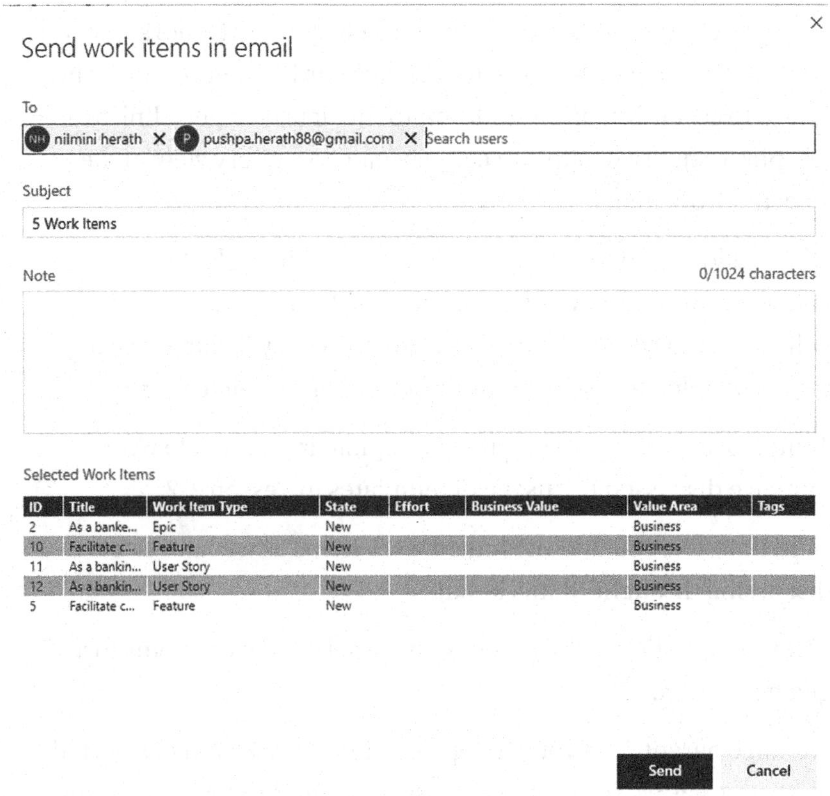

Figure 3-19. *E-mailing work items*

13. "New branch creation" allows you to create an Azure Git repo branch, which we will discuss in the *Hands-on Azure Repos* book of the series.

14. "Do exploratory testing" lets you explore the system based on the work item implementation and record test cases. We will discuss more about this in the *Hands-on Azure Tests* book of the series.

In this lesson, we discussed how to organize a backlog hierarchically using the backlog view of Azure Boards.

Lesson 3-3. Exploring Important Work Item Fields

You created a couple of work items of different types in the previous lesson, so it is good time to explore some important fields of a given work item.

Common Important Work Item Fields

Let's take a look at common and important work item fields available for all the work item types.

- **Id**: This is a unique ID for each work item across all projects in a project collection/Azure DevOps organization.

- **Title**: This is a short description of the work item.

- **Description**: You can provide in-depth information about the work item here.

- **Acceptance Criteria**: This is available in the Scrum template for the Epic, Feature, PBI, and Bug work items. It is useful to define the criteria for allowing the work item to evaluate for its completion with the Acceptance Critera before closing it.

- **Repro Steps**: You can write the bug-reproducing steps in this field. This is available in a Bug work item.

- **Area Path**: This is the team area or module of the work item.

- **Iteration Path**: This is the path of the iteration in which the work item belongs currently.

- **Assigned To**: The work item can be assigned to a team member, and the name of the current assignee will be recorded in this field.

- **Discussion**: The Discussion field allows multiple team members to discuss the work item by providing comments in the Discussion field. Each comment made in the Discussion field will be recorded with the date and time, and you are able to use rich text and images in the discussions to make them more useful.

- **Priority**: This is a subjective rating of the work items based on the relatedness to the business process. For example, you can set a value of 1 to denote that the priority is the highest; in other words, without the completion of this work item, the product is not shippable. A low value might indicate this work item can be considered as a "good to have" feature.

- **Risk**: This is the relative uncertainty on the completion of the story.

- **Severity**: This is the relative value considering the impact to the system.

- **Story Points (Agile)/Effort (Scrum)/Size (CMMI)**: This is the relative size of the work item. In Agile, the relative size is measured with story points.

- **Tags**: Work items can be added with tags, which are discussed in detail in Lesson 4-5.

Go to the user story backlog by selecting the "Backlog Work Item type" selection drop-down in the Backlogs view. Then you can use drag and drop or select "Move to position" in the context menu of the user stories to reorder them according to the business priority.

Open the topmost user stories by clicking each one's title, and fill out the story points. In Agile, you should get your team together and decide on the size of each user story. We will discuss this in Lesson 10-3 of this book. See Figure 3-20 for a sample backlog.

		Order	Work Item Type	Title	State	Story ...	Value Area
		1	User Story	> 📖 As a banking officer, I need to capture customer details so t...	● New	2	Business
+		2	User Story	> 📖 As a banking officer, I need to open a savings account f... •••	● New	3	Business
+		3	User Story	📖 As a banking officer, I need to perform initial cash depo... •••	● New	3	Business
		4	User Story	📖 As a banking officer, I need to perform final cash withdrawal...	● New		Business
		5	User Story	📖 As a banking officer, I need to close a savings account of a c...	● New		Business

Figure 3-20. Sample backlog

In addition, clicking a work item will open the work item in any view such as work items, backlog view, or boards view. The work item form can be used to edit a given work item's fields. There is a context menu in each work item to perform several actions for a given work item.

We discussed the most commonly used work item fields in this lesson. Throughout this book series, we will further discuss these fields.

Lesson 3-4. Selecting Work to Move to an Iteration

Now that you have created a backlog in Lesson 3-2, we'll show how you can move work to a time-bound iteration/sprint in this lesson.

Prerequisites: You need to work through Lessons 3-2 and 3-3 of this chapter and have a backlog created.

Open the backlog view for user stories. Then enable the side pane to show the planning view, as you learned in Lesson 1-4. To select stories for an iteration, you can simply drag them to the required iteration in the Planning side pane. See Figure 3-21.

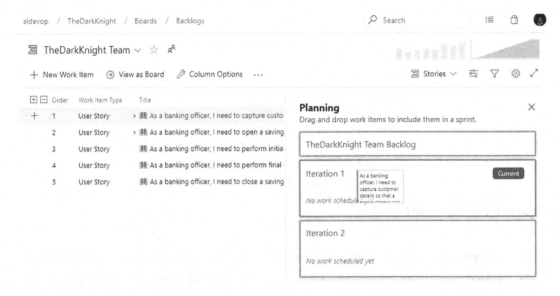

Figure 3-21. *Dragging and dropping stories onto an iteration*

Any child task defined in the user story will also be moved to the iteration automatically when you do this. Additionally, a work item can be moved to an iteration by using the work item's context menu option "Move to iteration" in work items, backlog view, or boards view as well as by changing the iteration path in a work item form.

In the Planning pane, the iteration will show you the number of stories and tasks selected for the iteration. See Figure 3-22.

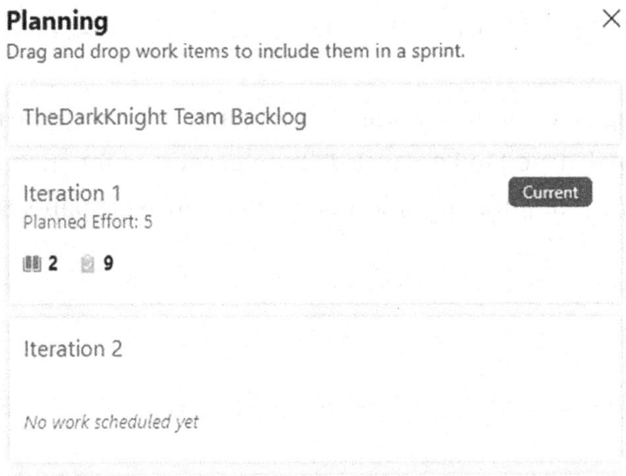

Planning   ×
Drag and drop work items to include them in a sprint.

> TheDarkKnight Team Backlog

> Iteration 1   Current
> Planned Effort: 5
>
> 📖 2   📄 9

> Iteration 2
>
> *No work scheduled yet*

Figure 3-22. *Stories and tasks selected for an iteration*

Now go to the iteration backlog view by clicking Sprints on the left-side menu in the Boards section. Click the Capacity tab and set up your team capacity as described in Lesson 2-6. See Figure 3-23.

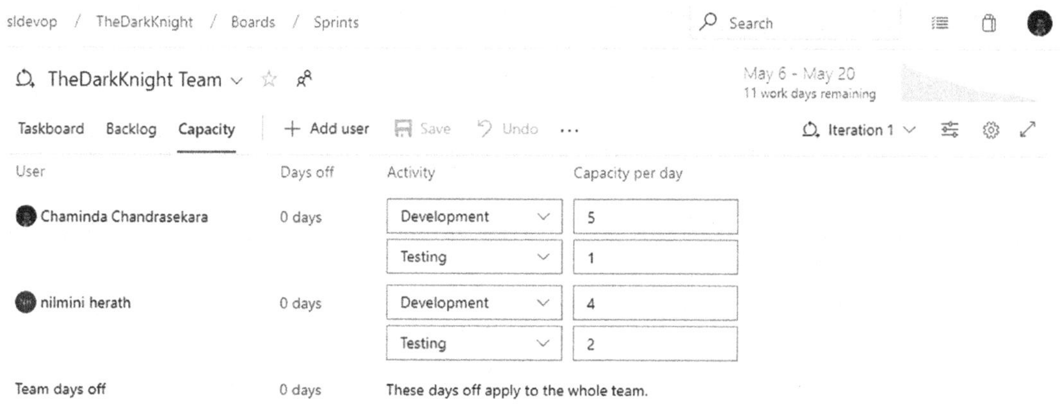

Figure 3-23. *Team capacity*

Go to the Backlog tab of the Sprint page, and you will be able to see the selected user stories for the current iteration. Expand one level, and you can see the tasks under each story. Enable the side pane with the work details, and you will be able to see the capacity of your team calculated depending on the number of days in each iteration and considering the activity type capacity of team members. See Figure 3-24.

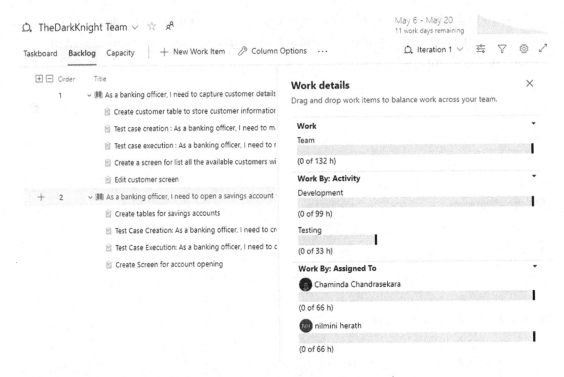

Figure 3-24. *Sprint backlog view with work details*

Now open each task selected for the iteration and define its activity type and remaining work. The "Remaining work" field in the task work item defines how much effort (generally in hours) is required to complete the task. See Figure 3-25. But it is possible for you to use your own unit as well instead of hours. The only condition is that the same unit of measurement should be used in both capacity and in remaining work to make it effective in Azure Boards.

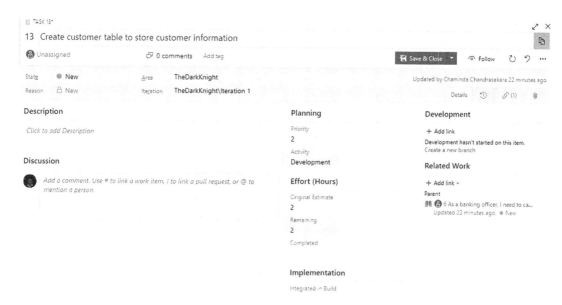

Figure 3-25. *Task activity and remaining work*

Once you define the remaining work and activity of each task, you will be able to see when the team's capacity is getting filled up and view the work by activity type in the "Work details" side pane. See Figure 3-26. However, you will notice that the team member capacity is not used yet. This is because the team members have not been assigned to any tasks as of now. You will explore how to assign tasks in the boards in Lesson 3-5, and then you can inspect the work details further to see whether a team member's capacity is getting filled with work. If the work assigned exceeds the capacity of the team or a member or an activity type, it will be highlighted and filled with red instead of green.

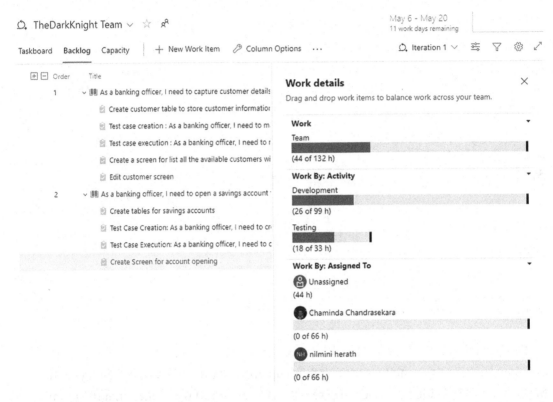

Figure 3-26. *Work details capacity*

In this lesson, you explored how to select work for a given iteration and how to use the work details to show the team's capacity with the activity type of each task.

Lesson 3-5. Using Kanban Boards and Task Boards

Now that you have created a backlog and have selected items for the current iteration, let's explore Kanban boards to understand how you can utilize them to perform the work of the team.

Prerequisites: You need to have worked through all the lessons in this chapter and previous chapters. You are ready with a backlog and have picked stories for the current iteration.

Kanban Boards

Click the Boards submenu under the Boards section and select the Epics view from the "Work item type" drop-down. You will be able to see the cards of each epic in the New state column. See Figure 3-27. You can drag and drop the cards to the relevant column, and the state will be automatically updated.

Figure 3-27. *Epics board*

When you move a work item from the New to Active column in a board, the work item's state changes to Active, and it gets assigned to the person who is logged in and making the change. See Figure 3-28. You can select a different assignee for the work item from your team members in the card itself. Once you make the change, it is automatically saved to the work item.

Figure 3-28. *Moving cards in the board*

As you can see in Figure 3-28, you can view and add the child work items in the card itself, and the count of child work items shows how many have been completed out of the ones available. Let's skip the features board and move to the stories board by selecting User Stories in the "Work item" selection drop-down of the Boards view. Move the topmost user story to the Active column, and you will see it is assigned to and similar to how the epics board displays the child tasks. See Figure 3-29. You can add tasks or mark them as complete in this view by checking the small box next to each child task; the task state will be changed to Closed. Additionally, notice that the size (story points) of the user story is shown in the card by default. We will discuss customizing the cards in Lesson 4-3.

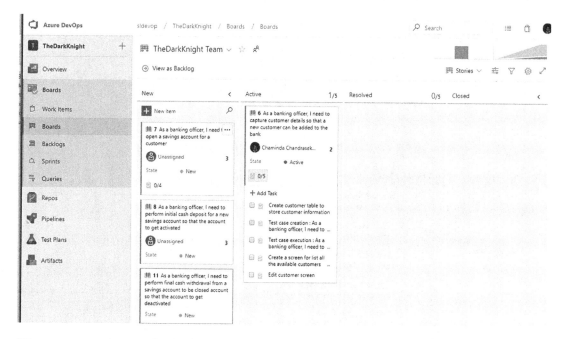

Figure 3-29. *Stories board view*

In Figure 3-29 notice that cumulative flow chart and velocity charts are already getting populated with values. We will discuss these charts in detail in Lesson 6-1. In addition, notice that Active and the other in-progress states such as Resolved show the count of cards in each column, with a preset allowing a maximum of five by default. This does not mean you cannot add more than five work items to Active. Once you add more than five work items, the number turns to red, indicating that you have exceed the limit of work items. Customizing these capacity settings and board columns will be discussed in Lesson 4-1.

In the stories board, you can click the context menu of a task to edit the title of the task, delete the task, or open the task. See Figure 3-30. Additionally, you can create a branch in Azure Repos, which we will discuss in the *Hands-on Azure Repos* book of this series. Even clicking the task title or story title in the card will open the relevant work item. This child context menu and the ability to click the title to open a work item's behavior are available for the epic and feature board cards as well.

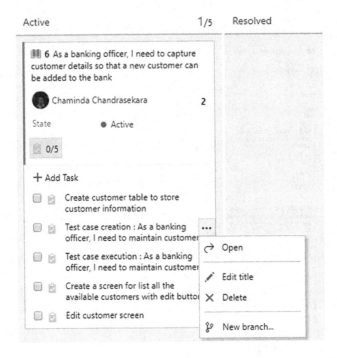

Figure 3-30. *Child work item context menu in boards*

Task Boards

Now let's move on to the sprint board view by clicking Sprints in the board section and selecting the Taskboard tab. The task board opens in expanded mode by default, and you can use filters as explained in Chapter 1 to find tasks easily. See Figure 3-31. The same drag-and-drop capability similar to the Kanban boards exists in the task boards.

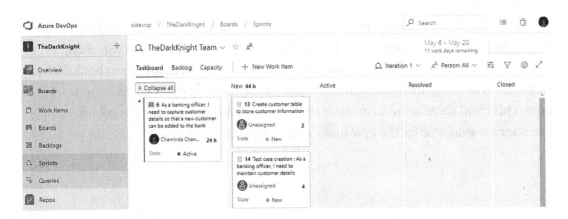

Figure 3-31. *Task board*

Once a task is moved to the Active column, it will be assigned to the user logged in, and it can be changed in the task card itself to another team member if required. You can enable the "Work details" side pane in the task board view. Notice that a team member's capacity starts filling up once tasks are assigned to the member. See Figure 3-32. Further, the green + sign in the New column for each story scope will allow you to add tasks for a given story in the board.

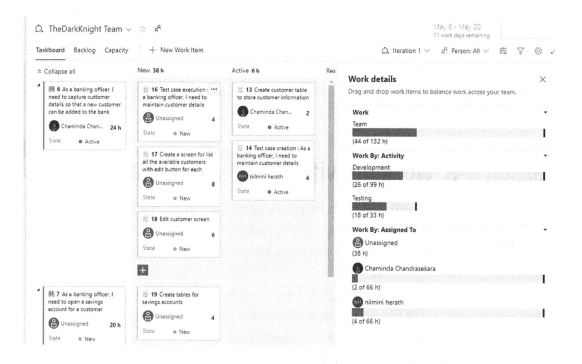

Figure 3-32. *Active tasks and work details*

Clicking Collapse All will show a summary view of all the stories in the iteration, and you can expand all of them or one by one individually. See Figure 3-33.

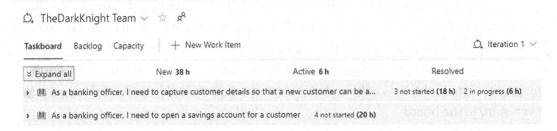

Figure 3-33. *Collapsed view of task board*

We explored the usage of Kanban and task boards in this lesson to use in the development process. Azure Boards offers you even richer capabilities with customizations to these boards via the board settings pages, which we will discuss in Chapter 4.

Lesson 3-6. Working with a Bug Work Item

You can define how you will work with Bug work items for each team in Azure Boards. You can track them at the same level as tasks, track them at the same level as requirements, or not track them at all. Let's quickly see how each setting works in this lesson.

You can set the preferences of bug behavior in a team's configuration settings on the General tab, as described in Lesson 2-2. Additionally, you can click the Settings cogwheel while you are in any backlog view or in a Kanban or task board view to open the Settings page. In the Settings page's general section, you will see the "Working with bugs" tab where you can specify your preferences. See Figure 3-34.

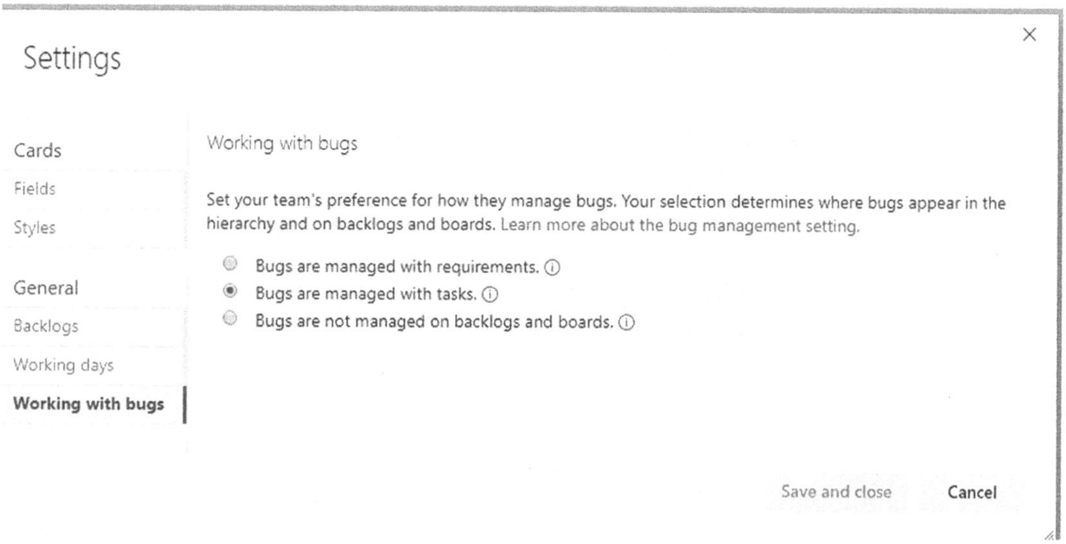

Figure 3-34. *Bug behavior settings*

Let's explore each behavior.

Managing Bugs with Tasks

By default, in an Agile project template, bugs are set to be managed with tasks. This means you can add bugs as child work items of stories via task boards (see Figure 3-35).

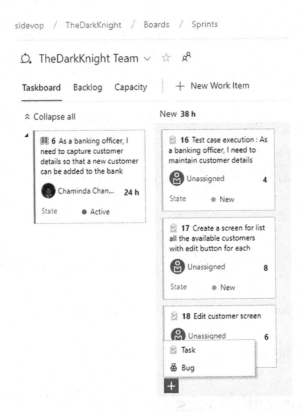

Figure 3-35. *Adding bugs in the task board*

Figure 3-36 shows how to add bugs in the stories backlog.

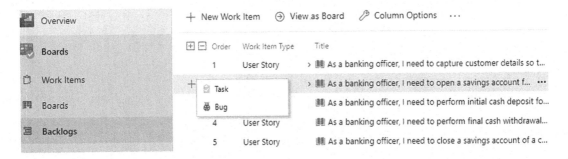

Figure 3-36. *Adding bugs via the stories backlog*

Managing Bugs with Requirements

Setting bugs to be managed with requirements will allow them to be added at the stories level in the stories board (see Figure 3-37).

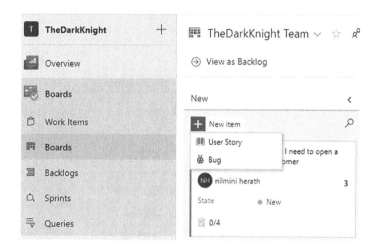

Figure 3-37.   *Adding bugs in the stories board*

They can also be added in the stories backlog (see Figure 3-38).

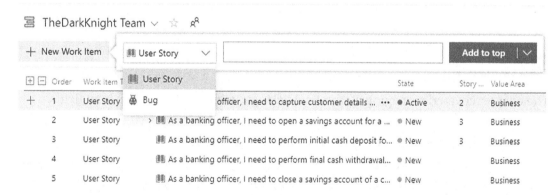

Figure 3-38.   *Adding bugs in the stories backlog*

Bugs Not Managed with Requirements or Tasks

With this setting, you can add bugs only on work items tab (see Figure 3-39) or while you perform testing, which we will discuss in the *Hands-on Azure Tests* book of this book series.

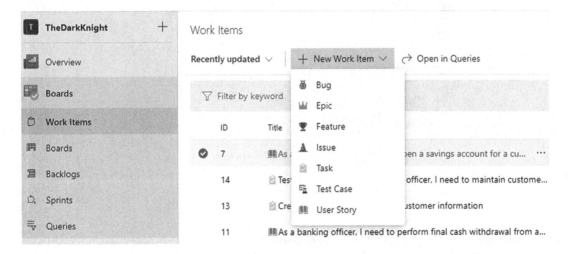

Figure 3-39. *Adding bugs in work items*

In this lesson, you explored the Bug work item behavior depending on the team's preferences.

Summary

The chapter covered managing hierarchal backlogs, using common work item fields, assigning work to iterations, and working with boards. Additionally, you explored the bug work item's behavior when team preferences are defined.

In the next chapter, we will show how to start customizing the boards to highlight the rich features you can enable to visualize information in Azure Boards to help your team to work productively.

CHAPTER 4

Work Item Notifications, Tags, and Customization

In the first half of this chapter, you will discover how to use tags in work items and how to subscribe to work item notifications in a team. In the next half of the chapter, you will focus on Azure Boards customizations. Azure Boards allows you to do multiple levels of customizations. In this chapter, you will be exploring how to customize cards in Kanban boards to emit valuable information. We'll also discuss how to change board columns and add boards to customize the workflow of Kanban boards.

Lesson 4-1. Setting Up Work Item Tags

Tags are markers on work items to denote their purpose or identify a specialty for a set of work items. This lesson explains how to add tags to work items and filter and search work items using the added tags.

Prerequisites: You need an Azure DevOps board with multiple work items.

Let's add a new tag first. This lesson shows how to add a tag to a user story. Open a User Story work item's card by clicking the title of it in the Kanban board.

Click the "Add tag" label next to the comments and add a tag value; for example, select Teller to denote this is related to a bank's teller operations. See Figure 4-1. Click the Save & Close button to save the changes. Use a meaningful value when adding the work item tags. For example, if the work item is related to an ATM withdrawal, you can add a tag called ATM.

© Chaminda Chandrasekara and Pushpa Herath 2019
C. Chandrasekara and P. Herath, *Hands-on Azure Boards*, https://doi.org/10.1007/978-1-4842-5046-4_4

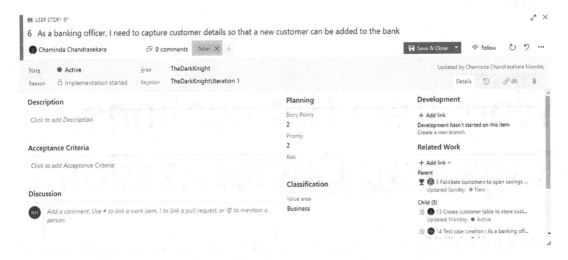

Figure 4-1.   Adding a tag to a work item

It is possible to add more than one tag to a work item. If you want to add more tags, click the + sign next to an added tag value. If you want to remove a tag value, click the X icon on the tag. Since you have learned how to add a tag to a work item, it is worth exploring the uses of tags.

You already know you can add hundreds of work items to a single project. If you need to find a few specific work items among these hundreds of work items, you need an easy way to do that. Azure DevOps provides a lot of filtering options to help you find a work item easily. Filtering by tag is one of the filtering options available in Azure DevOps. You can add your own tag names and filter work items using them.

Click the filter icon, and you will see there is an option to filter work items by tags. Also, you can filter values by selecting more than one filter at once. See Figure 4-2.

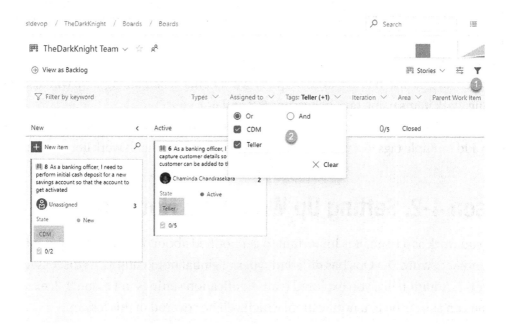

Figure 4-2. *Filtering work items using tags*

Azure DevOps allows to search work items with the tag values in addition to filtering. In the search box in Azure DevOps, type **Tags:** and then the names of tags within double quotes. You'll see a drop-down with suggestions on applying operators and filter fields. See Figure 4-3. After that, press Enter to start searching. You can give multiple tag values using operators.

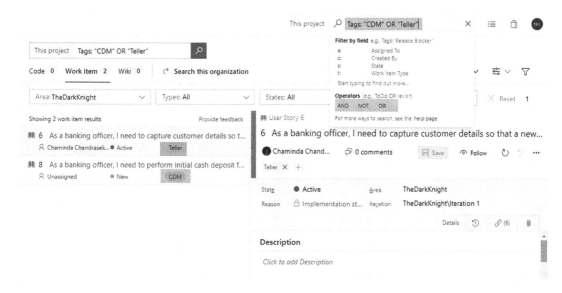

Figure 4-3. *Searching work items using tags*

Another feature available in Azure DevOps is that you can highlight these added tags by coloring them. This option is available only in Kanban board cards. Tag colors will be explained in Lesson 4-3 of this chapter.

Azure DevOps also has a feature to query work items based on tags. We will discuss querying work items using tags in Lessons 6-2 and 6-4.

We identified the use and importance of tags in this lesson. Additionally, you learned how to add multiple tags to a work item and how to filter and search work items using tags.

Lesson 4-2. Setting Up Work Item Notifications

When you work as a team, it is important to get notified about the changes happening in the project. Azure DevOps has different types of global notifications, as discussed in Lesson 1-7. Additionally, you explored team notification settings in Lesson 2-2, except how you can subscribe to a notification, which will be covered in this lesson.

Let's add a new notification and send a notification mail to selected members of the team when a work item changes.

Go to the project settings and select Notifications under Project Settings in the required team's scope. Then click "New subscription" to add a new notification. See Figure 4-4.

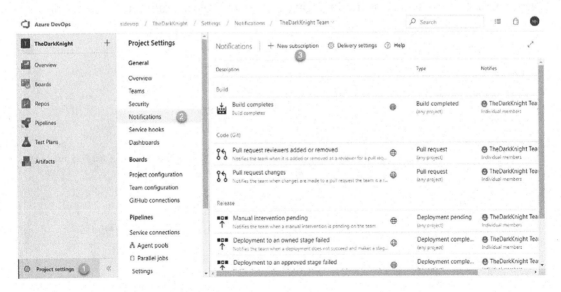

Figure 4-4. *Adding a new notification*

A new window will open. You can select a notification category and template from this window. To send a notification for work item changes, select Work in the Category section and select "A work item is changed" in the Template section. See Figure 4-5. Then click Next to move to the next step.

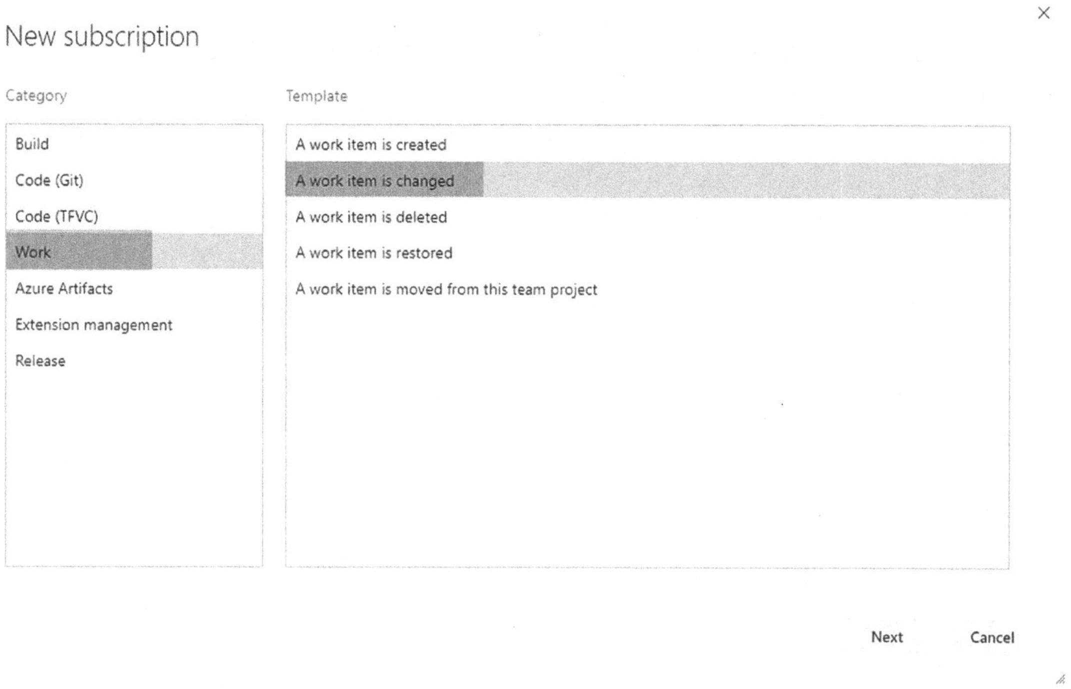

Figure 4-5. *Selecting a category to create a notification*

Let's identify the template items in the Work category.

- **A work item is created**: Mail receivers will be notified when a new work item is added.

- **A work item is changed**: Mail receivers will be notified when a work item is changed.

- **A work item is deleted**: Mail receivers will be notified when a work item is deleted.

- **A work item is restored**: Mail receivers will be notified when a work item is restored from the Recycle Bin of Azure Boards.

- **A work item is moved from this team project**: Mail receivers will be notified when a work item is moved from the team project to another team project.

After clicking the Next button, you will navigate to the window where you can select the notification receivers. See Figure 4-6.

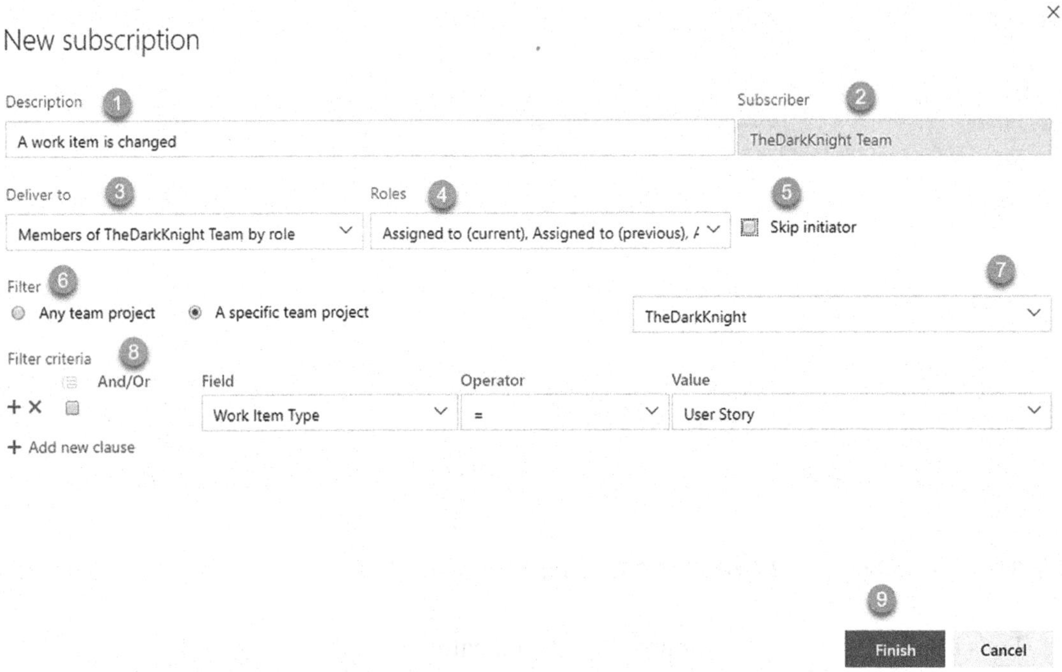

Figure 4-6. *Adding a notification receiver*

1. This is a description of the work item.

2. This is the creator of the notification.

3. Select the notification receivers from this drop-down. There are several options to select the notification e-mail receivers. See Figure 4-7.

Figure 4-7. *Drop-down to select notification receivers*

a. A notification is sent to the members of TheDarkKnight team, which has a selectable role. See Figure 4-8. As an example, the notification is sent to a previously assigned user of the changed work item.

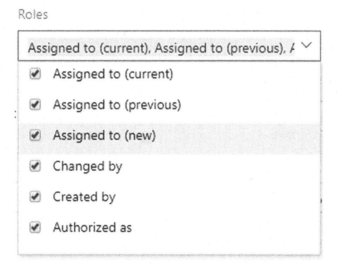

Figure 4-8. *Roles*

b. "Deliver to" recipients are determined by the delivery setting of the team or group.

c. A notification is sent to the custom e-mail addresses provided separated by a comma.

129

    d. All members of the team receive notifications.

    e. SOAP allows you to define a URL where you can develop a web app/API that can receive SOAP messages.

4. Here you give values for the "Deliver to" drop-down selections.

5. No notification is delivered to the user who initiated the event when "Skip initiator" is cheeked.

6. You can use the Filter options to select the team project.

7. Select the team project.

8. Add queries to define the filter criteria. You can add other fields and change the filter criteria to create a custom notification.

9. Create and save the notification.

You can find the newly added work item in the Notifications section. See Figure 4-9.

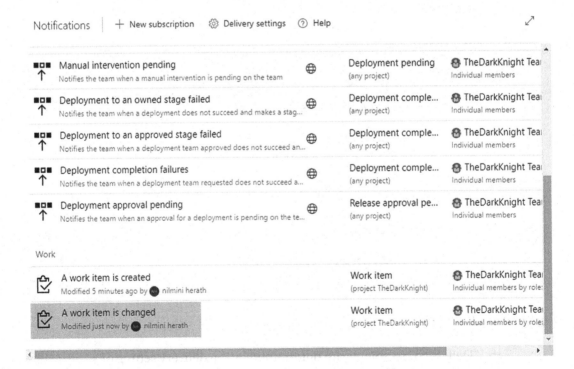

Figure 4-9. *Newly added notifications*

When you subscribe to notifications, you will receive an e-mail based on the notification settings. For example, you'll receive a notification that a work item has been assigned when someone else assigns you a work item. See Figure 4-10.

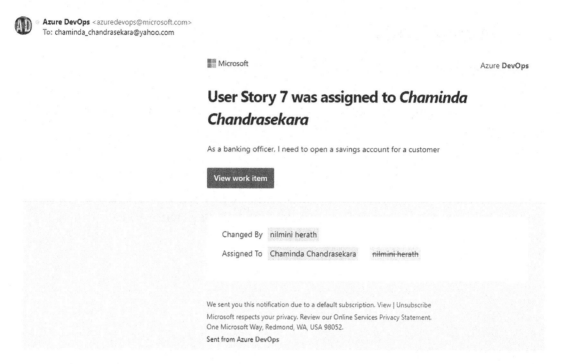

Figure 4-10. *Work item assigned a notification e-mail*

We discussed Azure DevOps team notifications in this lesson. You learned how to create a work item notification and verify notification was sent to the relevant receivers as defined.

Lesson 4-3. Customizing a Kanban Board's Card

Kanban board cards can be customized to visualize the information of the backlog effectively in Azure Boards. In this lesson, you'll learn about the Azure DevOps Kanban card customization capabilities.

Prerequisites: You need a backlog with work items.

Azure DevOps allows to customize epic, feature, and storyboard cards separately. You can have different card views for each board. The main purpose of card view customization is to track the project's progress easily at the team meetings such as the daily standups.

Go to the Stories board and click Settings.

The Board settings window will open. You can find the Fields section under Cards. Let's start with the field customization.

Customizing Fields

Azure DevOps provides various cards with customization options. You can select the fields that need to be displayed on the cards.

You will see two main sections in the field customization area. One is the core field area where default fields are displayed. The other area is the "Additional fields" area where you can add new fields to the cards.

There are core fields with a check box to the left of each field name. If you want to remove a core field from the card view, you can deselect the check box next to that core field.

Core fields are ID, assigned to, Story point, and tags. See Figure 4-11.

Figure 4-11. *Core fields*

You can add any field by clicking the + Field button and selecting a field name from the drop-down. If you want to remove a field, you can remove the field by clicking the red X to the right of the field value. At the bottom of the page you will see a check box that allows you to decide whether empty fields should be displayed on cards. See Figure 4-12.

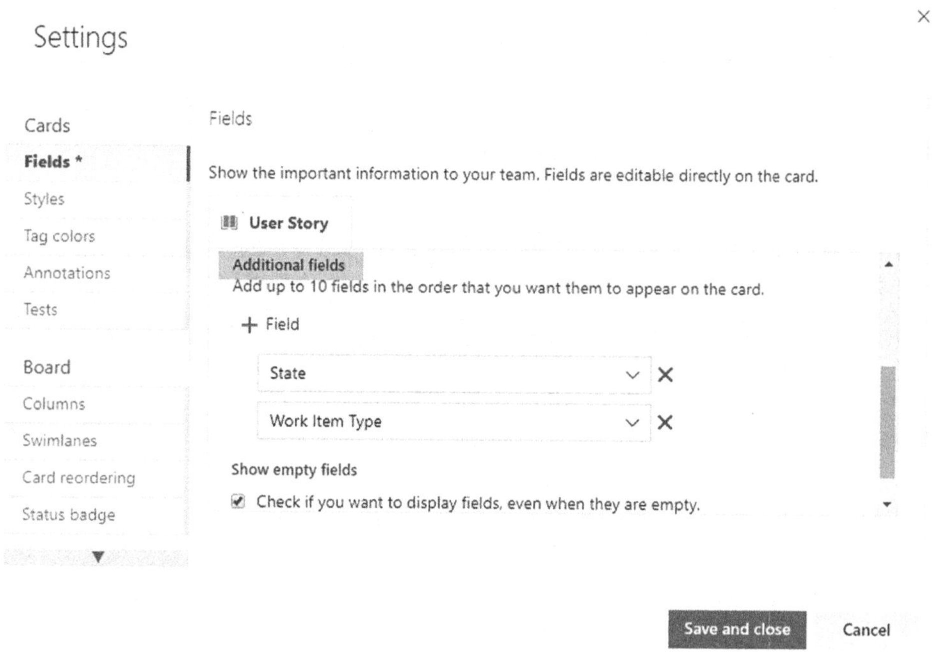

Figure 4-12.   *Additional fields*

In our example, we have four core fields and two additional fields in the storyboard cards. Let's go to the storyboard and verify the fields on the card. See Figure 4-13.

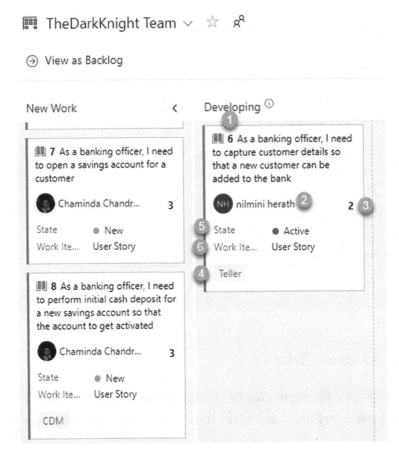

Figure 4-13. *Story board card fields*

1. Work item ID

2. Assigned team member

3. Story points

4. Tag value

5. Work item state

6. Work item type

You can see all the selected field values displayed on the story board. If you go to the epic or features board, these field values are not visible on the card.

So far, you have seen how to customize Kanban board cards. If you move to the task board of the sprint, you can add different customizations. Go to the settings of a task board. You can add the same rules to the task, bug, and user story of the task board. See Figure 4-14.

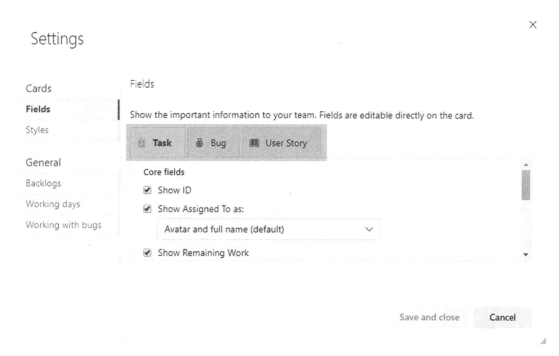

Figure 4-14. *Task board with multiple work item customizations*

You have learned about the different board card field customization options available with Azure DevOps. Now let's discuss how to add card-style rules.

Adding Card-Style Rules

Azure DevOps has a board customization feature that allows you to add styling rules to cards. When a work item matches the criteria of more than one rule, the first rule is used and applied to the card. Let's add a few rules to the work items.

Go to a story board and open the Settings dialog. Select Styles in the Cards section. Click the Styling rule to add a new rule.

For the name of the first rule, enter **No recent state change**. Set it up so that the work item card's color changes to red if the card stays in the same state for more than five days. See Figure 4-15.

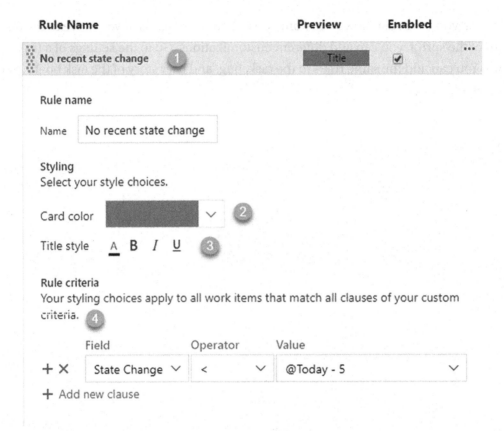

Figure 4-15. *Adding the card rule*

Let's identify each section of the rule.

1. This is the rule name. You can enter any meaningful name.

2. You can change the card color. The cards that meet the rule requirements change to this color.

3. You can change the card title fonts in this section.

4. You can add rule criteria in this section.

For the second rule, enter **Current Iteration Items for the name, and set up the** rule as shown in Figure 4-16.

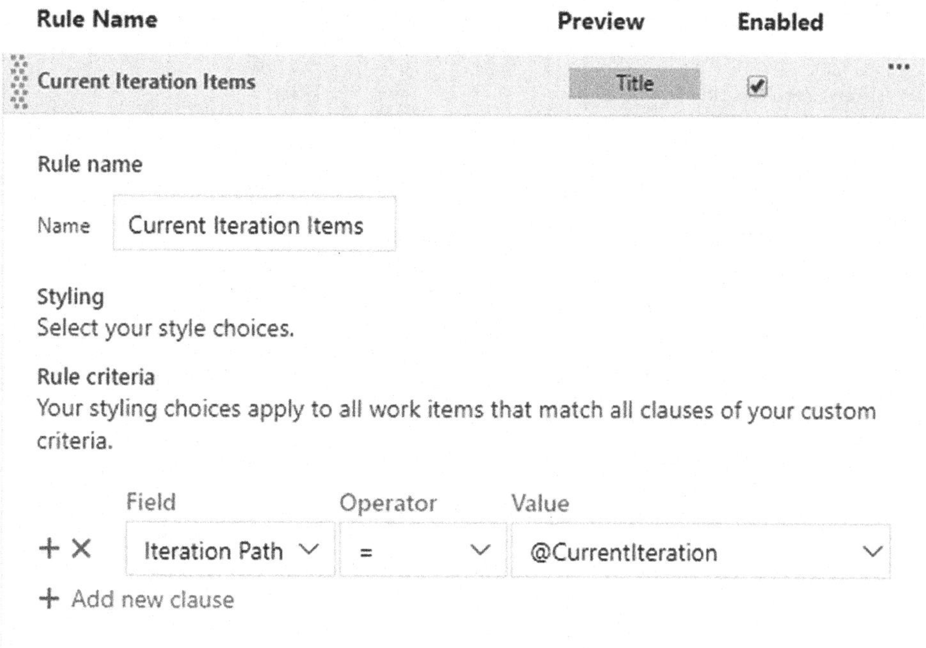

Rule Name   **Preview**   **Enabled**

Current Iteration Items   Title   ☑   ...

Rule name

Name   Current Iteration Items

Styling
Select your style choices.

Rule criteria
Your styling choices apply to all work items that match all clauses of your custom
criteria.

	Field	Operator	Value
+ ✕	Iteration Path ⌄	= ⌄	@CurrentIteration ⌄

+ Add new clause

Figure 4-16. *Rule to view current iteration items in blue*

For the third rule, enter **Current Iteration Title Font Change** for the name.
Set it up to change the title fonts and colors based on the current iteration. See
Figure 4-17.

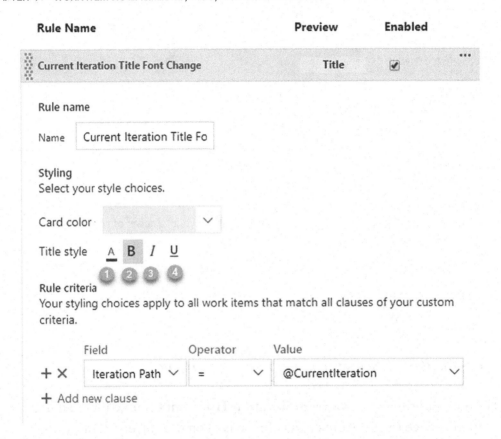

Figure 4-17. *Changing work item title fonts*

You can make the following changes to the work item's font:

1. Change the font color.

2. Use bold for the title text.

3. Use italics for the title text.

4. Underline the title.

You can add different style rules to the cards and keep rules in the disabled state. These rules are used only when they are in enabled mode. See Figure 4-18.

Figure 4-18. *Style rules list*

Click the three dots on a rule. Then you will be able to see the pane that allows you to perform three actions on the rules.

1. Delete the rule.

2. Create a clone of the rule.

3. Rule order is important because the first one applies when more than one matches for a work item. You can change the order of the rules using this option.

By adding these types of rules, you can easily identify the progress of a project. As an example, if there is a work item in the same state for more than five days, there may be a blocking issue to complete that work. If these types of items are displayed on the board in a different color, team members can easily identify the work item and take the correct action. See Figure 4-19.

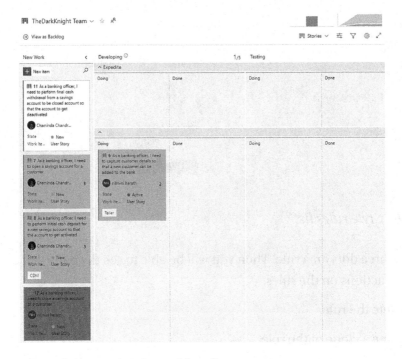

Figure 4-19. *Board customization with rules*

So far, we have discussed two card customization options. Let's see another available feature in Azure DevOps.

Go to Boards and open the Settings window. You will see the "Tag colors" section under Cards.

Setting the Tag Color

Click the "Tag color" icon.

Select the tag from the Tag drop-down and select the color of the tag. You can give colors to every tag available in the project backlog items. See Figure 4-20.

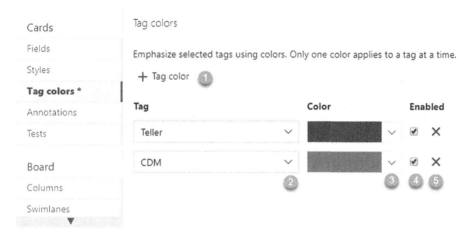

Figure 4-20. *Adding tag colors*

Let's identify each part of the page shown in Figure 4-20.

1. Add new tags.

2. Select a tag value from the drop-down.

3. Select the color.

4. Enable or disable the tag color.

5. Delete the tag color.

After adding the tag colors, save the changes. Go to the relevant board. You will be able to see that the tag colors have changed. See Figure 4-21.

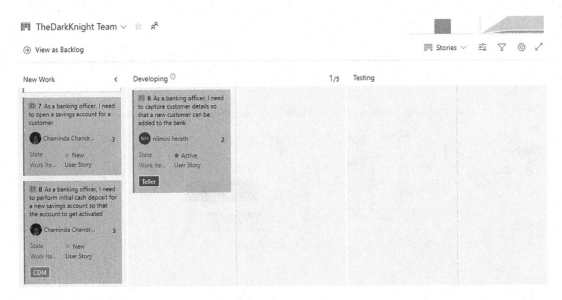

Figure 4-21. *Tag color changes on the board*

Let's discuss the Annotations section of the card customization options. You can find the Annotations section under Cards. Select Annotations.

By default, you will see three annotation values in the card customization section. They are Task, Bug, and Tests. See Figure 4-22.

Cards	Annotations		
Fields	Show visual cues on cards.		
Styles			
Tag colors	**Annotation**	**Visualization**	**Enabled**
Annotations *	Task	📋	☑
Tests	Bug	🐞	☑
Board	Tests	⚗	☑
Columns			
Swimlanes			

Figure 4-22. *Enabling and disabling an annotation*

We will discuss bug and tests in the *Hands-on Tests* book of this series. Note that we will discuss how a task's visual cues work here. You can decide whether tasks are displayed on the story card or not. You can enable or disable the task using the check box. If you disable a task from here, tasks are not displayed on the story board's cards. See Figure 4-23.

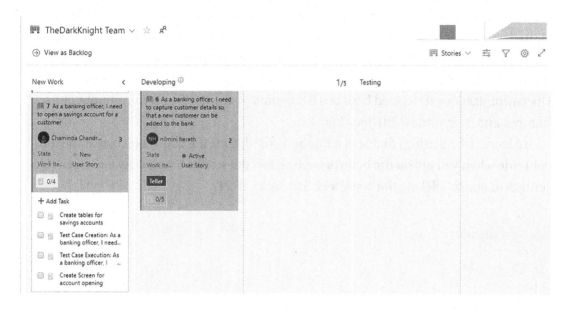

Figure 4-23. *Task displayed on the story items*

In the epic board, you can enable features as the child item to display on cards, while in feature cards you can display stories as the child item to display, similar to tasks in the story cards.

Customizing Tests

The Tests section in the card customization options will be discussed in the *Hands-on Tests* book of this series.

You learned different card customization features available in Azure DevOps in this lesson. You explored how to add new fields to a card, add card rules, and add tag colors. Finally, you saw how to customize annotations in this lesson.

Lesson 4-4. Customizing a Kanban Board's Settings

The Kanban board in Azure DevOps can be customized using the Settings dialog of the Kanban board. The customizations are limited but powerful when used in combination with the process customization at the project template (Agile/Scum/CMMI/Basic) level, which can be used to introduce new work items or to add new states and fields to work items. We will discuss these process customizations with project templates in Chapter 5. In this lesson, let's look at the available options in the Settings dialog that let you change the board's appearance by introducing new columns, splitting columns into ongoing and done lists, introducing swim lanes, reordering cards, and using status badges. The customizations described here can be applied to any backlog level, namely, epics, features, and user stories/PBI/requirements.

To launch the Settings dialog of a Kanban board, click the cogwheel icon at the top-right side when you are on the board's page. Select the stories board view and open the Settings dialog by clicking the cogwheel. See Figure 4-24.

Figure 4-24. *Launching the board's Settings dialog*

Customizing Columns

By default the Agile team backlog item process flow for epics, features, and user stories is New ➤ Active ➤ Resolved ➤ Closed. The New state is considered as belonging to the "Proposed state" category, and the Closed state belongs to the "Completed state" category. The in-between states, Active and Resolved, belong to the In Progress states. In the board's column customization settings, you are not allowed to alter the order or state used for the first column or for the last column in the board, which belong to the "Proposed state" and "Completed state" categories, respectively. The only context menu option available for the first column is Insert Right, which will add a new column to the right of the first column. The last column's context menu has an Insert Left option, allowing you to add a column to the left of the last column in the Kanban board. However, you can alter the name of the first and last columns of the Kanban board to suit your preferences. Let's rename the first column to New Work. See Figure 4-25.

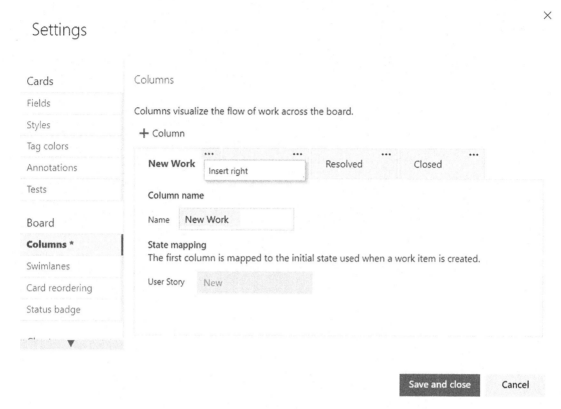

Figure 4-25. *Customizing the first column of the Kanban board*

Now let's move to the second column, Active, and do some comparison to the first column as well as some customizations. See Figure 4-26.

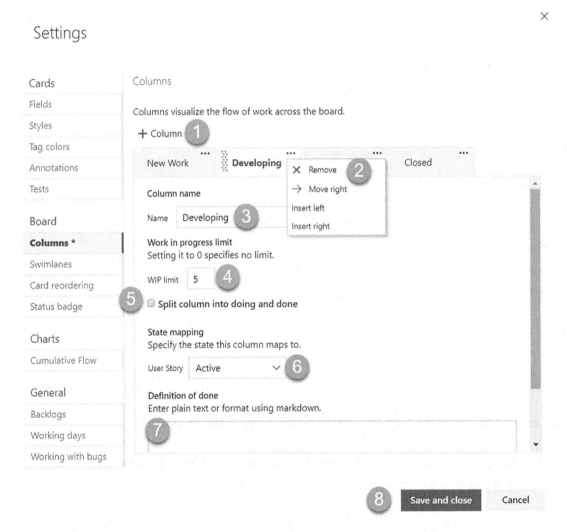

Figure 4-26. *Customizing the in-progress column*

1. This allows you to add a column to the left of the selected column. When you select the first column and click this button, the new column will be added to the right of the first column.

2. The context menu of the In Progress category columns will allow you to remove a column. You can move a column left or right (in Figure 4-26 the column can be moved only to the right since it is next to the first column), and you can insert another column to the left or right side of the current column.

3. You can rename the column to suit your preferences. Let's rename Active to Developing.

4. You can set a limit for the work in progress (WIP) for the column. This means you should not have more work items than the number specified for the WIP limit. However, this does not prevent you from adding more items to the Kanban board column than the specified limit. Rather, it will indicate the work in progress limit has been exceeded by changing the color of the number that appears on top of the column to red. See Figure 4-27.

Developing   4/3

Figure 4-27. *Exceeding the work in progress limit*

5. Splitting columns into Doing and Done helps you to identify two stages within the same column. Let's select "Split column into doing and done" for the Developing (Active) column.

6. The state mapping can be provided for the backlog work item type for the column. Dragging and dropping an item to a given column will make the state change to the specified state. This is useful when new states are introduced to work items that change the process flow, which we will discuss in Chapter 5. There can be multiple work item states to map. For example, if you are managing the Bug work items with the requirements (as you learned about in Lesson 3-6), you have to set both the work item states here. See Figure 4-28.

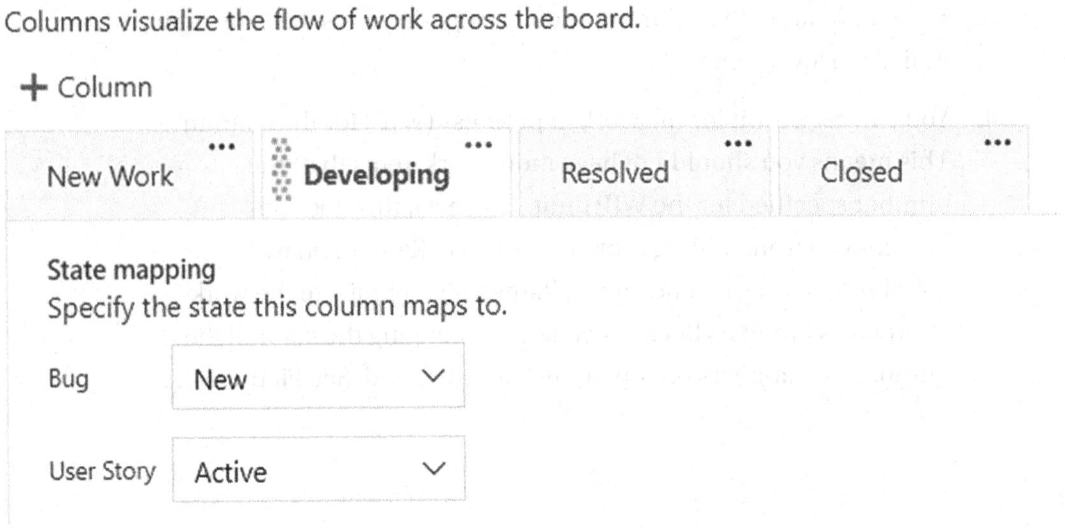

Columns visualize the flow of work across the board.

+ Column

New Work •••	⠿ **Developing** •••	Resolved •••	Closed •••

State mapping
Specify the state this column maps to.

Bug	New ⌄

User Story	Active ⌄

Figure 4-28. *Work item state mapping for column*

7. You can define a definition of done criteria for when you are considering a work item in this column done. When the item meets the criteria, it will be moved to the column on the right side or to the done area inside the column when it is split into Doing and Done. Let's add a definition of Done such as "All development tasks are closed by meeting the individual task acceptance criteria" to the Developing column. This will set a small information tag near the title of the column in the Kanban board, which will show the definition of Done for the column when you hover the mouse over that icon. See Figure 4-29.

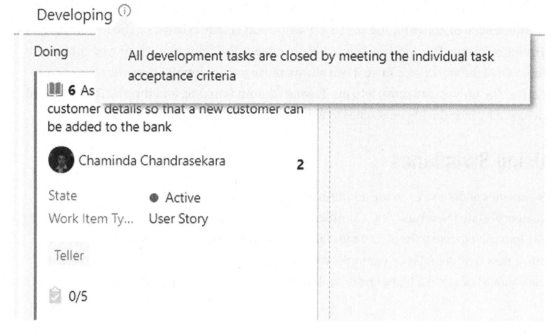

Figure 4-29. *Definition of Done in Kanban column*

Let's add another column in between Developing and Resolved and name it Testing. Set the user story's state as Active and split the column to Doing and Done.

8. Once all the changes are completed, click Save and Close to save the changes to the board columns. The board should look like Figure 4-30.

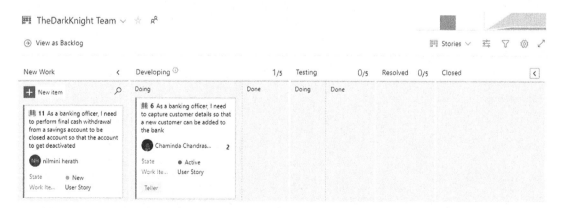

Figure 4-30. *Kanban flow modified*

Even though you successfully modified the Kanban workflow of the user story board, the same state of Active for the User Story work item is shared between the Developing and Testing columns. This makes it impossible to change the column to Testing by changing the state of the work item, since it will always move to Developing when the state is set to Active. The only way to move it to the Testing column is to drag and drop it. You can fix this behavior by introducing new states to work items, as will be explained in Lesson 5-3.

Using Swimlanes

Swimlanes allow you to create additional horizontal lanes in between the "Proposed category" state (New) and the "Completed category" state (Closed). In the Kanban board's Settings dialog, select the Swimlanes tab in the Boards section. Then click + Swimlane to add a new swimlane. As an example, you can name it Expedite to denote the work in this lane should be given a higher priority than the work items in other lanes. See Figure 4-31.

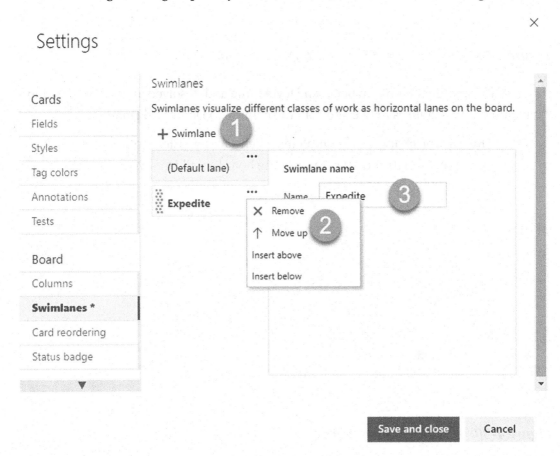

Figure 4-31. *Swimlanes settings for the Kanban board*

1. This allows you to add a swimlane above the currently selected swimlane.

2. You can remove a swimlane (Remove is not available for the Default lane), move a swimlane up or down, and insert a lane above or below the current lane options.

Let's move the newly added swimlane Expedite to the top and then save and close it. This will add the new Expedite lane to the Kanban board. You are able to collapse and expand when you have more than one swimlane in the Kanban board. See Figure 4-32.

Figure 4-32. *Swimlanes in Kanban*

Reordering Cards

In the Kanban board, the card reordering settings can be used to define the behavior of the card order when you drag and drop a card from a column to another column. To change the card reordering settings, select the "Card reordering" tab in the Boards section in the Kanban board settings. See Figure 4-33.

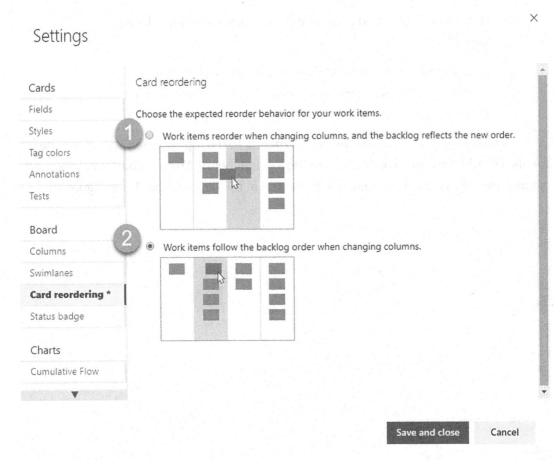

Figure 4-33. *Card reordering settings*

1. When you drag and drop the work item, depending on the place you are dropping, the work item will reorder in the backlog.

2. When you drag and drop, the work item will be automatically moved and positioned on the board depending on the order of work items set in the backlog. This will be the more desirable option if you are new to Azure Boards to prevent accidental reordering of backlog items.

Setting Up a Status Badge

A status badge can be used to quickly communicate the status of Azure Boards in dashboards. The "Status badge" settings can be changed in the Kanban board on the "Status badge" tab in the Boards section. See Figure 4-34.

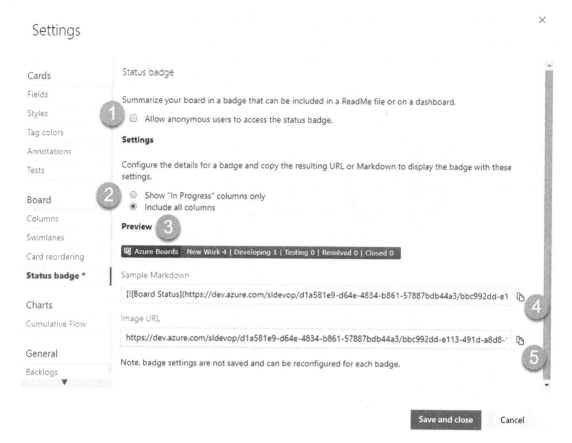

Figure 4-34. *Board's "Status badge" settings*

1. You can allow anonymous access to the status badge.

2. You can include all board columns or only the In Progress columns, which will omit the first and last columns from the badge.

3. A preview of the badge will be shown.

4. Copy the Markdown content, which you can use in the Markdown widget in the dashboard or in a team wiki page.

5. An image of the badge can be viewed using this URL.

The "Status badge" settings saved are not the ones getting applied when you are using it in wiki or dashboards. You can set your preferences and copy the Markdown or image URL and use the copied url in a web page or in a wiki page. Then change the preferences and get more Markdown code or an image URL. Both will work at the same time without any issues with different settings.

Let's copy the image URL of the status badge while allowing anonymous access and with all columns. Then paste it in a new browser window's address bar and press Enter. The badge will appear. Change the settings to the In Progress columns, open another browser window, and try accessing the URL. Now you will be able to see the status badge only with the In Progress columns in the board. See Figure 4-35.

Figure 4-35. *Status badge image in a browser*

The image URL can be used in a readme HTML file or in any other place where applicable to show the status of Azure Boards.

You can add the Markdown code of the status badge to a widget in the dashboard to enable users to view the badge in the dashboard. See Figure 4-36. We will discuss how to use the Markdown widget in a dashboard in Lesson 6-8.

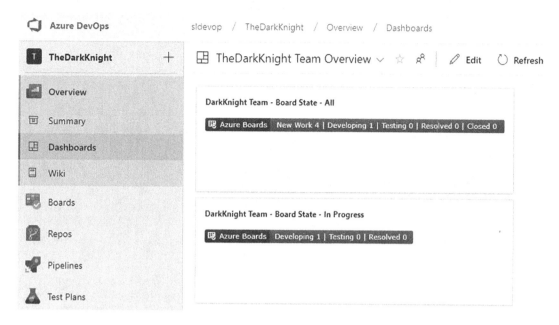

Figure 4-36. *Board status badge in the dashboard*

In this lesson, we discussed how to change columns, add swimlanes, reorder cards, and use status badges. However, you do use these options to customize the task boards (sprint/iteration boards). Customizations to task boards can be applied only via state changes to task work items, which will be discussed in Lessons 5-3 and 5-4.

Summary

In this chapter, we discussed how to subscribe to work item notifications in Azure Boards. Further, we showed how to set up Kanban board card style customizations including adding fields, changing colors, and using tag colors. We also showed how to change columns, add swimlanes, reorder cards, and use status badges.

In the next chapter, we'll proceed to the process customizations that will allow you to apply more changes to how Azure Boards and work items behave so that you can change Azure Boards to model how you want your process to flow.

CHAPTER 5

Customizing the Process

We discussed how to customize Kanban boards and cards in detail in the previous chapter. Adding on to that knowledge, this chapter will take you further through the journey of customizing Azure Boards. We'll discuss how to customize work items, change work item state flow, introduce new work item types, and show how to add top-level backlogs on top of epics, features, and stories. Additionally, custom work item rules can give you the capability to set up custom behaviors on work item fields to cater to various business scenarios. We will not cover the XML-based template customizations that are available for on-premises versions of Azure DevOps.

Prerequisites: You are the collection admin of the Azure DevOps server or services. (Setting up security will be discussed in Chapter 9.)

Lesson 5-1. Creating an Inherited Process

To customize an inherited process, you first need to create an inherited process template from the existing process templates. There are four process templates available in Azure Boards out of the box, namely, Agile, Scrum, CMMI, and Basic. You can inherit from any these templates to create a custom process.

Since you have used the Agile template throughout the previous chapters, in this lesson you'll create an inherited template of the Agile template. Go to the Azure DevOps home, select your desired organization if you have multiple organizations, and then click "Organization settings." See Figure 5-1.

© Chaminda Chandrasekara and Pushpa Herath 2019
C. Chandrasekara and P. Herath, *Hands-on Azure Boards*, https://doi.org/10.1007/978-1-4842-5046-4_5

Figure 5-1. *"Organization settings" item*

Under Organization Settings on the left, select Process in the Boards section. See Figure 5-2.

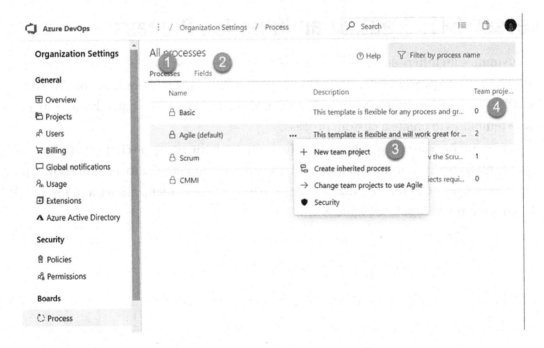

Figure 5-2. *Process item*

Let's identify the areas on the Processes page.

1. This shows the process templates available. Out of the box there are four templates.

2. All the fields in the work items are listed here. We will discuss this tab in Lesson 5-2.

3. In the process template's context menu, you can create a new team project with the template, create an inherited process template, change existing projects to use the template, and manage the security of the template.

4. This shows the number of projects that are using the process template.

Let's go ahead and create an inherited process template of the Agile process by clicking "Create inherited process" in the context menu. A dialog box will open, and you can enter a name like **DemoAgileCustom** and a description for the inherited template. Then click the "Create process" button to create the new inherited template based on the Agile process template. See Figure 5-3.

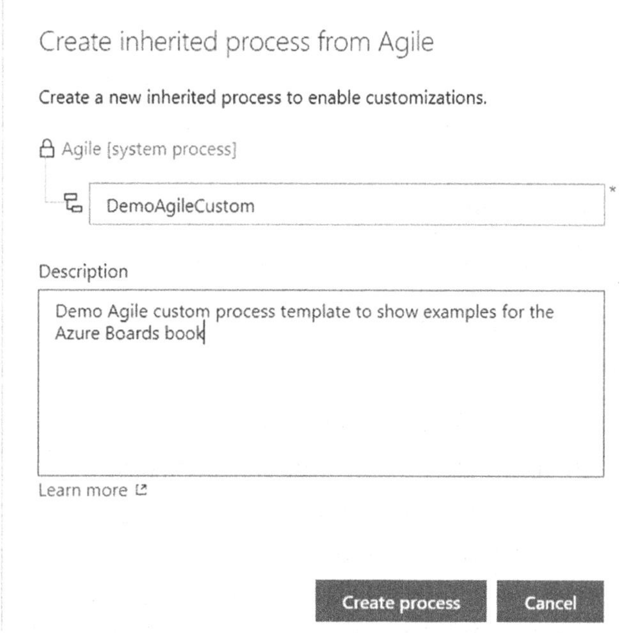

Figure 5-3. *Creating an inherited process*

Let's inspect the context menu of the newly created inherited process template. See Figure 5-4.

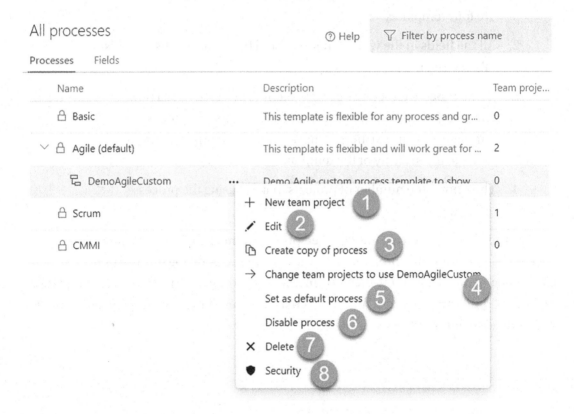

Figure 5-4. Inherited process template context menu

1. Create a new team project with the process template.

2. Edit the name and description of the process template.

3. Create a copy of the current template as an inherited template of the parent template.

4. Change a project that is in the parent (Agile in this case) process template or in any of the inherited templates of the parent template to use the current template. You cannot change a project in one of the other parent templates to use the inherited or parent template of the current selection. For example, the Agile template or its inherited templates can be used, but only by the team

projects that are already using Agile or its inherited processes. Moving a project from one of the default templates to another default or its inherited processes is not allowed.

5. Set the template as the default for the organization, which will be selected as the default template when you try to create a new team project from the organization home page or on the Projects tab of the organization settings, as described in Lesson 1-2. The "Set as default process" menu option is available in any template context menu other than the current default template context menu.

6. You can disable any process template other than the default one. Any existing team projects using the template will work fine after disabling the template. However, you will not be able to create new projects or change existing projects to use a disabled template. Nevertheless, you will be able to create an inherited process from a disabled template if it is an out-of-the-box one, or you can copy the process if it is an inherited one. The context menu options will change once a process template is disabled, and it will let you enable the process via the context menu instead of the disable option.

7. Deleting is possible for any inherited custom process template as long as the template is not set as the default template for the organization and the template is not used by any of the team projects.

8. Security for the process template can be set here. We will be discussing security options in Lesson 8-4.

Let's try to change the existing team project you have been using throughout this book to use the new custom inherited template by clicking "Change team projects to use DemoAgileCustom." In the dialog that appears, you can select the required project from "Available projects" and click OK to change the process template to the new inherited template. See Figure 5-5.

Change process

Change team projects to use the **DemoAgileCustom** process.

Available projects

☐ AgileTarget [Agile]

☑ TheDarkKnight [Agile]

Projects that will change process

TheDarkKnight

Learn more ⬈

Ok   Cancel

Figure 5-5. *Changing a project to use a given template*

You explored the ability to create an inherited process template from the out-of-the-box templates available in Azure DevOps in this lesson. Further, you selected a project that was using the Agile template and changed it to use the inherited Agile custom template.

Lesson 5-2. Editing Work Item Types

You can define how your work item type behaves, how the work item form should look, and what fields are shown in the work item by modifying the work item in the inherited process template. It is possible to introduce new fields to work items or make modifications to fields. Let's explore the options to modify work item types in this lesson.

Editing the Work Item Color and Icon

Clicking the name of the inherited process on the Process tab in the organization settings will open the process's "Work item types" tab. See Figure 5-6.

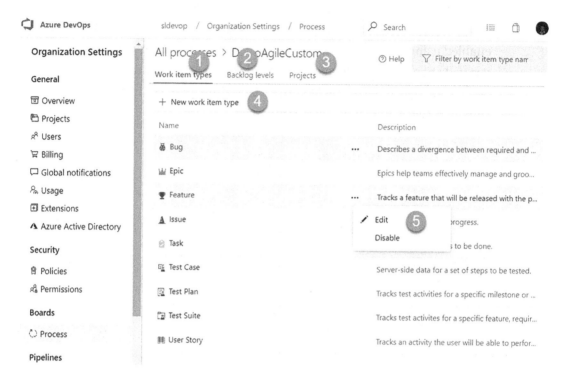

Figure 5-6. *Process template work item types*

1. This is the "Work items types" tab, which will list all the work item types.

2. These are the backlog levels of the process template. We'll explore this tab in Lesson 5-5.

3. Projects using the template are listed on this tab.

4. You can start creating a new work item type by clicking "+ New work item type," which we will discuss further in Lesson 5-4.

5. The work item type context menu will let you disable any work
    item type except Test Case, Test plan, and Test Suite. When a work
    item type is disabled, any project using the template cannot create
    new work items of the disabled work item type. However, any
    existing work items in a team project of the disabled work item
    type can still be used and updated. Disabled work items can be
    enabled using the same context menu once disabled; the menu
    text will change to Enable instead of Disable. Clicking Edit will
    open a dialog where you can edit the description, icon color, and
    icon of the work item type. See Figure 5-7.

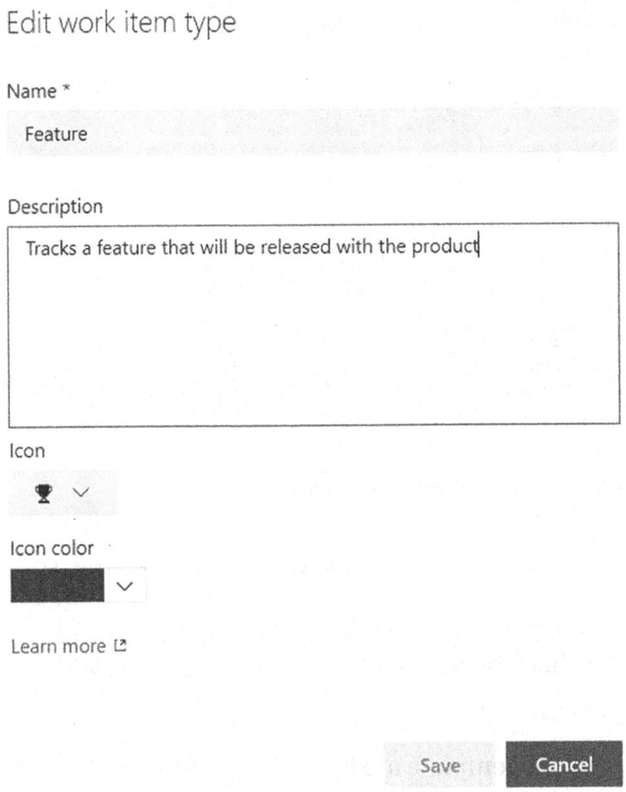

Figure 5-7. *Editing the work item type*

Modifying the Layout of the Work Item Form

Clicking a work item type name shown on the "Work item types" tab of the process template (see Figure 5-6) will take you to the Layout tab of the work item type. Let's open the layout of the User Story work item. You can see there is a page named Details and three columns in the layout. See Figure 5-8.

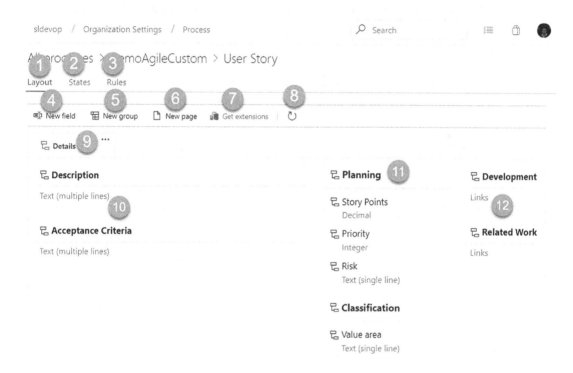

Figure 5-8. *Work item layout*

1. This is the Layout tab of the work item.

2. This is the States tab where you can change the state workflow of the work item type, which we will discuss in Lesson 5-3.

3. This is the Rules tab for defining custom rules for the work item type, which we will discuss in Lesson 5-6.

4. You can add a new field, which we will discuss later in this lesson.

5. You can add a new group, which we will discuss later in this lesson.

6. You can add a new page to the work item layout, which we will discuss later in this lesson.

7. You can use extensions from the marketplace in the work item layout, which we will discuss in Lesson 10-2.

8. You can refresh the layout.

9. This is the Details page. It has a context menu, which allows you to click Edit and open a dialog to edit the name of the page.

10. The Description and Acceptance Criteria fields both have a context menu, which allows the fields to be hidden from layout and allows you to edit the field's label. However, it is not possible to move the field out from the group that the field is in since it is an inherited field from the parent process. See Figure 5-9. Any other inherited field such as Story Points, Priority, and so on, has the same context menu and has the same restriction that you cannot change the group or column the field is appearing in by default.

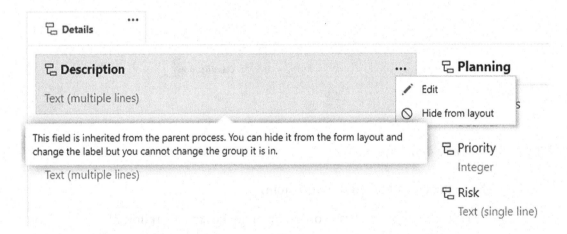

Figure 5-9. *Inherited fields context menu*

11. The Development and Related work fields can be hidden from the page layout but cannot be edited or moved to another position.

Editing an Inherited Field

Click Edit in the Description field's context menu. You will be able to edit only the label. See Figure 5-10.

Figure 5-10. *Inherited field label editing*

On the Options tab of the Edit field, you can set the field to be required and provide a default value for the field. See Figure 5-11.

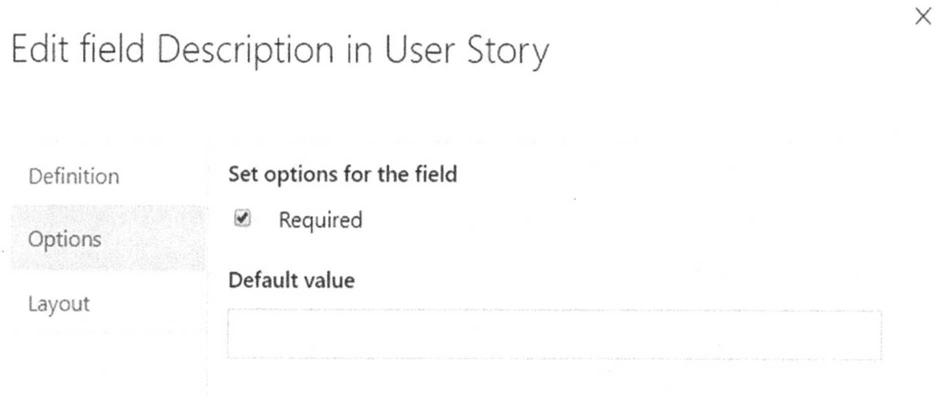

Edit field Description in User Story

Definition

Options

Layout

Set options for the field

☑   Required

Default value

Figure 5-11. *Inherited field options*

167

The information—namely, the name, type, or description—on the Definition tab of an inherited field cannot be edited.

Editing an Inherited Group

Inherited groups such as Planning have a context menu (see Figure 5-12) that allows you to add a new field to the group and edit the group name via a dialog. However, you can only edit the name of the inherited group and the column; where the group is currently positioned cannot be changed.

Figure 5-12. *Inherited group context menu*

Adding a New Page to the Layout

On the Layout tab of the work item, you can click "New page" (see Figure 5-8) to add a new page. You can provide a name for the page in the pop-up dialog and click OK to create a new page in the work item layout. The newly created page has a context menu with two options. Edit will allow you to edit the name of the page, and Remove will remove the page. See Figure 5-13.

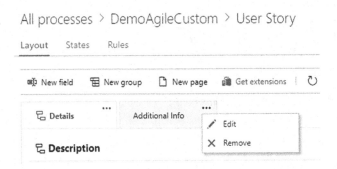

Figure 5-13. *New page in layout*

Adding a New Group to the Layout

You can click "New group" while you are in a layout page (see Figure 5-8) to add a new group to the page that is selected. A pop-up window will open, and you can provide a name for the group, select the page to add the group, and define the column that the group should be added to. See Figure 5-14.

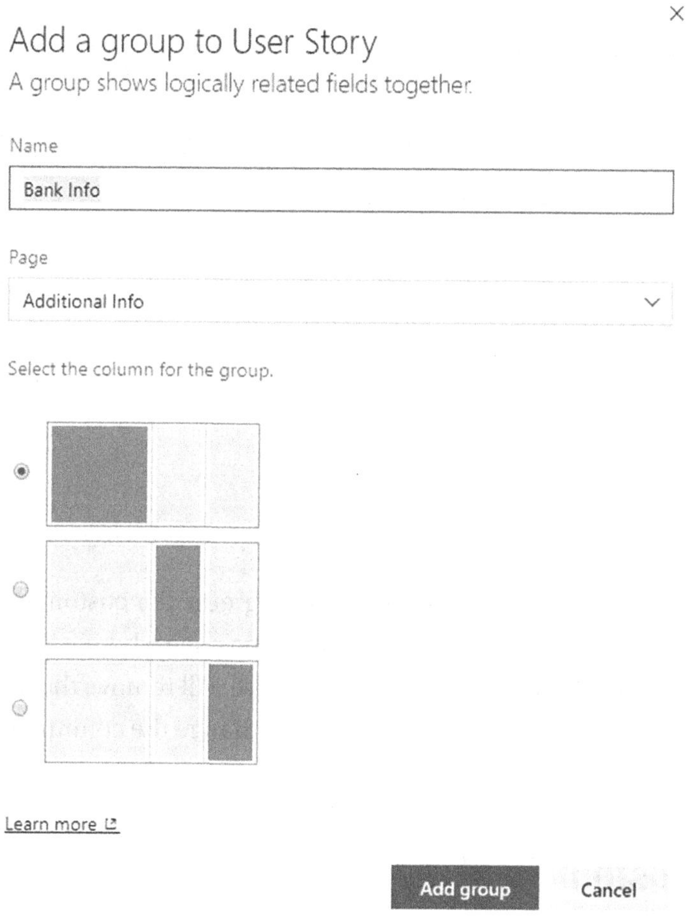

Figure 5-14. Adding a group

In a group, a few context menu options are available. See Figure 5-15.

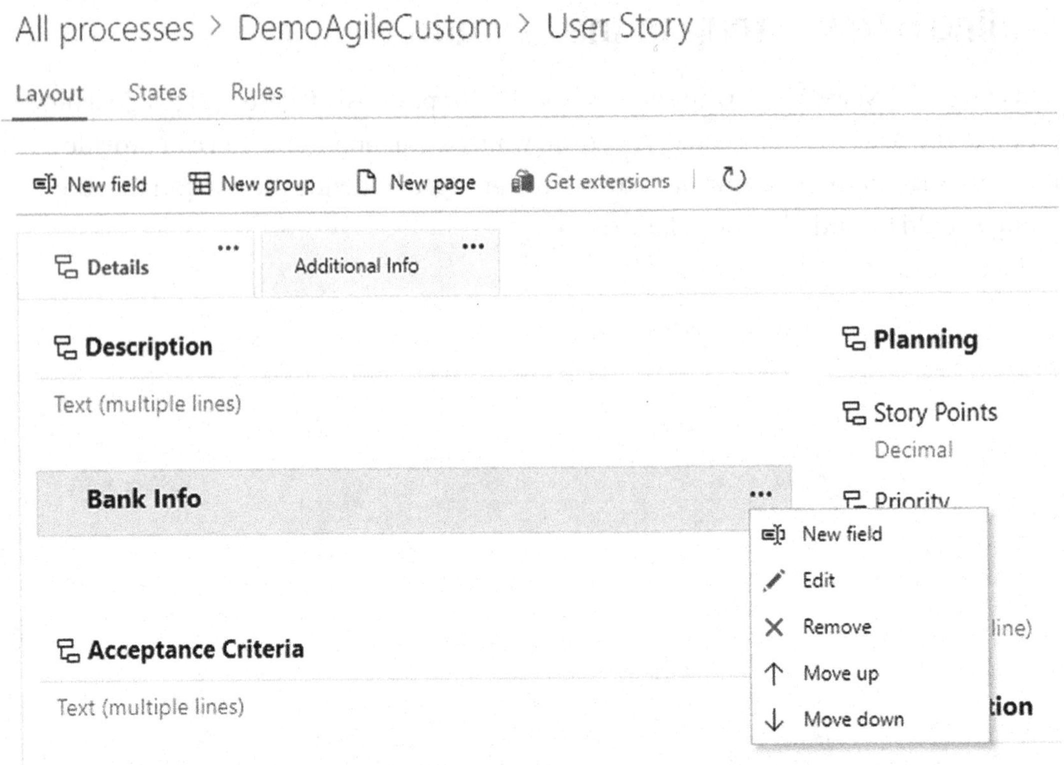

All processes > DemoAgileCustom > User Story

Layout   States   Rules

🖉 New field   ⊞ New group   🗋 New page   📇 Get extensions | ↻

| 🗀 Details   ··· | Additional Info   ··· |

🗀 **Description**   🗀 **Planning**

Text (multiple lines)   🗀 Story Points
                                                                   Decimal

   Bank Info   ···   🗀 Priority

🖉	New field
/	Edit
✕	Remove
↑	Move up
↓	Move down

🗀 **Acceptance Criteria**

Text (multiple lines)   **tion**

Figure 5-15. *Custom group context menu*

"New field" allows you to add a new field to the group. For custom added groups, you can edit and change the name, page, or column of the page where it is added. Edit can change the page of the group such as Details. Remove will remove the group. "Move up" and "Move down" or drag and drop can be used to change the column or position of the custom group within a layout page.

Adding a Custom Field

Let's add a new field to a User Story work item type group. For this you can click the New field in the group context menu or click "New field" on the layout page. On the Definition tab you can specify a name and select the type of data and provide a description. See Figure 5-16. Instead of adding a new field, you can add an existing field that is not already in the work item layout. If you are using an existing field, you are not allowed to change the data type or description. For this example, select a new field, type **Operation Area** for the name, and select "Picklist (string)" for the type. See Figure 5-16.

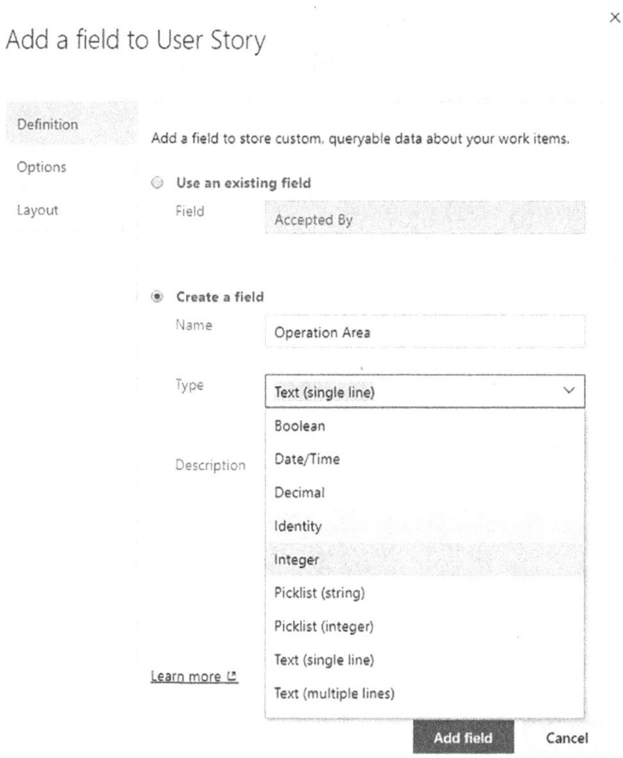

Add a field to User Story   ×

Definition   Add a field to store custom, queryable data about your work items.

Options   ○ Use an existing field

Layout   Field
                           Accepted By

                    ◉ Create a field
                    Name
                           Operation Area

                    Type
                           Text (single line)   ∨

                           Boolean

                           Date/Time

Description   Decimal

                           Identity

                           Integer

                           Picklist (string)

                           Picklist (integer)

                           Text (single line)

Learn more ⤢   Text (multiple lines)

                                                    Add field   Cancel

Figure 5-16. *Adding a new custom field*

When a pick list is selected, you can define values for the picklist. See Figure 5-17.

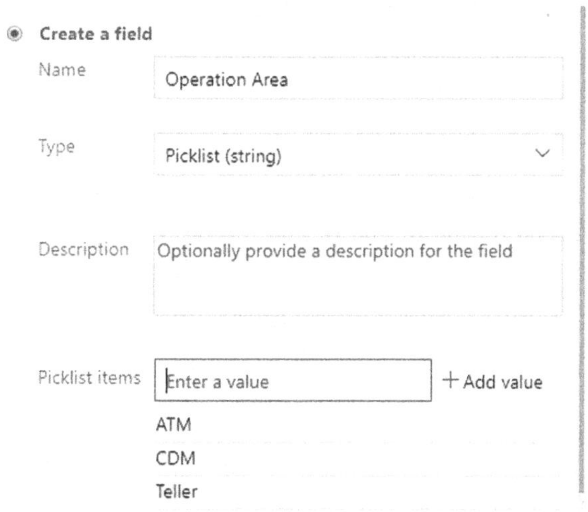

◉ Create a field
Name
       Operation Area

Type
       Picklist (string)   ∨

Description   Optionally provide a description for the field

Picklist items   Enter a value   ＋ Add value
                  ATM
                  CDM
                  Teller

Figure 5-17. *Picklist type custom field*

On the Options tab, you can set the field as required if necessary and set whether to allow user input other than the values in a picklist. Additionally, you can set a default value for the field. See Figure 5-18.

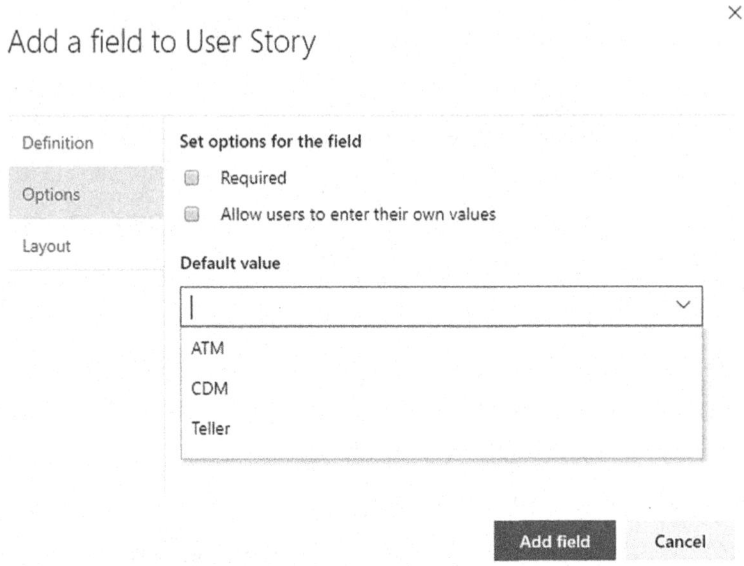

Figure 5-18. *New field options*

The Layout tab of the new field dialog allows you to define where the new field should be positioned by selecting the page and the group in the layout. You can even create a new group from here and add the new field to it. See Figure 5-19.

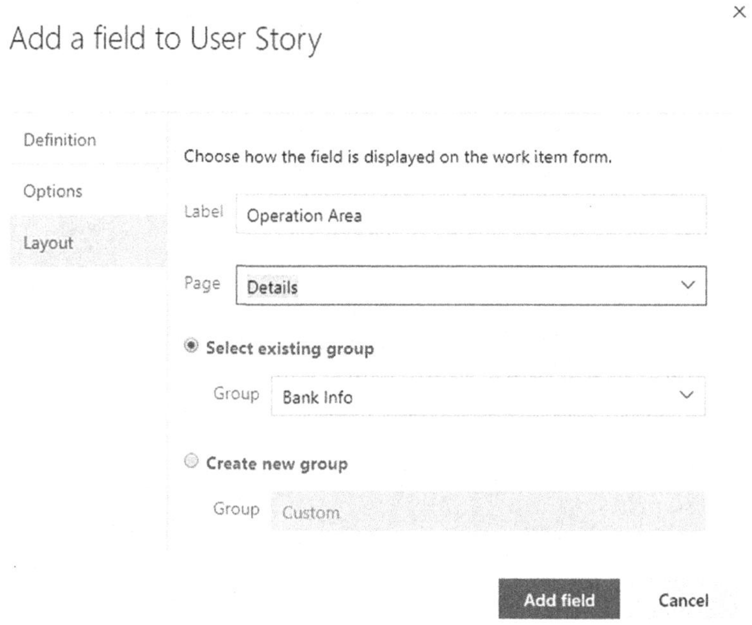

×

Add a field to User Story

Definition

Options

Layout

Choose how the field is displayed on the work item form.

Label   Operation Area

Page   Details   ∨

◉ **Select existing group**

Group   Bank Info   ∨

○ **Create new group**

Group   Custom

[**Add field**]   Cancel

Figure 5-19. *New field layout*

You can add or remove values for the picklist data type after creating the field using the Edit field in the field's context menu. However, once a new field is added, it cannot be renamed, and the data type cannot be changed. All other values such as whether it's required, the default value, and layout options can be changed by editing the field. Add the new field and inspect a User Story work item in a team project that is using the template that you modified. The new field should be visible in the work item. See Figure 5-20.

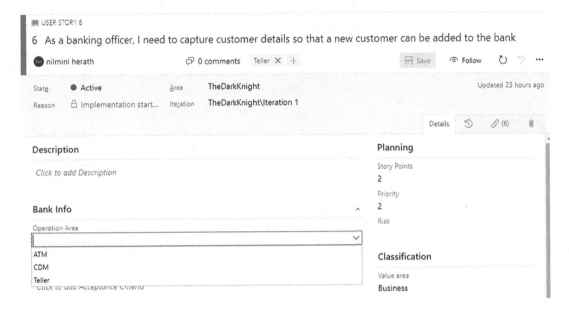

Figure 5-20. *New field in user story*

In this lesson, you looked at the work item layout change options and how you can add new custom fields to work item types.

Lesson 5-3. Changing the State Workflow of a Work Item

With the knowledge gained in the previous chapter, you know how to introduce a new workflow using Kanban columns. However, we discussed the issue of not being able to make the workflow changes effective when more than one Kanban column is sharing the same state. The change of state will always move the work item to the leftmost column in the board that is utilizing that state. To create effective state workflows, it is useful to have the ability to add or remove states in a work item type.

In Lesson 4-4, we added In Progress Kanban columns called Developing and Testing instead of Active and shared the Active state in both columns. Let's now create the actual Developing and Testing states for the User Story work item.

In the process template, select the User Story work item type and go to the States tab. You can see that the states are categorized into the groups Proposed, In Progress, Completed, and Removed. See Figure 5-21.

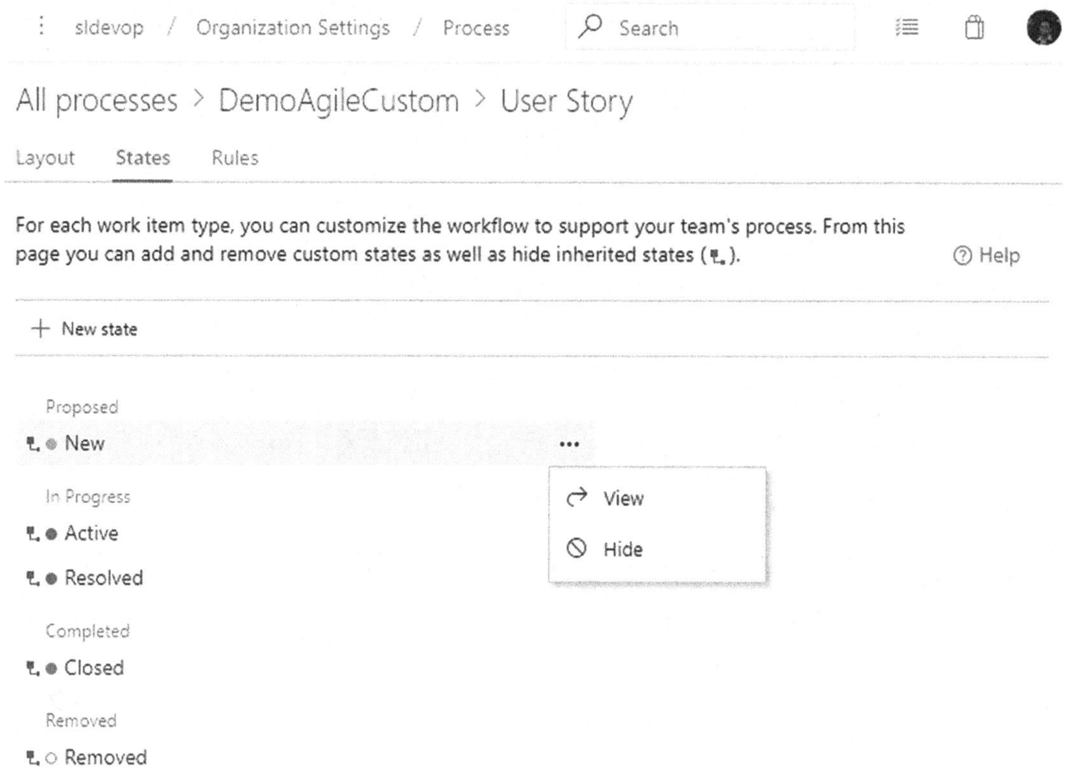

⋮   sldevop   /   Organization Settings   /   Process   🔍 Search   ☰   🗂   ⬤

All processes > DemoAgileCustom > User Story

Layout   States   Rules

For each work item type, you can customize the workflow to support your team's process. From this
page you can add and remove custom states as well as hide inherited states (⚑).   ⑦ Help

+ New state

Proposed
⚑ ● New   •••

In Progress   ⟶ View
⚑ ● Active
                                               ⊘ Hide
⚑ ● Resolved

Completed
⚑ ● Closed

Removed
⚑ ○ Removed

Figure 5-21. *Work item type states*

A context menu allows you to hide any out-of-the-box state except the Closed state.
But you must have at least one state available in each state category. Click the "+ New
state" button to add a new state. See Figure 5-21. A dialog will appear allowing you to
select the existing state name or provide a new state name; select the state category and
the color for the state. See Figure 5-22.

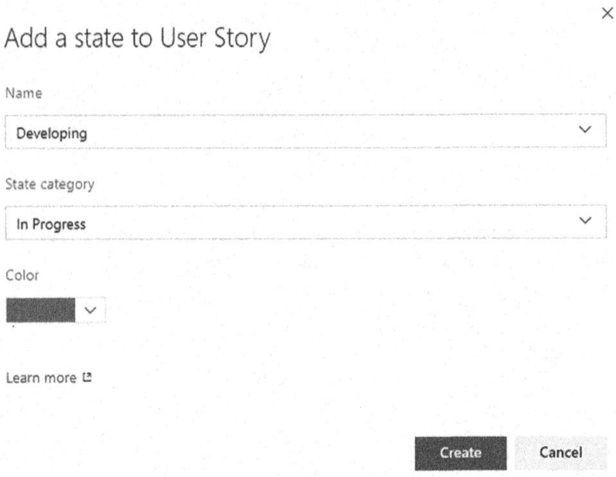

Figure 5-22. *Adding a new state*

Let's add new two states, Developing and Testing, to the Progress category and hide the Active state. See Figure 5-23.

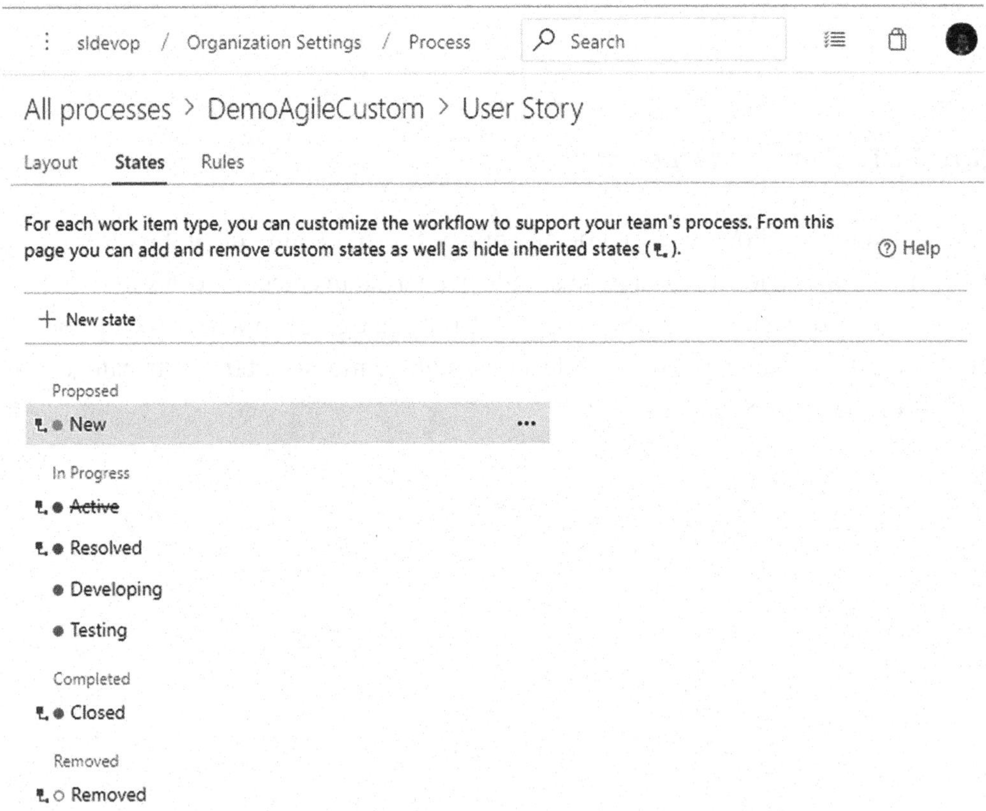

Figure 5-23. *Modified user story states*

When you view the user stories board in a team project that is using the changed process template, it will display an error message since you have hidden the Active state for the user story while it is already in use in the board columns. See Figure 5-24.

Figure 5-24. *User stories board in error*

You can follow the instructions in Lesson 4-4 and select the correct states using the Kanban board's Settings page for the columns Developing and Testing. This correction will make the Kanban board work. However, you will notice that the user stories that were in the Active state have disappeared from the board. You can go to the Work Items tab of the team project's Boards section to filter for all the user stories that are in the Active state. See Figure 5-25.

Work Items

Recently updated ∨ | + New Work Item ∨ ↗ Open filtered view in Queries ✏ Column Options ···

▽ Filter by keyword   **User Story** ∨   Assigned to ∨   **Active** ∨   Area ∨   Tags ∨   ✕

ID	Title	Assigned To	State
6	As a banking officer, I need to capture customer details so that a ne...	nilmini herath	● Active

Figure 5-25. *Active state user stories*

Then you can bulk edit and change them to either the Developing or Testing state appropriately so that they appear on the user's stories board. See Figure 5-26.

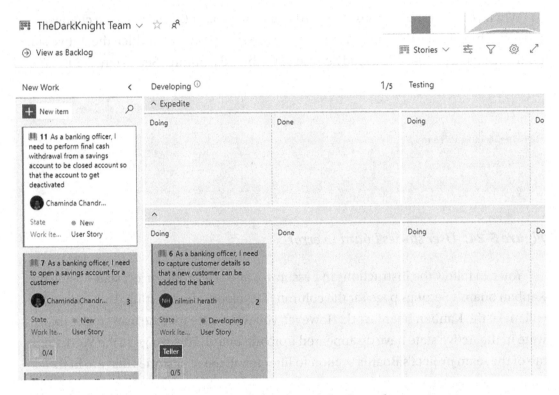

Figure 5-26. *Stories in new states appearing in the board*

In the same way, you can edit the state workflow of any other work item type such as Epic, Feature, or Bug. As explained in Lesson 4-4, the task board does not have the ability to add columns via the Settings page of the task board. However, if you change the state fork flow of the task work item, it will be automatically get applied to the task board columns. See Figure 5-27.

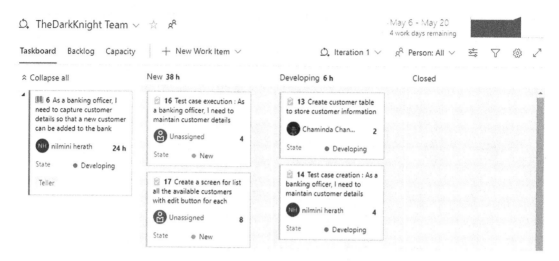

Figure 5-27. *Task board with state workflow changed to include Developing state*

We discussed how to change the state workflow of work item types in this lesson using inherited process templates.

Lesson 5-4. Adding New Work Item Types

Sometimes your teams may not find the exact type of work items you are looking for in the out-of-the-box templates. For example, you may need a work item to keep track of follow-up work. Or you may want to add a backlog level.

In this lesson, let's try to add a new work item type to the inherited Agile process template named Initiative that you can use in Lesson 5-5 to add as a new backlog level.

On the process template's "Work item types" tab, click "+ New work item type." See Figure 5-28.

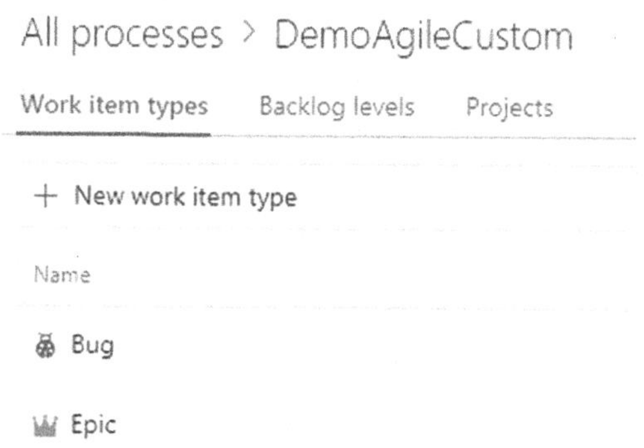

All processes > DemoAgileCustom

Work item types   Backlog levels   Projects

+ New work item type

Name

🐞 Bug

👑 Epic

Figure 5-28. *Clicking "+ New work item type"*

Provide a name and description and select an icon and color for the new work item in the pop-up dialog. See Figure 5-29.

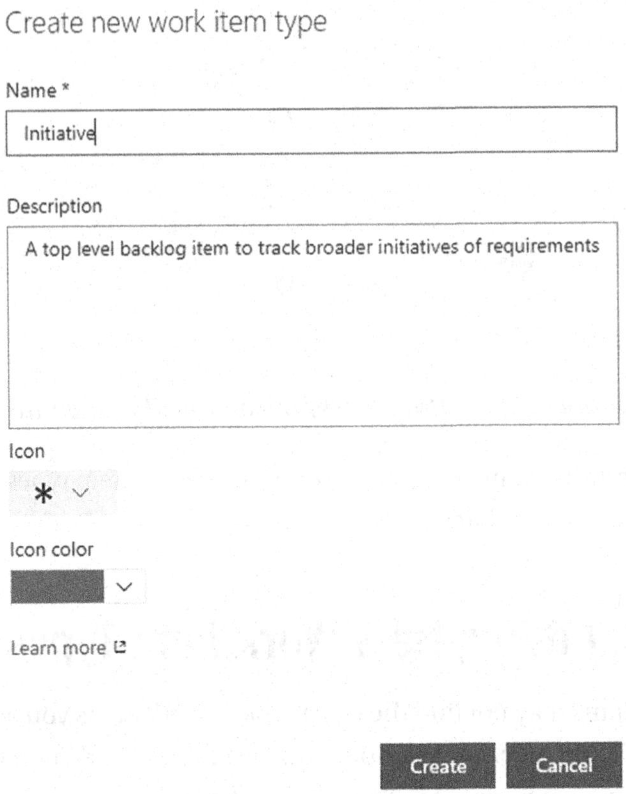

Create new work item type

Name *

Initiative

Description

A top level backlog item to track broader initiatives of requirements

Icon

* ∨

Icon color

∨

Learn more ↗

Create   Cancel

Figure 5-29. *Creating a new work item type*

Once the new work item type is created, you will see the layout page of the new work item. There you can add new fields from existing ones or as new custom ones as per the instructions in Lesson 5-2. Change the state workflow based on your preferences using the instructions in Lesson 5-3. In the Work Items tab of a team project using the modified template, now you can see the new work item type is available for you to add and use. See Figure 5-30.

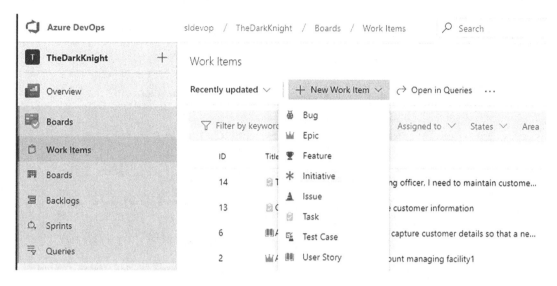

Figure 5-30. *New work item type*

In this lesson, you explored how to create a new work item type using an inherited process template.

Lesson 5-5. Adding a Top-Level Backlog

If you are handling a large project, you may want additional grouping levels for your backlog. With the new work item called Initiative created in Lesson 5-4, let's check how you can get it added as a top-level backlog.

Click the "Backlog levels" tab in the inherited process template. See Figure 5-31.

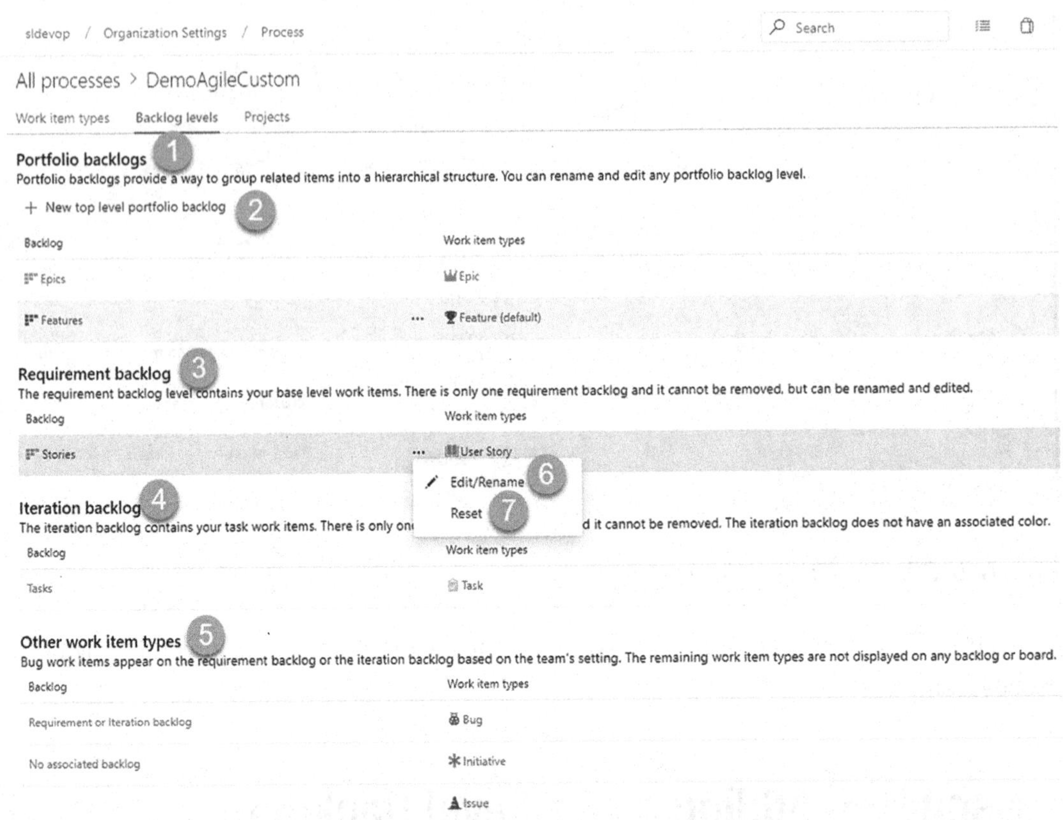

Figure 5-31. Backlog levels

1. This is the portfolio backlog level with the epic and feature levels out of the box.

2. You can add more top-level backlog levels to the portfolio backlog level.

3. This is the requirements backlog.

4. This is the iteration backlog.

5. This section contains other work item types. Note that the Bug work item is special, and it can be in a requirement or iteration backlog level. The newly added work item is also in the other backlog levels.

6. A context menu is available for the portfolio, requirement, and
    iteration backlog levels. Edit/Rename will open a dialog box
    where you can change the backlog level name, add available
    work items to the backlog level, and set a default work item type
    for the backlog level. Clicking "+ New work item type" in the
    "Edit backlog level" dialog lets you add a new work item type by
    providing a name icon and an icon color. See Figure 5-32.

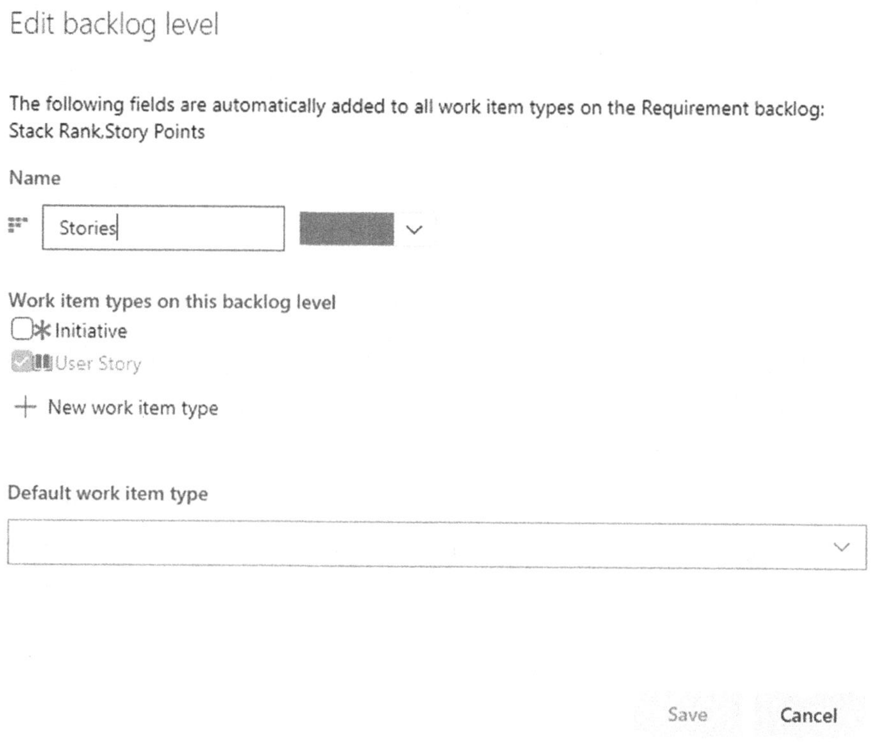

Edit backlog level

The following fields are automatically added to all work item types on the Requirement backlog:
Stack Rank.Story Points

Name

Stories

Work item types on this backlog level
Initiative
User Story

+ New work item type

Default work item type

Save   Cancel

Figure 5-32. *Editing the backlog level*

7. The Reset menu option will remove all custom changes made to
    the backlog level.

Let's click "+ New top level portfolio backlog" to create the Initiatives top-level
backlog for the Initiative work item you created. In the dialog box that opens, provide
a name for the backlog level, select a color, and check the Initiative work item. You can
select the default work item of this level as Initiative. Click Save to add the backlog level.
See Figure 5-33.

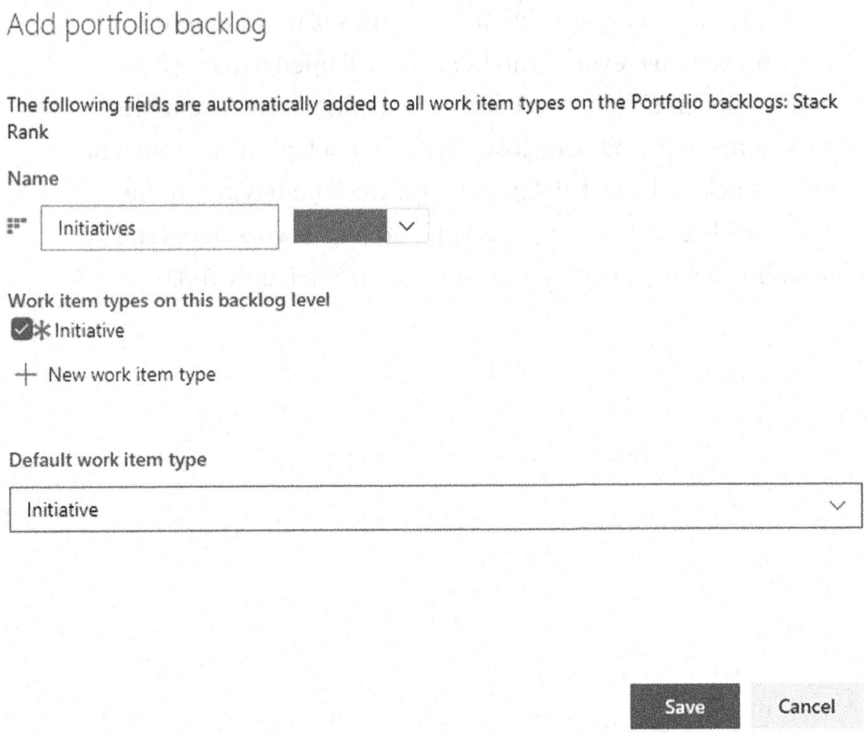

Add portfolio backlog

The following fields are automatically added to all work item types on the Portfolio backlogs: Stack Rank

Name

Initiatives

Work item types on this backlog level
☑ ✳ Initiative
+ New work item type

Default work item type

Initiative

Save   Cancel

Figure 5-33. *Creating a new top-level portfolio backlog*

Once the backlog level is added in a team project that is using the modified process template, go to the board settings, and on the Backlogs tab of the General section, select the new backlog level for the team. Save and close the Settings page. See Figure 5-34.

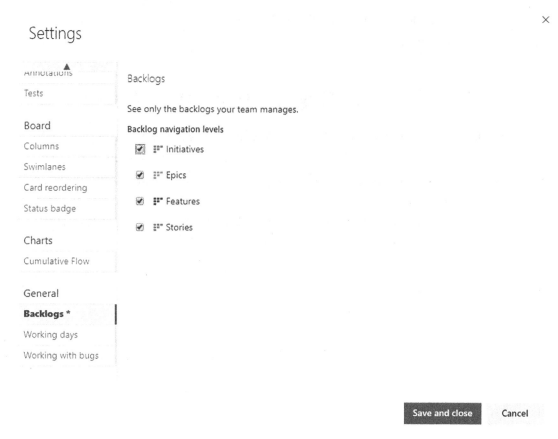

Figure 5-34. *New backlog level in board settings*

The Initiatives backlog will be available for the team, and you will be able to add child Epic work items to it. See Figure 5-35.

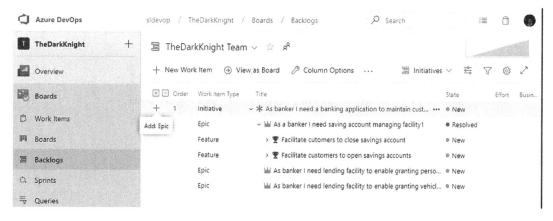

Figure 5-35. *New backlog level in use*

In this lesson, you learned how to add work items to backlog levels and how to create a top-level portfolio backlog level.

Lesson 5-6. Defining Custom Work Item Rules

As another level of customization to the process, you can define custom rules for each work item type in Azure Boards. The custom rules may help to control flow or make it mandatory to capture some valuable information based on the business requirements.

Prerequisites: You need to have performed all the previous lessons in this chapter.

In this lesson, let's explore how to define custom rules. Click the inherited process template User Story and select the Rules tab. See Figure 5-36.

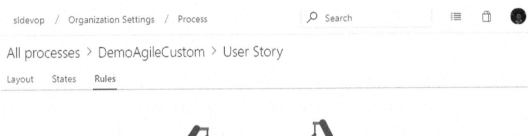

Figure 5-36. *Work item rules*

Clicking "New rule" will show the rule setup page. See Figure 5-37.

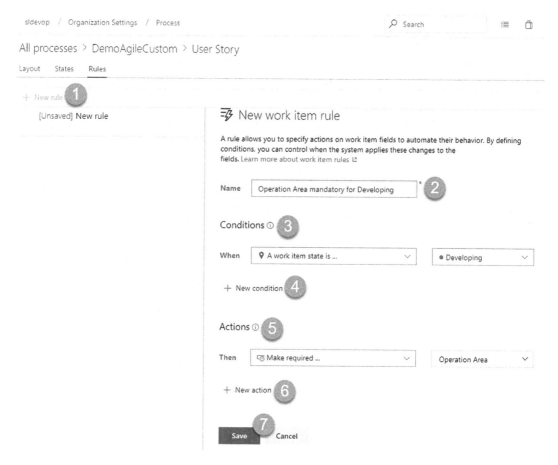

Figure 5-37. *Custom work item rule*

1. Once the first rule is added, "+ New rule" can be used to add more rules.

2. You can enter the name of the rule.

3. These are the conditions of the rule. You can select conditions from a predefined set of conditions available in the drop-down.

4. You can add additional conditions with an AND operator to the conditions.

5. These are actions to perform when the condition is true. Actions can be selected from a predefined actions set.

6. You can add more actions.

7. Save the rule.

As an example, select the condition that states when a user story state is Developing, make the new custom field Operation Area be a required field, and save the rule. If you haven't added the custom field, make the Description field required. In a team project where the modified process template is used, try to change a user story state to Developing without selecting the Operation Area/Description field. When trying to save the story, you will see an error saying the Operation Area/Description field cannot be empty. See Figure 5-38.

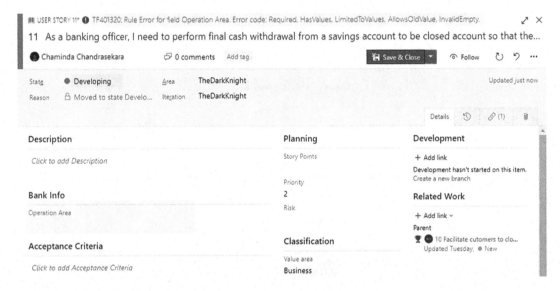

Figure 5-38. *Custom rule applied to user story*

Once you fill in the Operation Area/Description field, you will be able to save the story with a Developing state.

In this lesson, you explored how to define custom work item rules.

Summary

In this chapter, you learned about doing process customizations such as changing the work item layout, adding new custom fields, adding new work item types, and adding portfolio backlog levels. These lessons will be useful when creating your own process flow with Azure Boards.

In the next chapter, let's look at visualizing data using out-of-the-box reporting and using various custom queries, charts, and dashboards.

CHAPTER 6

Visualizing and Reporting in Azure Boards

Visualizing and analyzing your team's work in the various reports and charts that are available in Azure Boards will help you to decide how to improve the way your team works. There are several out-of-the-box chart types available in Azure Boards, such as velocity, cumulative flow, burndown, and so on, that allow you to monitor and track the progress of your team's work and forecast the future deliveries based on trends. In the first lesson of this chapter, you will discover the out-of-the-box reports and charts in Azure Boards. In the next few lessons of the chapter, you will focus on queries and visualizing project progress with different types of reports and charts that you can create based on the queries. You will explore how to write queries, how to create charts using queries, and how to add the generated charts to the Azure DevOps dashboards. Finally, we will discuss the dashboard widgets available in Azure DevOps, which are useful for visualizing various aspects of your project.

Lesson 6-1. Exploring the Out-of-the-Box Reporting of Azure Boards

Azure Boards provides really useful charts that display a team's progress, and those charts are an important part of monitoring team progress and predicting trends.

Prerequisites: You need to have a board in Azure Boards with work items on it.

Go to Azure Boards. You will see two charts in the top-right corner of the page. See Figure 6-1.

© Chaminda Chandrasekara and Pushpa Herath 2019
C. Chandrasekara and P. Herath, *Hands-on Azure Boards*, https://doi.org/10.1007/978-1-4842-5046-4_6

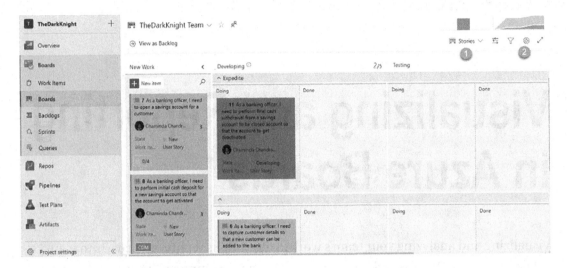

Figure 6-1. *Azure Boards charts*

1. **Velocity chart**: This type of chart shows fully completed and done
   stories and bug fixes, and the accumulated size gives the velocity
   of the iterations that have been completed. In Azure DevOps,
   the velocity chart provides information on completed sizes as
   well as in-progress sizes. It is arguable whether team velocity
   for a completed iteration should be considered in the progress
   velocity as well. However, in reality, in-progress work adds no
   value to the customer, and considering that, a team's velocity has
   no validity. This chart further helps you to identify how much
   work your team can complete during a sprint. By referring to the
   data in the velocity chart, you can identify the average velocity of
   the team, which makes it possible to make decisions such as how
   much work your team can handle during a future iteration. The
   velocity chart also shows how a team has progressed over a couple
   of iterations. See Figure 6-2. You can see the completed work
   displayed in green and the remaining work in blue. Sprint 2017.32,
   which is a completed iteration, has met a velocity of 135 points,
   while 14 points are in progress, so the actual team velocity for the
   iteration is 135 points.

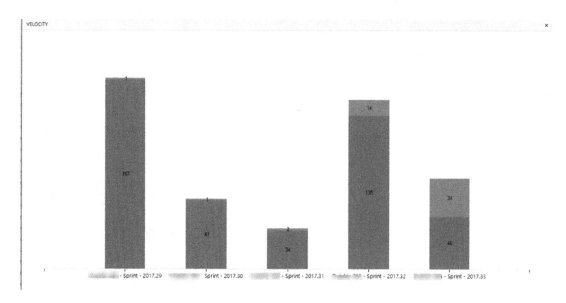

Figure 6-2. *Velocity chart*

There is a widget that provides more insights into the velocity, which we will discuss in Lesson 6-9.

You can use the average velocity in the forecast of the backlog to predict how many iterations will be required to complete a prioritized and sized backlog. Enable Forecasting in the View options and provide the average velocity to see the forecasting. See Figure 6-3.

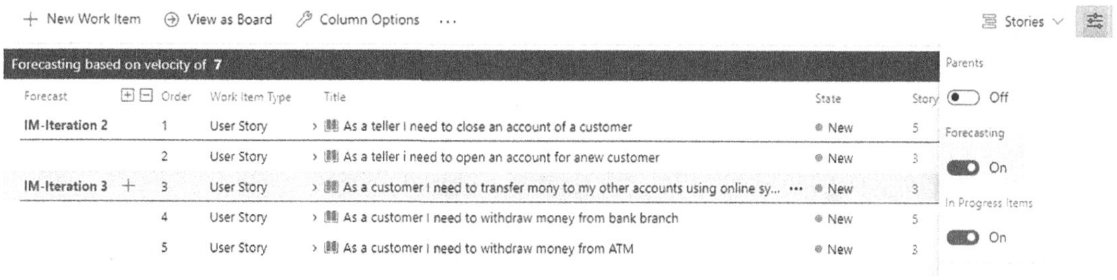

Figure 6-3. *Forecasting*

2. **Cumulative flow chart**: This type of chart shows the progress of the count of work items in each column of the Kanban board over time. It shows how many New, Developing, Testing, Resolved, and Closed work items are in the board as of a given date. See Figure 6-4.

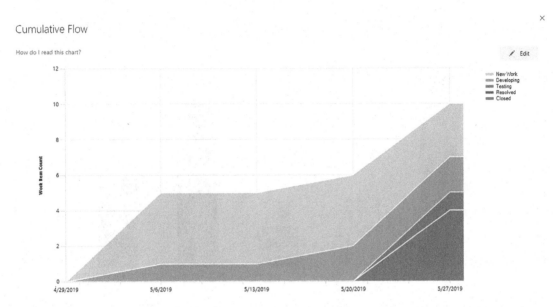

Figure 6-4. *Cumulative flow chart*

You can click Edit in the cumulative flow chart to configure the chart with your preferences in the Cumulative Flow Diagram settings. You can set a date to start the chart drawing. This date should be a date within the last 30 weeks because the maximum allowed period to show in the chart is 30 weeks. You can define whether to include the first and last columns of the Kanban board in the chart using the settings. See Figure 6-5.

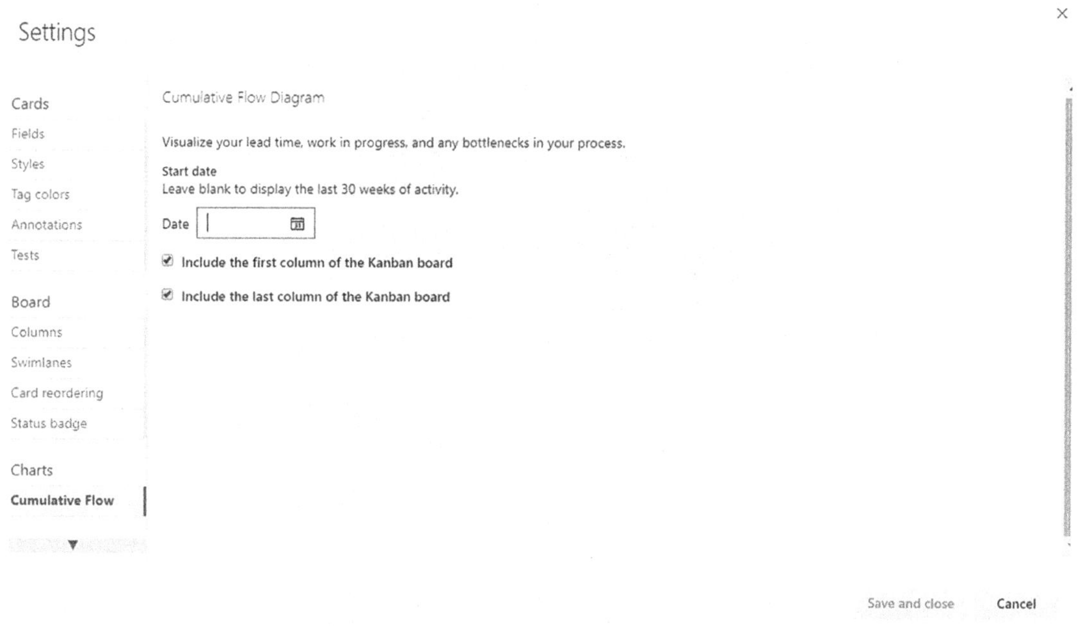

Figure 6-5. *Cumulative flow chart settings*

The cumulative flow chart settings allow you to understand a team's progress via several aspects. Let's take a look at each option.

How the Work Is Progressing?

In general, work in progress should have mostly thin parallel lines because of the principle of limiting work in progress in Agile practices. The last column should be increasing, gradually showing the work getting completed. If there is a widening gap in the work in progress (WIP), that indicates work is not getting completed, and the team is working on too many items in parallel. In other words, it is not a good sign. The team should take action to get work completed together as a team without starting on other new work. See Figure 6-6.

Figure 6-6. *WIP increasing in cumulative flow*

Bulges in Cumulative Flow

When some part of the work is not getting completed as expected, bulges may occur in the cumulative flow. For example, a bulge may occur in the development completed state if testing work is happening more slowly than the development work. Normally a bulge indicates an issue in the next stage (state) of the process rather than the state the bulge is shown in. In this example scenario, you could support your testing team members by having the development members also participating in the testing activity. This is a major reason that cross-functional and multiskilled teams are valuable in Agile practices. See Figure 6-7.

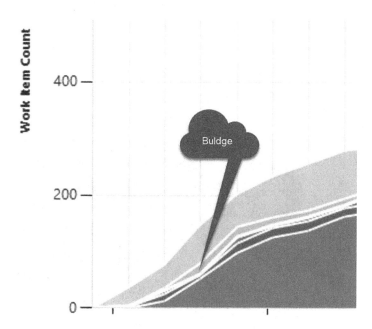

Figure 6-7. *Budge in cumulative flow*

Flat Lines and Scope Changes

A flat line in a cumulative flow diagram (CFD) may occur when the team takes more time than planned to get work moving from one process state to another. It could be that a team has not updated the work items regularly, which may have caused the flat lines. A similar effect can happen even in burndown and burn-up charts if a team does not update work items regularly, which we will discuss later in this lesson. You should always encourage the team to drag the work items to the relevant column in the Kanban boards, and the daily Scrum meeting is a good time to check whether a work item is in the right column. Flat lines occur when multiple process states are not progressing as planned, and if one state progresses while the other is not, then a bulge as explained in the previous section may occur. See Figure 6-8.

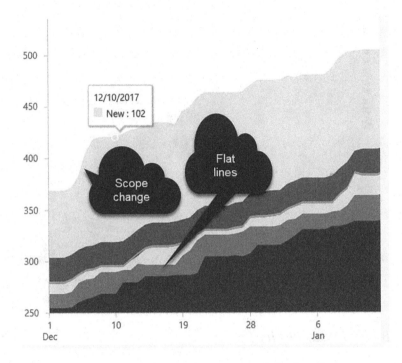

Figure 6-8. Scope changes and no progress in cumulative flow

If you go to sprint section, you will be able to see another important chart display in the top-right corner of the Sprints page. This is the sprint burndown chart. It shows the remaining work of a sprint. The burndown chart will help the team to figure out whether they are on track to complete all the work items in the sprint. Let's look at the maximized view of this sprint burndown chart. See Figure 6-9.

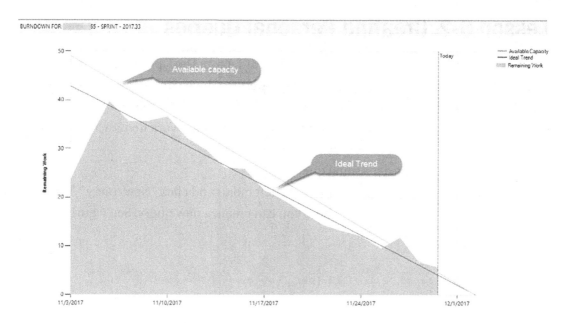

Figure 6-9. *Sprint burndown chart*

You will see the chart has two lines. One is the available capacity line. It shows the team's total capacity for the sprint and how it will change over the sprint. In other words, it shows how many working hours remain to complete the team's work.

An ideal trend line shows how much work should take place in each day in order to complete all the work planned for the sprint. If your team's actual remaining work is maintained below or close to the ideal trend line, it indicates that the sprint is progressing as planned, and you will be able to complete all the work. When the actual remaining work is above the ideal trend line, it indicates the team has not progressed as expected because of some reason that should be rectified as soon as possible. If the actual remaining time or ideal trend line goes above the available capacity line, it indicates that the team capacity is not sufficient for the workload.

Charts provide you and the team with valuable information on how well your team is progressing with the work. It is important that you communicate to the team the meaning of these charts and how to interpret them. By understanding the information in these charts, the team can make the required improvements to add value to your end users (clients) rapidly and with quality.

Lesson 6-2. Creating Personal Queries

In this lesson, let's discuss the querying capability of Azure DevOps. In Azure DevOps, you are able to create your own queries as My Queries, which you can save for your use only. You may need to filter work items for different purposes. For this purpose, you can create your own queries and save and reuse them to filter work items according to different needs.

Let's see how to create a personal query.

Go to Queries in the Boards section in the left menu and click "New query." Then navigate to the My Queries section where you can create a new query. See Figure 6-10.

Figure 6-10. *Adding a new query*

1. You can move to the Results page where the results of the query will be displayed.

2. The editor allows you to add/edit queries.

3. You can create charts from the query results, and those charts will be displayed on the charts page.

4. You can run a query using the "Run query" icon.

5. You can add new work items by clicking the New icon and selecting the work item type. Then the work item creation window will open, where you can give values and create a work item.

6. After you add the query filters, you can save the query by clicking the "Save query" icon. After clicking the "Save query" icon, a pop-up will open where you can give the query name and the location. See Figure 6-11.

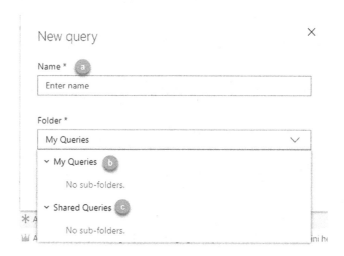

Figure 6-11. *Saving the query*

   a. Provide a name for the query.

   b. From the folder, you can select the location to save the query. If you select My Queries, the query will be saved as a personal query.

   c. By selecting the Shared Queries option, you can save the query as a shared query that can be accessed by other team members.

  7. You can revert the changes done to the query by clicking the "Revert changes" icon.

  8. Query results display in tabular form, and you can add or remove columns from the results using this "Column options" section.

  9. After running a query, you will be able to see the filtered results. Sometimes you may need to edit the values of these filtered work items by using the work item context menu's Edit option or by clicking each work item and editing them on the review pane. When such an edit is made, you can use the "Save items" button to save changed work items.

  10. When you click the three dots, you will get access to more commands. See Figure 6-12.

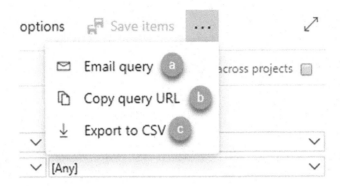

Figure 6-12. *More commands*

a. You can send the query results through mail using the "Email query" option. A pop-up window will open. See Figure 6-13.

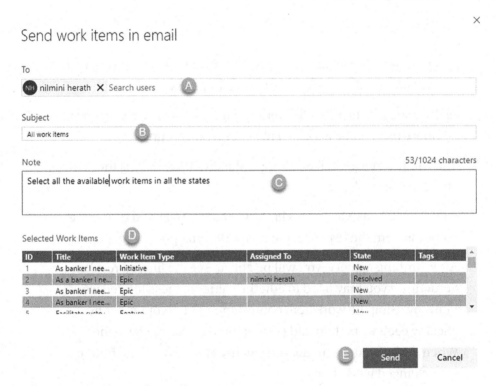

Figure 6-13. *Query result mail*

    A. Provide the mail receivers.

    B. Give a subject for the mail.

    C. Add a note to the mail.

    D. These are the filtered work items returned by the query.

    E. Send the mail by clicking this button.

    We have discussed how to send a query result mail. Now let's
go back to the commands section.

b. "Copy query URL" allows you to copy the URL of the query. After clicking
this icon, a window will open where you can copy the query URL. See
Figure 6-14.

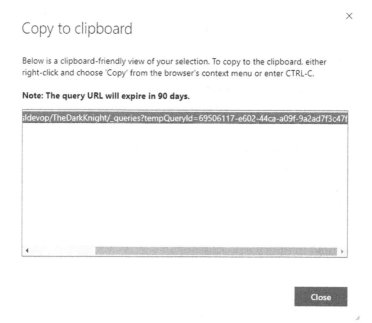

Figure 6-14. *Copying the query URL*

c. You can export the work items to a CSV file by clicking the
Export to CSV icon.

11. You can expand the page by clicking this icon.

12. Select the check box next to "Query across multiple projects" to create queries to filter the values of all the projects.

13. Select the query type. Azure DevOps has three query types. See Figure 6-15.

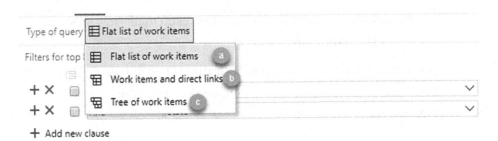

Figure 6-15. *Type of queries*

  a. Flat list of work items

  b. Work items and direct links

  c. Tree of work items

  These are three different ways to write queries. We'll discuss these in Lesson 6-4.

14. You can remove the query lines by clicking the red X, and you can add query lines by clicking the green + sign.

15. Select the field to query.

16. Select the operator to query.

17. Select the value for the filter.

18. Add a new field to the query.

In this lesson, you learned about the options available for you to create a query in Azure Boards.

Lesson 6-3. Sharing Queries with the Team

This lesson will explain you how to create a query and share it with the team. We discussed the features available in Azure DevOps to create a query. You can create queries that can be used by the creator of the query only, or you can create queries to share with team members. Let's see how to create a shared query.

Go to the All tab of Queries. You will be able to see the My Queries section and the Shared Queries section. If you hover the mouse over My Queries or Shared Queries, you will see dots that you can click to access more actions. See Figure 6-16.

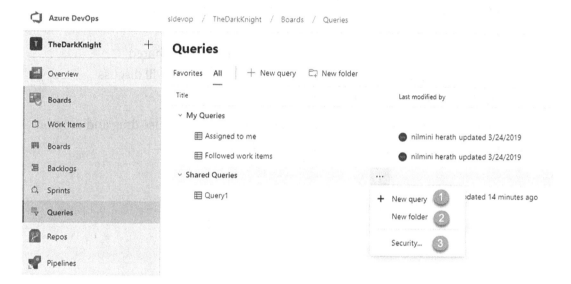

Figure 6-16.   *Queries*

1. Click to add a new query to any shared query section.

2. After clicking this, a window will open that allows you to create a new folder in the My Queries or Shared Queries section. See Figure 6-17.

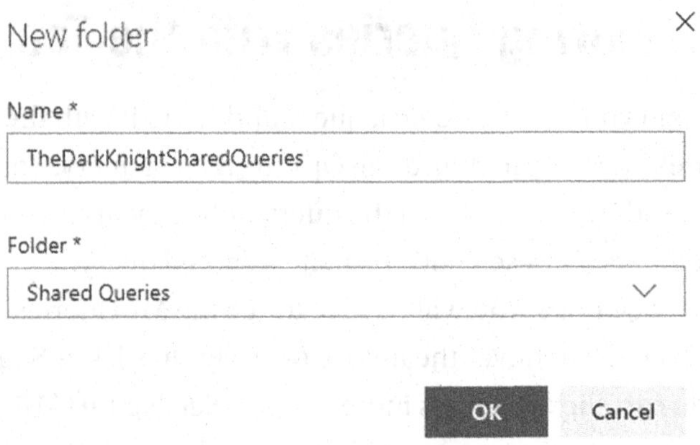

Figure 6-17. Creating a new folder in the Shared Queries section

3. You can navigate to the security control window of the shared queries by clicking the Security drop-down option. We will discuss more about security in Chapter 8.

To move a query from My Queries to Shared Queries, you can use drag and drop on the All queries tab of the Queries page. See Figure 6-18.

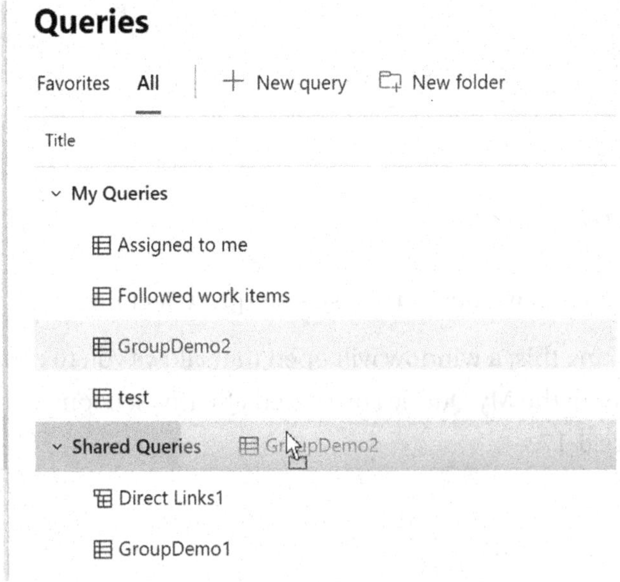

Figure 6-18. Dragging and dropping to Shared Queries

You can drag and drop a query from Shared Queries to My Queries as well. However, this should be done only if you want to other team members to not to see a query in Shared Queries anymore.

Favorite Queries

In addition to My Queries and Shared Queries, there is an option to make a query your favorite or a team favorite. A query can be set to be on your favorites list by clicking the star that appears next to each query. Using the context menu of shared queries, you can add a query to the team favorites. See Figure 6-19.

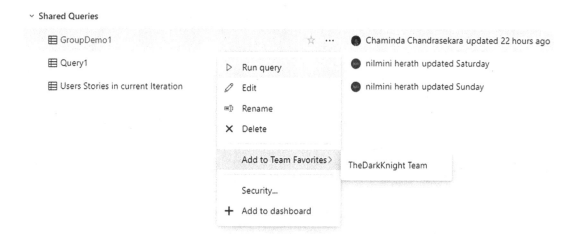

Figure 6-19. *Adding to the favorites*

You can remove a query from the team favorites once it is added as a team favorite in the same context menu. Your favorite queries can be added and removed by clicking the star. The favorite queries are shown on the Favorites tab of the Queries page.

In this lesson, you learned how to share queries with teams and add and remove queries to and from your favorites and the team favorites.

Lesson 6-4. Writing Complex Queries

So far, we have discussed the basic querying features available in Azure DevOps. This lesson will guide you to create complex queries to filter work item values. There are three types of queries in Azure DevOps.

- **Flat list of work items**: Using this query type, you can filter user stories in the New and Closed states with Teller or CDM tags. Also, you can filter bugs in the Developing and New states with Teller or CDM tags. See Figure 6-20.

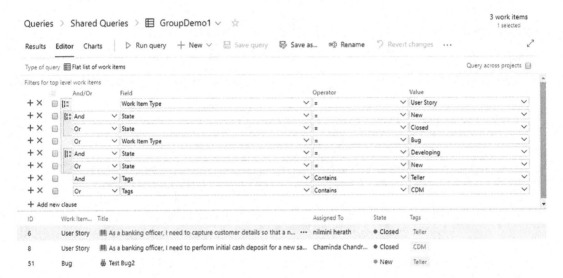

Figure 6-20. *Flat list query*

- **Work items and direct links**: Work item direct links allow you to create a query in two levels. You can define the top query level criteria and define another criterion for the second level. The first and second levels can be linked with the relationships available in work items. See Figure 6-21.

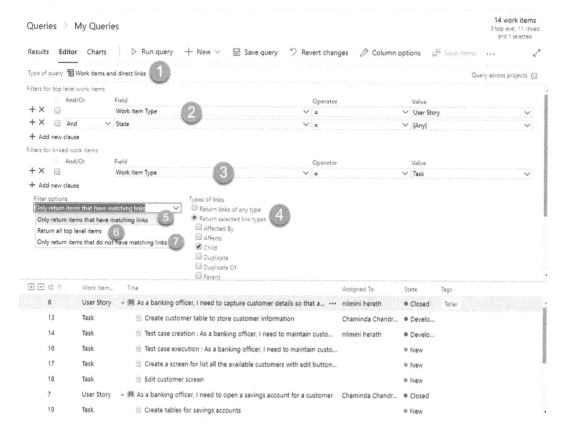

Figure 6-21. *Work items and direct link query*

1. This is the type of query selected as a work item and direct links.

2. This is the query criteria for the top level.

3. This is the query criteria for the second level.

4. This is a list of link types of the top and second levels. You can set this to use any link type or select specific link types based on your preferences.

5. Considering the link type, only the top-level items with matching link types will be returned.

6. This returns all top-level items matching the top-level query criteria regardless of whether they have a matching link in the second level.

7. This returns top-level items that do not have matching linked items in the second level.

- **Tree of work items**: The "Tree of work items" type allows you to write queries that can retrieve work items as a hierarchical structure depending on their Parent/Child or Duplicate Of/ Duplicate link types. See Figure 6-22.

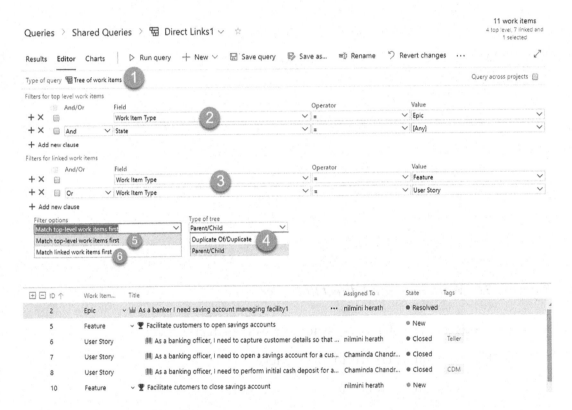

Figure 6-22. *Tree of work items*

1. The type of query is set to "Tree of work items."

2. This is the top-level query criteria.

3. This is the second-level query criteria.

4. The link type is Parent/Child or Duplicate Of/Duplicate.

5. The top-level criteria is applied first, and then the matching items are found for the second-level criteria satisfying the link specification. This will make all top-level items be returned with or without second-level criteria items.

6. The second-level criteria is matched first to find the work items of the top-level criteria that satisfy the link specification. This will return top-level work items only if the second-level criteria items are found with the links.

In each type of query, you can use multiple groupings of criteria to create complex queries.

In this lesson, you explored how to set up three different query types: flat list, work item direct links, and tree of work items. These queries are useful to retrieve work items with various criteria to visualize them in a useful way.

Lesson 6-5. Creating Charts with Queries

You created several queries in the previous lessons. Now let's see one of the most important uses of queries, which is to create charts. You can use queries to filter work items in different ways, and Azure DevOps has features to visualize these query results as charts.

Go to Queries and select a query. Then move to the Charts tab and click "New charts" to create a new chart. The chart creation window will open. See Figure 6-23.

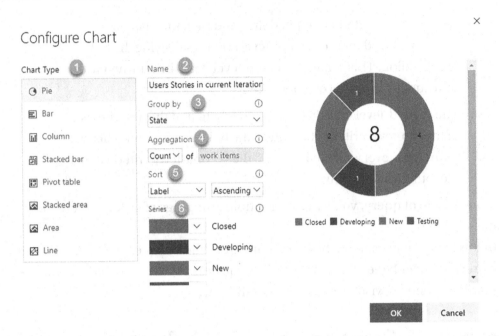

Figure 6-23. Creating a query chart

1. Azure DevOps provides a facility to create different types of charts. Here you can see the different types of charts that you can create.

2. This is the name of the query.

3. You can select how you group your data using this drop-down. When you create a pie chart, you can group work items by the "Assigned to," State, and "Work item" types or other output columns in your query.

4. You are going to create a chart for the work items count. This shows up in the Aggregation section.

5. You can sort chart values using labels or values in ascending or descending order.

6. You can customize the colors of each section of the chart.

Note   A pivot table chart lets you select row and column fields, which allows you to count the work items matching both fields.

In this lesson, you learned how to create a chart using a query in Azure DevOps.

Lesson 6-6. Adding Charts to the Dashboard

We discussed how to create a chart from a query in the previous lesson. This lesson will explain how to use the created chart in a dashboard. You can add only shared queries to a dashboard as private queries in My Queries are visible only to you.

Go to the Charts section of the query. Hover your mouse over the chart, and you will see three dots appear. Click the dots to see the configuration options. See Figure 6-24.

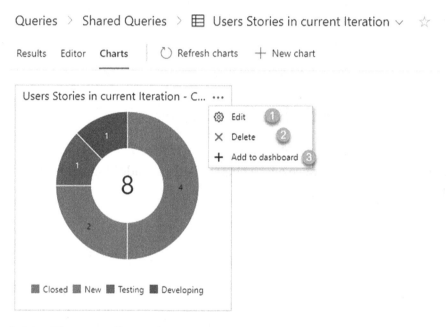

Figure 6-24. *Chart configuration*

1. Click the Edit icon to edit the chart.

2. Click Delete to delete the chart.

3. Click "Add to dashboard." A pane will open on the right side of the page. Select the dashboard from the drop-down where you need to display this chart and click OK. See Figure 6-25.

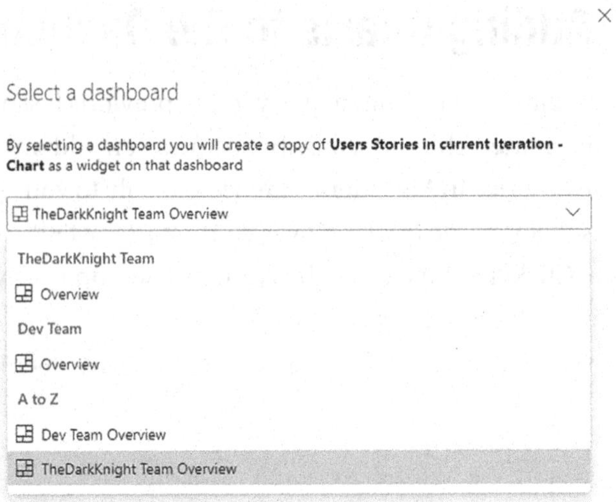

Figure 6-25. *Selecting the dashboard to add a chart*

Now if you move to the relevant dashboard, you will be able to see the chart. See Figure 6-26. Hovering your mouse over a chart will display additional information, and if you click the chart, the query will be opened.

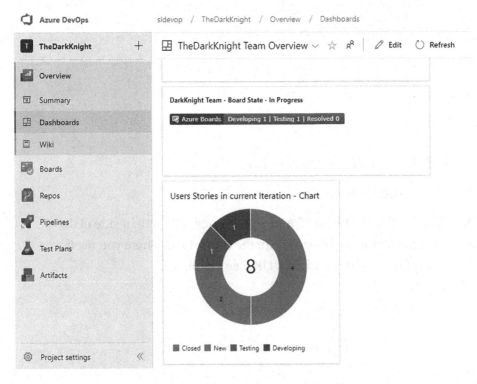

Figure 6-26. *Added chart on TheDarkKnightTeam dashboard*

In this lesson, we discussed how to add charts to dashboards to enable the visualization of the work item queries you have created for your team. These visualizations will allow you to create a holistic view of the team progress.

Lesson 6-7. Creating Dashboards

Azure DevOps lets you add multiple dashboards to the project. This allows a team to visualize their performances or progress in different ways. As an example, teams can have a dashboard to display CI/CD pipeline data and another one to display work item details. Also, it is possible to create separate dashboards for each team. Each team can decide how they want to visualize team performances and progress.

Let's see how to create new dashboards.

Go to Dashboards and select "New dashboard" from the drop-down. See Figure 6-27.

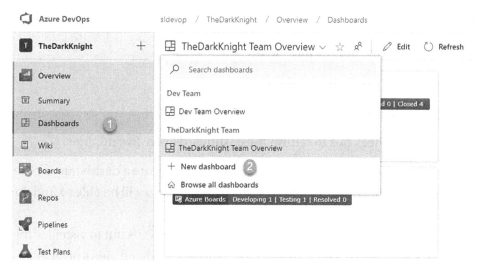

Figure 6-27.   *Creating a new dashboard*

After clicking "New dashboard," a window will open where you can provide the details to create the new dashboard. See Figure 6-28.

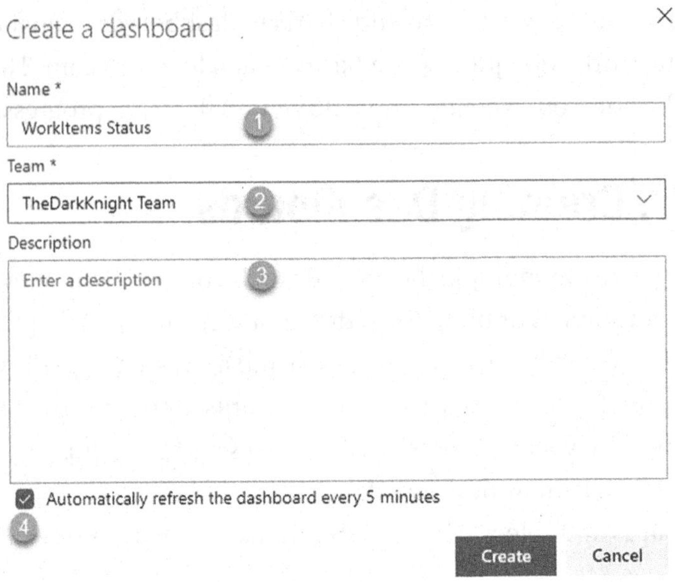

Figure 6-28. *Creating the dashboard*

1. Provide a name for the dashboard.

2. Select the team of the dashboard.

3. Add a description for the dashboard.

4. Select the check box to refresh the dashboard every five minutes.

After providing the dashboard details, click Create to create a dashboard for the selected team. After successfully creating the dashboard, you will be able to find the dashboard in the dashboard drop-down.

Having multiple dashboards as described in this lesson is useful to visualize the progress of each team separately as well as to create consolidated views of all teams and to visualize different aspects of work such as work items, CI/CD pipelines, test execution, and so on. Note that we will discuss CI/CD and test execution visualizations in the other books of the series.

Lesson 6-8. Adding Widgets to a Dashboard

We discussed how to create a new dashboard for a team. This lesson will discuss how to add widgets to a dashboard.

Open the dashboard you need to add widgets to and click the Edit button. See Figure 6-29.

Figure 6-29. *Dashboard's Edit button*

Dashboard edit mode will enabled, and you will see the side pane where you can search for widgets and add them to the dashboard. See Figure 6-30.

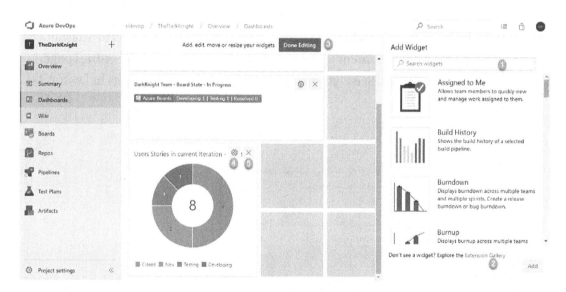

Figure 6-30. *Dashboard's edit mode*

1. Search for widgets using a search text box or select from the list below and click the Add button to add widgets to the dashboard.

2. If you can't find the widget you want from the given list, you can click "Extension gallery." This will take you to the marketplace where you can find more widgets. Adding extensions will be discussed in Chapter 10.

3. You can save and exit from edit mode using this button.

4. After clicking the cogwheel icon, the chart's configure pane will open. You can edit the basic chart configurations in this pane, and you can change the size of the chart.

5. Remove the chart from the dashboard.

If you want to change the location of the chart, you can do it in the dashboard's edit mode by dragging and dropping the chart to your preferred location. Some widgets allow you to customize how many blocks of squares you want the chart to use as its width and height.

Let's add the Azure Boards badge as a widget to learn how to add a widget to a dashboard. You can find the Markdown content of the board's badge on the board's Settings page. Copy the Markdown content. See Figure 6-31. We discussed board settings in Lesson 4-4.

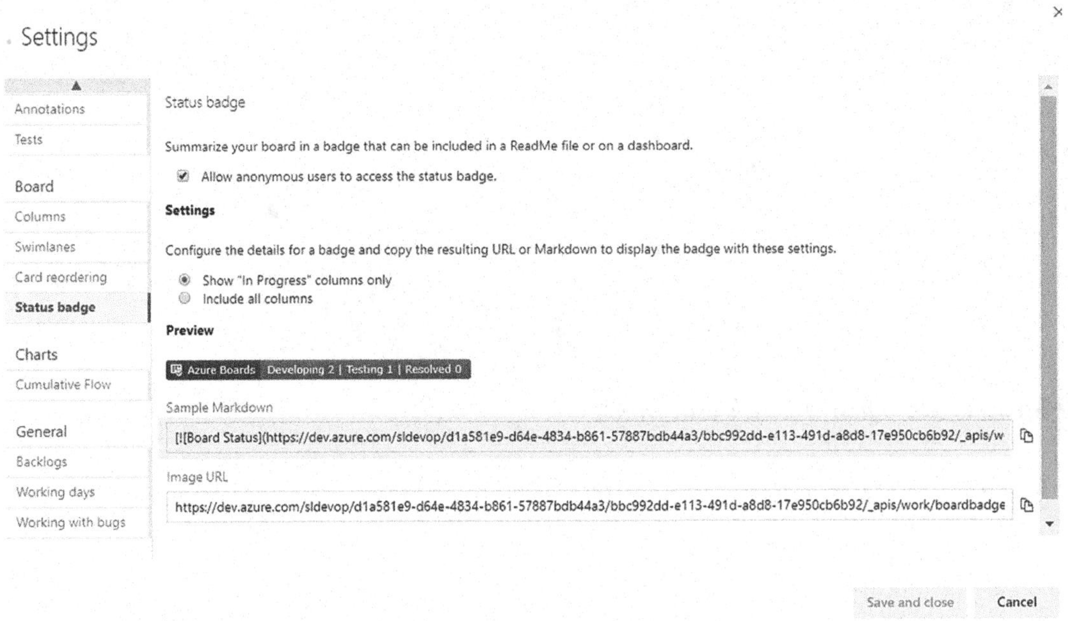

Figure 6-31. *Status badge of Azure Boards*

In the team dashboard, click Edit. Then in the widgets, search for Markdown, select the Markdown widget, and click the Add button. Then click the cogwheel icon to configure the widget. Add the title for the badge with the Markdown syntax and paste the Markdown content copied from the board's Settings page. See Figure 6-32. Define a size for the badge and click the Save button to add the Azure Boards status badge widget to the dashboard.

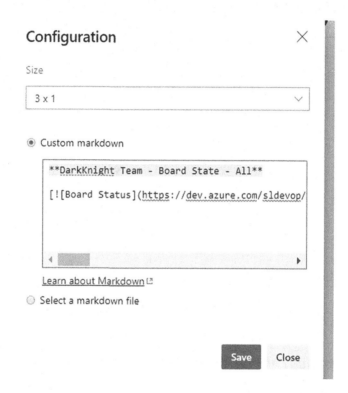

Figure 6-32. *Adding Azure Boards status badge to the dashboard*

If you click the status badge in the dashboard, it will open the relevant Azure Kanban board.

In this lesson, you explored how to add widgets to dashboards to use them to visualize work.

Lesson 6-9. Using Widgets to Visualize Work Items

Various useful widgets are available in the Azure DevOps dashboards, which can help teams to visualize team information on the dashboard.

- **Chart for work items**: This widget visualizes work items using the shared work item queries. The chart in Figure 6-33 displays the work items in the current iteration.

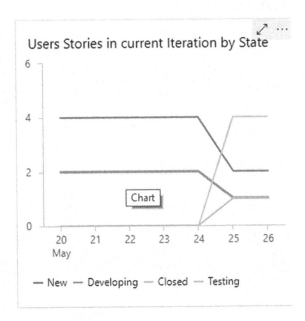

Figure 6-33. *Pivot chart of work items in current iteration*

- **Cumulative flow**: We have already discussed the cumulative flow diagram in the first lesson of this chapter. You can add the cumulative flow widget to the dashboard in addition to the cumulative flow diagram available by default in the boards and backlogs.

- **Velocity**: This widget allows you to visualize more information about the velocity of the team than the out-of-the-box chart available in the team backlogs and boards. You can configure date thresholds to consider work as planned or completed late in this widget. The chart shows you planned, completed, and completed late work as well as incomplete work. See Figure 6-34.

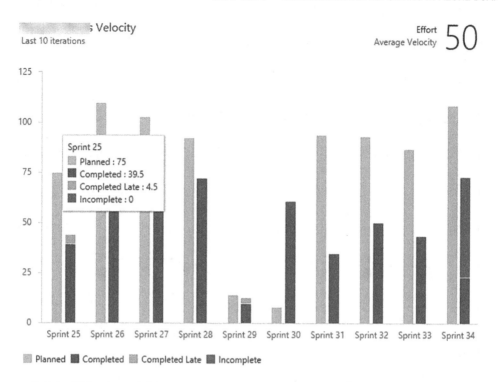

Figure 6-34. *Velocity widget*

- **Lead time and cycle time widgets**: Identifying the lead time and cycle time of your team helps you to determine how long it takes for work to go through the development and testing process to get it completed. You will be able to see the deviations from the median cycle and lead times in the charts. The bigger the work item type colored circles in the charts in Figures 6-35 and 6-36, the higher the work item counts. If you click any chart work item colored circle, you will be taken to a custom query that is autogenerated and filtered to the relevant work items.

- **Cycle time**: This is the time taken to complete the work item from the time that active work was started on it. See Figure 6-35.

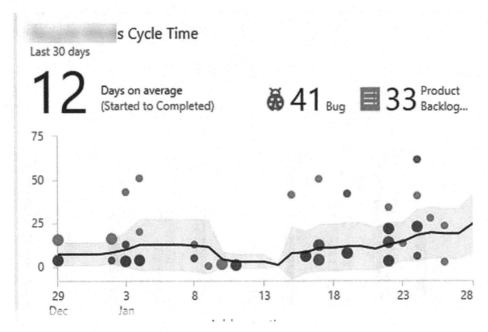

Figure 6-35. Cycle time

- **Lead time**: This is the total time taken to complete the work item
  from the time it was created. See Figure 6-36.

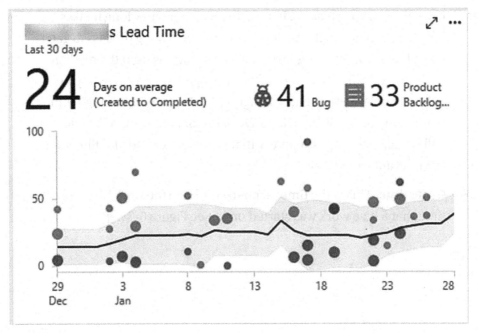

Figure 6-36. Lead time

- **Burn Down and Burn Up**: The burndown and burn-up widgets provide many options to display valuable information about your team's progress such as release burndown and so on. It is important to configure these charts as per your team requirements and understand the meaning of each of the values and lines shown.

  - **Total Scope**: The scope changes of the project are shown when considering the completed work as well. In Figure 6-37, there is a significant increase in scope shown.

  - **Burndown**: The burndown line plotted in the chart shows how fast your team completes the work. In Figure 6-37, the average burndown shows as a minus value because the burndown rate has decreased as an average due to increased remaining work or a significant scope increase in the project.

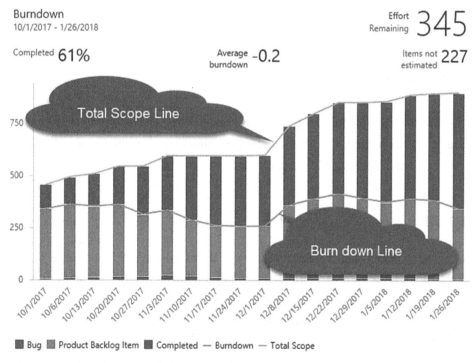

Figure 6-37. Burndown widget

The burn-up chart provides another view of how the work has progressed over the said period. Even though the scope has increased, the team has completed a significant amount of work. The total scope increase is almost 50 percent, which justifies the minus burndown average in Figure 6-38.

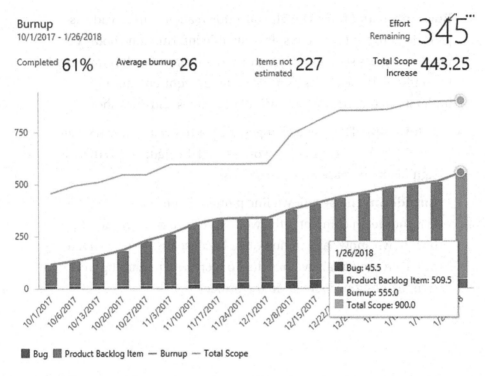

Figure 6-38. *Burn-up chart*

We discussed a few useful widgets in this lesson. You can explore more work item widgets and even get work item widgets as extensions from the Visual Studio marketplace. We will discuss adding extensions in Chapter 10.

Summary

In this chapter, we discussed visualizing work in different ways. You explored the out-of-the-box charts and creating work item query-based charts. Further, we explained how to use dashboards and add custom charts and widgets to them. Additionally, we explored a few of the useful widgets to give you more insights into the visualization capabilities of Azure Boards.

In the next chapter, we'll discuss how to configure Azure Boards to handle large teams, which will be required when you have to work with much larger application implementations.

CHAPTER 7

Handling a Large Team in a Team Project

Agile principles and modern iterative software development practices suggest that a software development team should consist of six to nine members. However, because of the complexity or size of a software project or the demanding client deadlines, you might have to accommodate more team members to meet the required targets. In this sort of a scenario, what Agile practices suggest is to divide the software project into modules, which can be handled by ideally sized Agile teams of six to nine people. This means multiple teams work together to achieve the project goal.

In this chapter, we'll first cover the needs of large teams and how to organize a large team into multiple subteams effectively. Then we'll cover how you can utilize the capabilities of Azure Boards to organize and manage a group of teams to achieve a single project goal.

Lesson 7-1. Understanding the Requirements of Multiple Teams

In some scenarios, you have to manage a pretty large team, maybe because of the complexity or because of the tight deadlines of the project/product. Large teams aren't recommended by Agile practices, because they can lead to various complications in terms of teamwork, collaboration, communication, and other issues.

Dividing the work among subteams is the best way to handle the situation when a team gets too large and the amount of work to be delivered is huge or critical. You might choose a technical approach to divide the work into multiple teams, such as allowing one team to handle database changes, another team to handle the back-end code writing such as data access logics, another team to write business modules, and another

© Chaminda Chandrasekara and Pushpa Herath 2019
C. Chandrasekara and P. Herath, *Hands-on Azure Boards*, https://doi.org/10.1007/978-1-4842-5046-4_7

to take care of the user interface implementation. However, this sort of division of work is not recommended and often results in unsuccessful projects. In addition, these sorts of technical-focused teams are a total violation of the concept of Agile, which recommends having a multiskilled and cross-functional team. For example, when you have a team of experts only working on the database, the other teams have to wait to get started until the database team completes their work. This siloed mind-set will be created and lead to less collaboration to get the work completed to achieve the requirement.

Hence, make sure you focus on business modules rather than technical reasons when you divide teams. You want teams that are cross-functional and can focus on getting a business requirement done on their own. The individual team's contributions should create components in a much larger software system and should be loosely coupled with the other teams' work as much as possible.

It is also essential that you make sure to monitor the work in progress for all teams at all times. If you do not, it is likely that you will miss the deadlines or that you will run into last-minute impediments or risks within the software development process. Miscommunication among stakeholders from different subteams is another thing to keep an eye on. It is dangerous not to have a clear vision of where the project is heading. Also, when the teams start to release each of the components of the system and do the integrations between them, if you did not lay the proper plans well in advance, things can get worse. In the following lessons, we'll discuss how to divide a large team and manage it effectively and efficiently while leveraging the features of Azure Boards.

As we discussed in Chapter 2 for small teams, you start by creating the team project. This step is pretty much the same regardless of your team size. As we discussed, you can choose any out-of-the-box templates (Agile, Scrum, Basic, or CMMI) or use any custom process template to create the team project. To avoid managerial complexities, you must decide how to execute the project/product development in the early stages of the process. For instance, let's assume the project is complex and has several modules, such as membership management, events management, finance management, case management, and so on. In such scenarios, what is the ideal way to proceed? You should modularize the development process so that all application modules are developed in parallel by multiple teams. Having said that, the challenge is to decide on how to divide your team to deliver modules in parallel. There are various ways of doing this, and we'll discuss the best solution that gives the most business value quickly to your product/ project end users. Technically inspired team members might want to divide the team based on the technical aspects. For instance, they might want to divvy up the work into categories like the following: front-end development, business process and plugin development, database development, and so on. The danger of this approach is that the whole team might eventually lose the focus of the project's business purpose and continue to focus only on its technical aspects. At all times, the aim of the team should be to deliver value to the end users. With divisions like this, you and the team are not releasing the value to the end users. Instead, your team is focused on merely completing the work assigned to them. As a result, the integration becomes tedious and causes unnecessary delays.

Therefore, the most appropriate way of dividing a team is based on the business functions of the project. For instance, you can create different teams to develop membership management, finance management, case management, events management, and so on. Each team has its own set of developers and testers and its own Scrum master. You can create two different teams to handle development work and support work. Similarly, you can create the relevant teams under the main team project and assign the team members to each team you created. You may want to have both a development subteam and a support subteam for each team. See Figure 7-1.

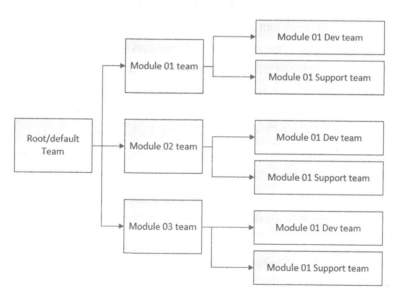

Figure 7-1. *Nested team structure*

However, nested teams are not a possibility in Azure Boards, which means you cannot have a team structure like the one shown in Figure 7-1. In fact, it is not necessary to have such a complex team structure. Obviously, for a large team and a complex project, you might be able to have one or two separate support teams that are working on all modules' support activity. So, you could set up a team for each module and then set up a support team or two under the root team. Having said that, what should you do if you really want to have both a dev team and a support team for each of the modules because you are handling each individual module in a totally decoupled manner technically and each has independent release cadences of its own? A work-around for this is to create all required teams with areas assigned to them and then move the required module dev or support team areas under the relevant module areas as children. Does this sound confusing? Let's simplify it in the next lessons of this chapter by practically implementing a solution.

As with ideally sized teams, you must define the delivery cadence for the project/product development for large teams. Remember, this is tricky since different teams are going to be working on the features of each module they are assigned to, and the work they undertake might have different levels of complexity. Some of the teams might demand a longer delivery cadence based on the functionality on which they are working. For example, one team might like to have a three-week delivery cadence, and another team might like to have a four-week delivery cadence. Even though Azure Boards supports different lengths of iterations, if you do not properly set up iterations and manage the work, your project delivery targets and quality of delivery may well end up in chaos. So, to make your work simpler, you can set up a delivery cadence of the same length that every team will be aligned with. This is handy when it comes to integration because you will be releasing fully baked goods to the clients. However, this decision again depends on the technical architecture and platforms your team chooses to deliver to the project. It is important to plan well and define what the delivery cadence is for each of your teams before you start the project. For this, you need to get the support of your technical teams and consider all aspects; for example, if you have a loosely coupled module design that has the ability to support previous versions of other modules with newer versions of a different module, you can consider having different delivery cadences for each module. Or, you might want to work with different iteration cycles in each module but maintain the same delivery cadence for all modules. For this, you can share one level of iterations with all modules to denote releases and then have different child iterations for each module team. These are just a few ideas, but to make your iteration setup really work, you need to figure out how you want it and then manipulate Azure Boards to behave the way you want the iterations to behave. Let's practically set this up in next lessons of this chapter so you can understand the possible implementations in practical terms.

When you start executing the project/product development work, it is extremely important to know the current status of your teams. When you are executing large projects, it is vital to identify any setbacks or delays as early as possible so you can take corrective actions to mitigate the issues. As explained in Chapter 6, Azure Boards comes with a set of reporting tools such as queries, charts, Kanban boards, and dashboards; these enable you to stay in touch with your teams.

Lesson 7-2. Configuring Areas and Teams to Isolate Backlogs

You can isolate the backlogs of each team in a single team project using the area path setup. Even though nested teams are not supported, the area path can be used as a work-around to achieve a hierarchical team structure. Further, you can share the area path with multiple teams to share a common backlog. Let's explore the options to set up a large project's team structure using areas and teams in a team project.

Isolating the Backlogs

Let's try to isolate the backlog of each team using area paths. For this, first create a new team project named **TheEndGame**. Then in the project setting of the team project, go to the Teams tab in the General section and click New Team. Name the team **Avengers**. Make sure to create an area path with the name of the team. See Figure 7-2.

Figure 7-2. Creating a new team

Create another team named **IronMan** with an area path with the team name. You should have three teams in the team project now: the TheEndGame team, which is the root team (the default team of the team project) of the team project, and the two new teams you just created, Avengers and IronMan. See Figure 7-3.

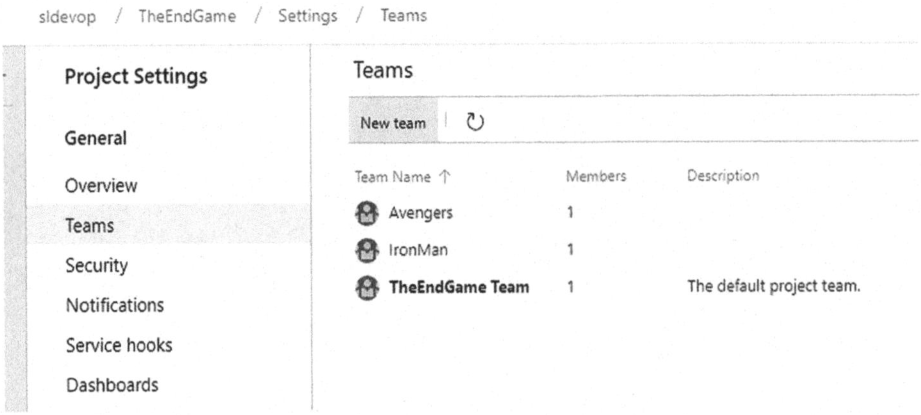

Figure 7-3. Teams

Let's inspect the area path setup in the team project by selecting "Project configuration" and going to the Areas tab. You should see the root area path is set to TheEndGame, and there are two child areas, Avengers and IronMan. See Figure 7-4.

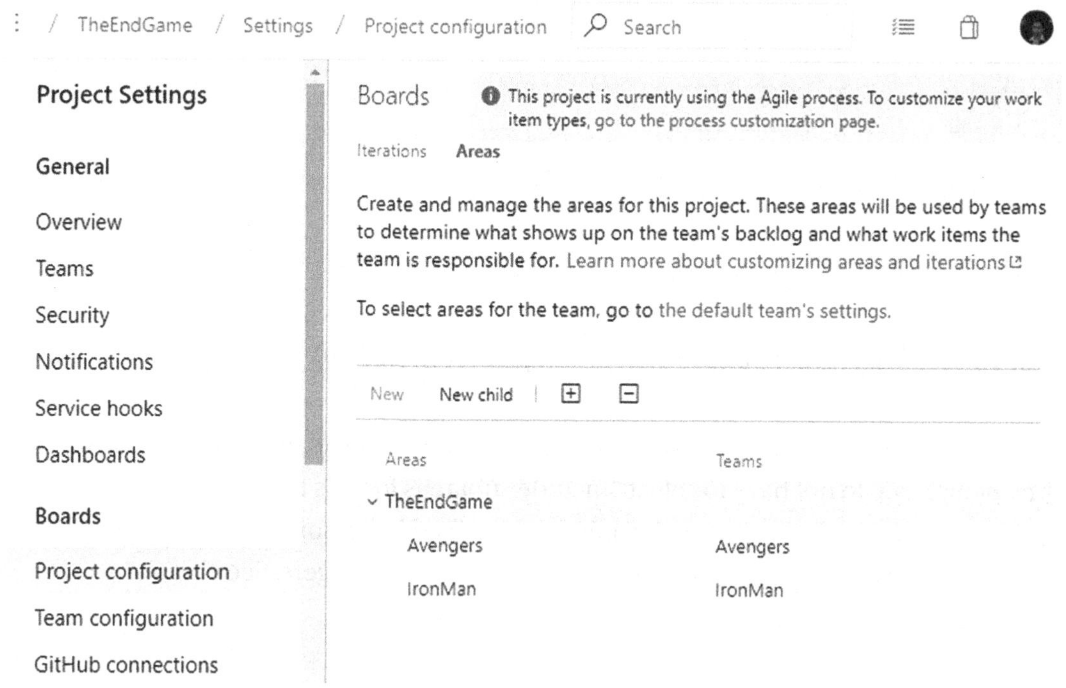

Figure 7-4. *Project area configuration*

Then select "Team configuration" and select the TheEndGame team, which is the default or root team. The default area for the team should be set to TheEndGame, and it is already selected under the selected areas of the TheEndGame team. Let's click the context menu of the selected area TheEndGame and click "Include sub areas" to make all the backlog items in this team project visible to the TheEndGame team. When you include subareas, there will be a warning message appear saying all work items of the team project will be shown in this team. Click OK because this is the desired behavior you are going to implement. The resulting area configuration of the TheEndGame team should be similar to Figure 7-5. You are making every backlog work item visible to the root/default team so that you can monitor the overall project progress from the perspective of the default team, TheEndGame.

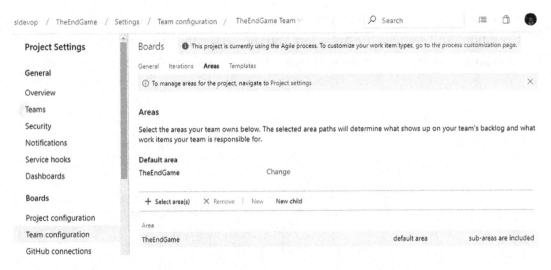

Figure 7-5. *The root/default team area path set to include subareas*

Select the Avengers team to view the Areas settings of the team Avengers. For the time being, you do not have to select "Include subareas for this team" because you are not yet going to implement nested teams, as described in Lesson 7-1. Just make sure the Avengers team has the default area set to TheEndGame\Avengers. See Figure 7-6.

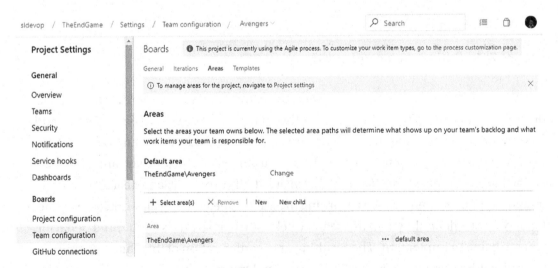

Figure 7-6. *Avengers team area setup*

Verify the Ironman team area path is set to use TheEndGame\IronMan as the default area path and that subareas are not included.

Go to the Iterations tab of the default team, TheEndGame, and set the Default iteration to TheEndGame by changing the current selection, which is @currentiteration. You are doing this because you want the new backlog items to be in the Backlog iteration, which is the root-level iteration TheEndGame, instead of the current active iteration. See Figure 7-7. We have described these options in detail in Lesson 2-2.

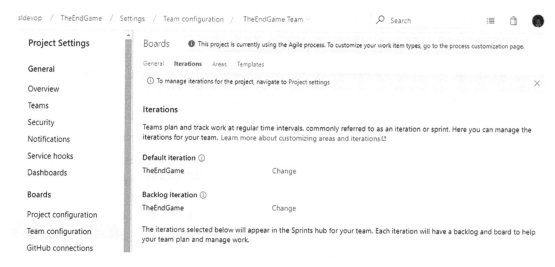

Figure 7-7. *Root iteration set as default and backlog iterations*

TheEndGame should be set as the backlog and default iterations for the two teams Avengers and IronMan as well, as shown in Figure 7-7. This will make sure any item you added from any team will have the iteration path set to the root iteration, which is TheEndGame. Do not worry about the selected iterations for any of the teams yet since we will discuss sharing common iterations to follow the same delivery cadence for all teams in Lesson 7-3. We will discuss having a separate delivery cadence for each team using separate iteration paths in Lesson 7-4.

Now let's add a few backlog items to the team TheEndGame. For now, you can skip the Epic and Feature work items and add just user stories to the backlog using the board or the backlog view. For example, see Figure 7-8.

☰ TheEndGame Team ⌄ ☆ ⅋ᴿ

+ New Work Item   ⊕ View as Board   ✎ Column Options   ···

	Order	Work Item Type	Title	State
+	1	User Story	📖 As a teller I need to close an account of a customer ···	● New
	2	User Story	📖 As a teller i need to open an account for anew customer	● New
	3	User Story	📖 As a customer I need to transfer mony to my other accounts using online system	● New
	4	User Story	📖 As a customer I need to withdraw money from bank branch	● New
	5	User Story	📖 As a customer I need to withdraw money from ATM	● New

Figure 7-8. *Stories for the system in the root team backlog*

Let's say from the backlog the teller module is developed by the Avengers team and the customer module is a transaction module is developed by the IronMan team. If you inspect each team's backlogs, you will not be able to see any user stories as of now in the Avengers team or in the Ironman team's backlog view. See Figure 7-9.

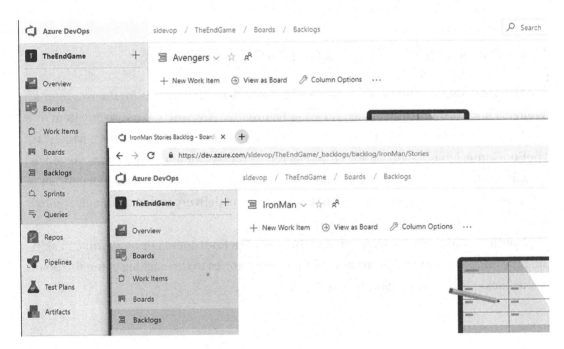

Figure 7-9. *Empty backlogs for Avengers and IronMan*

Let's move back to the boards of the TheEndGame team and assign the teller user stories to the Avengers area path and the customer user stories to the IronMan team area. Even after assigning them to the teams, the stories still appear in the root team's backlog, as you have set up the root team to show all work items of the subareas of the root area. See Figure 7-10.

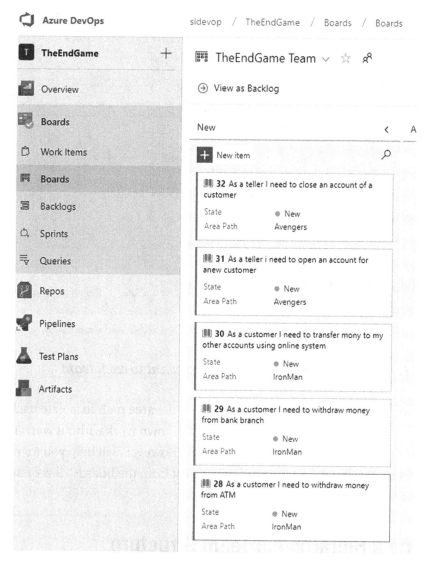

Figure 7-10. *Stories assigned to respective team areas*

If you now inspect the backlogs of the Avengers and Ironman teams, you will be able to see only the relevant stories appear in their backlogs, as per the area settings for each team. See Figure 7-11.

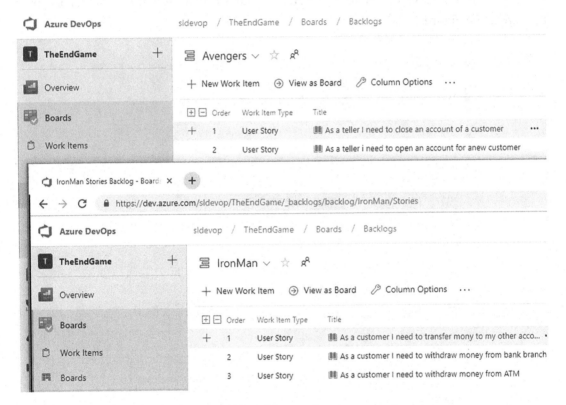

Figure 7-11. *Teams showing only backlogs relevant to each team*

This example scenario shows how you can use the area path to isolate backlogs from each individual team and let the team focus on their own work without worrying about another team's work items. The root/default team, however, will help you to track the entire project and review the progress of the project from the boards view or any charts, and so on, in dashboards.

Achieving a Hierarchical Team Structure

Let's look at a scenario where both the Avengers team and the IronMan team that you have used need to have separate developer and support teams, as we discussed in Lesson 7-1. To achieve that nested team structure , which is not available for teams, you can use hierarchal areas. First create another four teams, AvengersDev, AvengersSupport, IronManDev, and IronManSupport, and create area paths for those teams. This will create a flat team structure under the TheEndGame team area. See Figure 7-12.

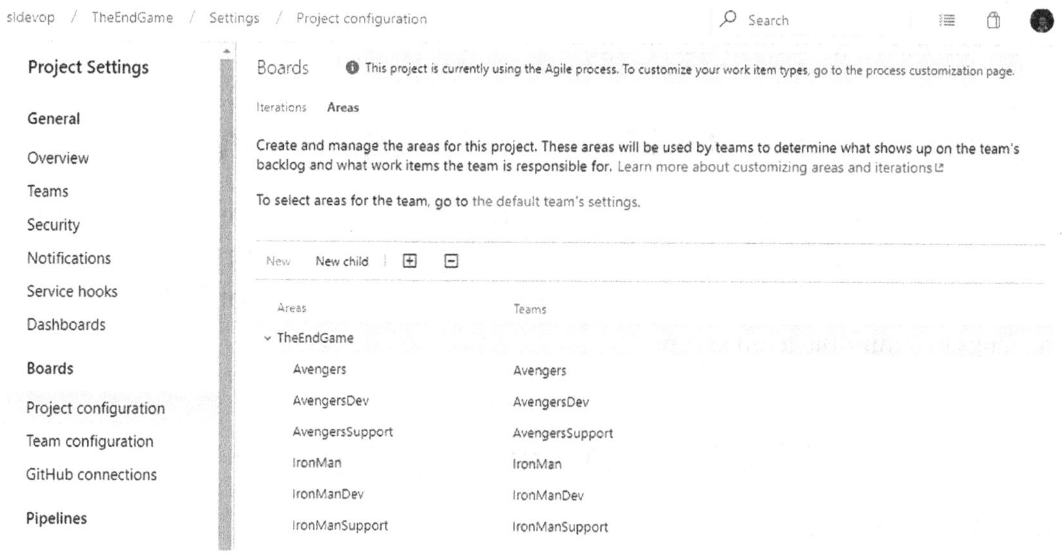

Figure 7-12. *Project team areas*

You can drag and drop the AvengersDev and AvengersSupport areas to the Avengers area and drag and drop the IronmanDev and IronManSupport areas to the IronMan area to create a hierarchical area structure, as shown in Figure 7-13.

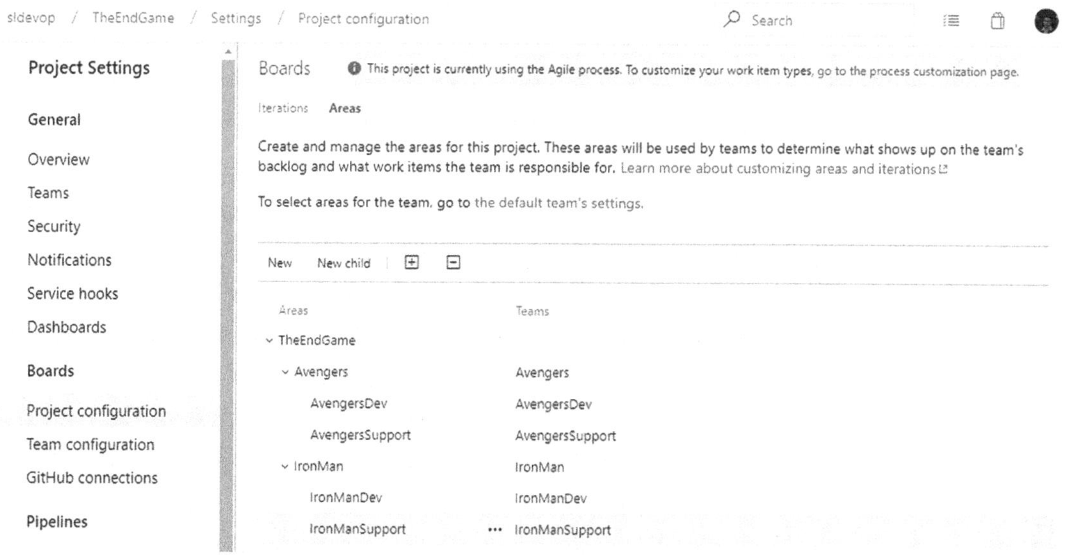

Figure 7-13. *Hierarchical area structure*

Now you have to go to the team area settings of the Avengers team and the IronMan team and include subareas for the selected team area in each team. This change will allow you to monitor any work assigned to AvengersDev or AvengersSupport from the Avengers team. The same is true for the IronMan team. The TheEndGame team can be used to monitor the entire project progress.

Sharing the Same Backlog with Multiple Teams

If you need to share the same backlog with multiple teams and let them work on any of the work items, you can do so by selecting the same area path for both teams.

In this lesson, we discussed how you can use the area path to isolate or share backlogs in a multiple team setup.

Lesson 7-3. Sharing the Same Iteration with Multiple Teams

Sharing the same delivery cadence with different teams can make monitoring the overall project much easier. You will learn how to share a common delivery cadence with iteration paths in this lesson.

Let's go to the project settings, select "Project configuration," and go to the Iterations tab to set up the iteration's hierarchy, as shown in Figure 7-14.

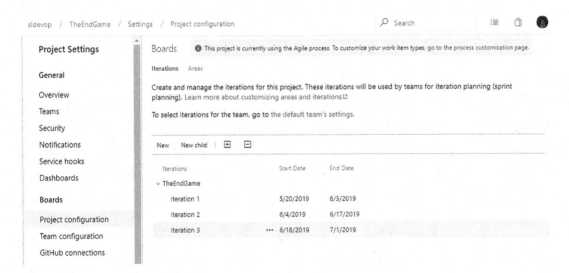

Figure 7-14. *Project iterations*

Then go to each team and select the defined iterations for the teams. For example, the Avengers team's iterations can be set as shown in Figure 7-15.

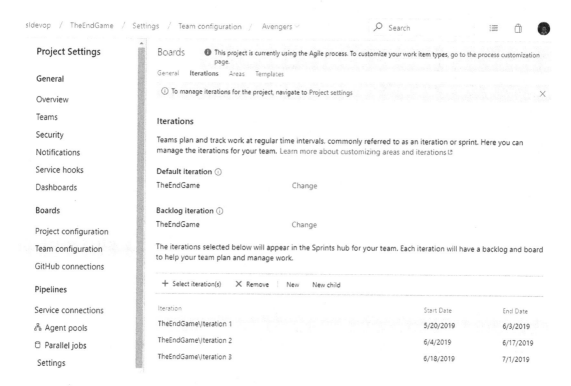

Figure 7-15. *Iterations selected for Avengers*

Once all teams are set up with iterations, you can define the capacity for each team. Here you can add all the members of all teams to the root/default team. Then you can add individual team members. This helps you to set up the capacity planning for the whole project iteration as well as individual teams. In Figure 7-16, for simplicity's sake, only two members were added to each team ,and all four members were added to the root team. Then the capacity for iteration 1 is planned correctly considering the activity type as well as all three teams. You learned how to set up capacity in Lesson 2-5.

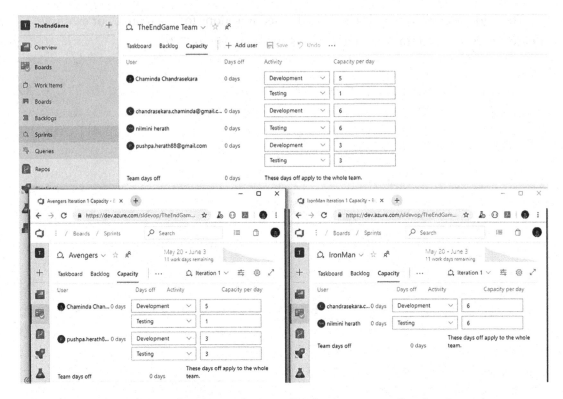

Figure 7-16. *Capacity planning when multiple teams are sharing iterations*

Now move all the stories you defined in Lesson 7-2 to iteration 1 from the TheEndGame team. Then go to each team iteration board and add a few tasks for each story with remaining work and the relevant activity type. See Figure 7-17, for example. You learned how to add tasks and work with boards in Chapter 3.

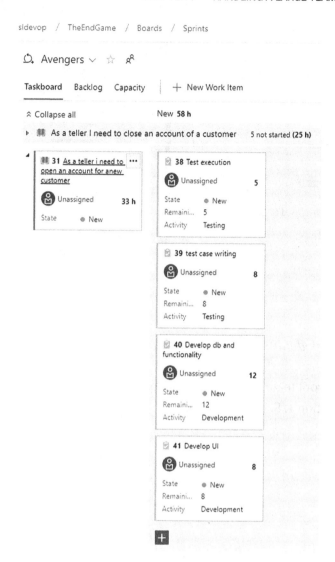

Figure 7-17. *Tasks added to team's user stories*

Now when you look at the work details for iteration 1 in the teams Avengers and IronMan, you can see the capacity and added work by work type. If you start working in the iteration by assigning tasks to members, each individual capacity usage also will be shown. See Figure 7-18.

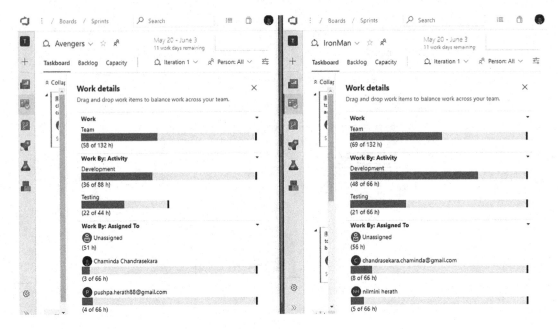

Figure 7-18. *Work details of individual teams*

In the default/root team, you will be able to see an overview of both teams' capacity and usage for iteration 1. See Figure 7-19.

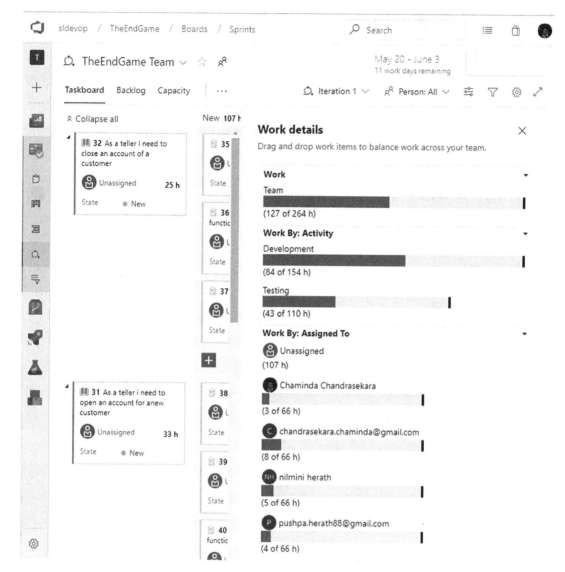

Figure 7-19. *Overall capacity and usage view for iteration*

You now understand how to share iterations with multiple teams and set up capacity planning to allow you to use the default team to enable an overview of the subteams' progress. You can use the same approach for hierarchical teams and get an effective overview of each team by following the same principles when sharing the same release cadence.

Lesson 7-4. Working with Different Release Cadences for Teams

Let's try to implement a different release cadence for the same two teams you used in Lesson 7-3.

As a prerequisite, move all the backlog items back to the backlog from iteration 1 using the root team. See Figure 7-20.

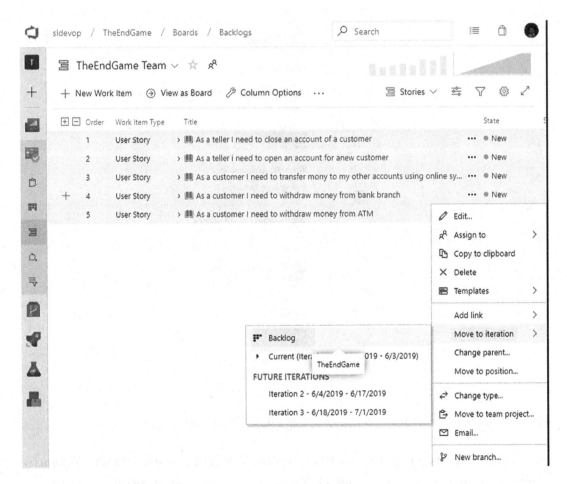

Figure 7-20. *Moving all work items to the backlog*

Set up the iterations for the team project configuration, as shown in Figure 7-21. The prefix is used to identify the team that the iteration belongs to.

sldevop / TheEndGame / Settings / Project configuration   🔍 Search   ☰   🛍   ⚫

Project Settings

General

Overview

Teams

Security

Notifications

Service hooks

Dashboards

Boards

Project configuration

Team configuration

GitHub connections

Pipelines

Service connections

🔗 Agent pools

Boards   ℹ️ This project is currently using the Agile process. To customize your work item types, go
to the process customization page.

Iterations   Areas

Create and manage the iterations for this project. These iterations will be used by teams for
iteration planning (sprint planning). Learn more about customizing areas and iterations ↗

To select iterations for the team, go to the default team's settings.

New   New child | ⊞   ⊟

Iterations	Start Date	End Date
⌄ TheEndGame		
⌄ Avengers Iterations		
A-Iteration 1	5/20/2019	6/3/2019
A-Iteration 2	6/4/2019	6/17/2019
A-Iteration 3	6/18/2019	7/1/2019
⌄ IornMan Iterations		
IM-Iteration 1	5/20/2019	6/10/2019
IM-Iteration 2	6/11/2019	7/1/2019
IM-Iteration 3	7/2/2019	7/22/2019

Figure 7-21. *Iterations for teams with different cadences*

Then you can select the individual team iterations (see Figure 7-22) and set up the
capacity and work items in each team (Avengers and IronMan) separately. You can
obtain each team's work details progress within an individual team. However, obtaining
a consolidated view for the capacity is not possible when you have a different delivery
cadence in each subteam.

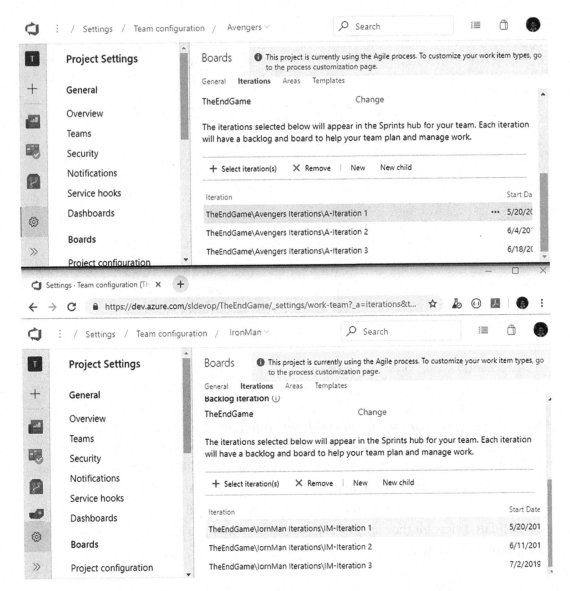

Figure 7-22. *Different iterations for each team selected*

You can set up the root team to use iterations from both teams. See Figure 7-23.

This allows you to see both iteration views, such as work details and planning, via the root team as well. Even though this is not as useful as the consolidated view when using the same delivery cadence, it is still useful information.

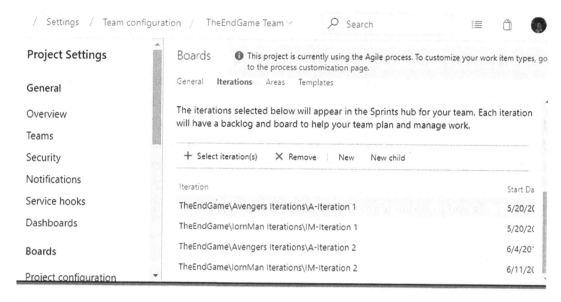

Figure 7-23. *Iteration selection in the root team*

In this lesson, you learned how to set up different release cadences for individual teams. However, this approach should be avoided as much as possible, as we discussed in Lesson 7-1. Further, setting up a different delivery cadence will not allow the consolidated view, which is useful for a single software project's planning and execution. However, if an organization is handling multiple projects within one team project using different teams, the ability to have different release cadences is useful. Then a project team can be considered the root team, and it may have subteams using area path hierarchies so that each project can have consolidated views of subteams' iterations of that given project team, using the same concepts explained in Lesson 7-3.

Lesson 7-5. Sharing a Team Member Across Multiple Teams

Sharing team members across multiple teams can be useful when you don't have enough skilled resources, even though Agile principles do not encourage you to share resources across teams. However, for practical needs, you may have the same team member working in different teams.

Let's look at what you need to consider when assigning the same team member to multiple teams.

Adding a user to any team is really straightforward, and Chapter 8 gives you more details on how to set up security. As long as the user is added to the relevant team, the user will be able to work with the work items in that board.

However, the capacity of a single person per day is limited. If you are using hours as your work unit, Agile practices recommend using a maximum of 6.5 hours for planning capacity for a given day as the rest of the time in the day might be required to balance the time it takes for Agile ceremonies such as sprint planning, daily standups, reviews, and retrospectives. So, when you set the total capacity, be mindful of how the capacity assigned in each team adds up for a single person. For example, the user Chaminda in Figure 7-24 is assigned to both the Avengers and IronMan teams, but the total capacity is less than 6.5 hours.

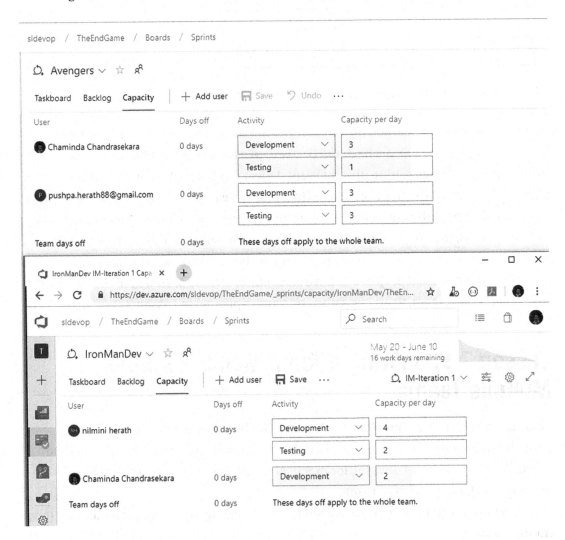

Figure 7-24. *Assigning multiple teams' capacity*

In this lesson, you looked at the considerations when assigning the same person to multiple teams. However, it is recommended not to do this as much as possible since it will make the person less productive due to context switching, as well as the difficulty of focusing on work in multiple teams and so many other reasons as mentioned in Agile practices recommendations.

Summary

In this chapter, you explored the reasons you may need to set up multiple teams to handle larger projects in a single team project. The options to isolate backlogs and obtain consolidated views with shared iterations were explained in detail. Further, we discussed setting up different delivery cadences along with sharing team members across multiple teams. Using the knowledge gained in this chapter, you can try different setups of the area path and iteration path to come up with solutions that meet your specific needs. Azure Boards is flexible and customizable; by using teams, areas, and iterations, you can solve almost any need a modern software development team may come across.

In the next chapter, you will look at the available security options in Azure Boards; you will learn how to set up proper access rights in each area such as teams, projects, or even groups to properly organize the permission structure.

CHAPTER 8

Azure DevOps Security Options

Azure DevOps comes with a wide range of access control and security features. You can control who accesses projects, teams, source code, build-deployment pipelines, work items, and so on, with the Azure DevOps permissions, which are applicable to individuals and groups of users. The permissions in Azure DevOps range from organization-level permissions to team project permissions to team permissions to individual user permissions. Additionally, each feature area has security-related options. For example, area paths, iteration paths, and queries come with their own security settings and permissions.

In this chapter, you will look at each of the security and permission options available related to the Azure DevOps organizations, team projects, and teams, as well as the overall permissions related to Azure Boards. We will skip the other permission areas such as pipelines, repos, and test management since we will be discussing them in the relevant books of this series.

Lesson 8-1. Adding Users to Azure DevOps

This lesson will explain how to add users to Azure DevOps and how to manage different access permissions for each of those users.

Under Organization Settings, select Users in the General section. You will see the user management page. See Figure 8-1.

© Chaminda Chandrasekara and Pushpa Herath 2019
C. Chandrasekara and P. Herath, *Hands-on Azure Boards*, https://doi.org/10.1007/978-1-4842-5046-4_8

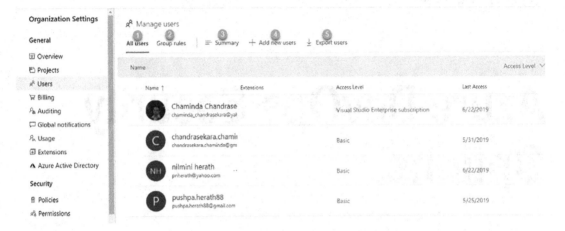

Figure 8-1. *User management of an Azure DevOps organization*

1. In this section, you will see all the existing users of the Azure DevOps organization.

2. You can define group rules, and those group rules will be displayed here.

3. The left pane will show a group rule summary.

4. Click the "Add new users" link to add new users to the Azure DevOps organization. A pane will open where you can enter details for the new user. See Figure 8-2.

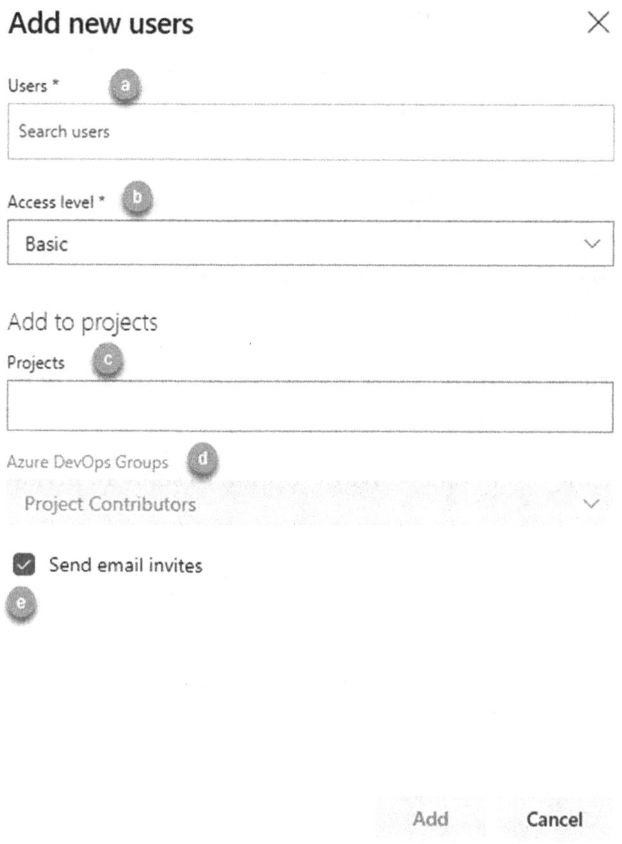

Figure 8-2. *Adding new users*

a. Enter the username. You can search by username or by e-mail address.

b. Select the access level.

- **Basic**: Get basic-level user access to features such as version control and tools for Agile, Java, and build and release management.

- **StakeHolder**: This access permission allows users to manage work items and approve builds and releases.

- **Visual Studio subscriber**: At this permission level, users get all the access, including basic-level feature access. For example, the test management feature is allowed in addition to the basic user features for Visual Studio subscriber users.

c. Select a project from the list.

d. Select the Azure DevOps group where this user needs to be added. The following are the available groups:

- **Project contributor**: The user has permission to contribute to the project code and work item tracking.

- **Project Readers**: The user has permission to view project information but no permission to modify it.

- **Project Administrators**: The user has permission to administer all teams and projects.

e. Enable the "Send email invites" option to send an invitation to the added user.

5. The "Export users" option allows you to download the user details as a CSV file.

When you select the group policy section, you will see that the menu items have changed. See Figure 8-3.

Figure 8-3. *Group rule menu items*

Click the "Add a group rule" link to add a new group rule. After clicking it, the left-side pane will open, and you can enter the group rule details. See Figure 8-4.

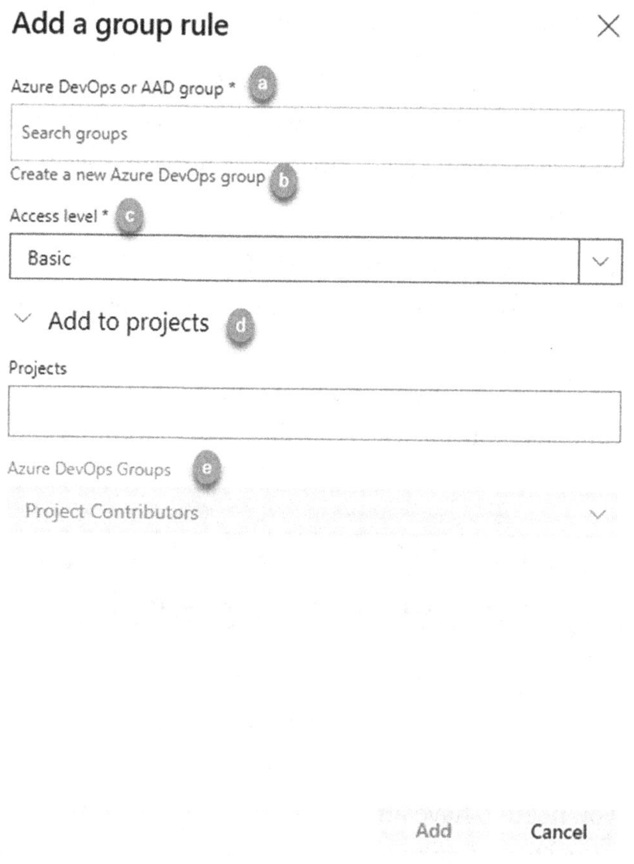

Figure 8-4. *"Add a group rule" pane*

a. Create a new Azure DevOps group or select a group in Azure
    DevOps or Azure Active Directory (AAD).

b. Change the options to add users to the group from AAD and Azure
    DevOps.

c. The group rule can have three access levels.

    - **Basic**: Get basic-level user access to features such as version
      control and tools for Agile, Java, and build and release
      management.

    - **StakeHolder**. This access permission allows users to manage
      work items and approve builds and releases.

    - **Visual Studio subscriber**. At this permission level, users get all
      the access.

    d. You can select and add a project to the group rule.

    e. After selecting the project, the Azure DevOps groups section will be enabled. You can select the user permission—Project Contributors, Project Readers, and Project Administrators—from the drop-down.

The "Re-evaluate rules" option allows the facility to reevaluate the rules. If there are any changes in AAD, the changes will affect the group after re-evaluating it. This process takes about ten minutes to complete.

In this lesson, we discussed how to add users to Azure DevOps and how to define group rules, which will help you set access levels based on groups.

Lesson 8-2. Setting Up Azure DevOps Organization-Level Security Policies and Permissions

Azure DevOps allows you to control security with different levels. For example, you can control security at the organization level or the project level. This lesson will explain the security features available at the organization level.

Prerequisites: You need to have an Azure DevOps organization.

Go to the Azure DevOps organization settings. You will see a security section with Policies and Permissions items. Select the Policies section to identify the policy capabilities. You will see the "Application connection policies" and "Security policies" sections on this page. See Figure 8-5.

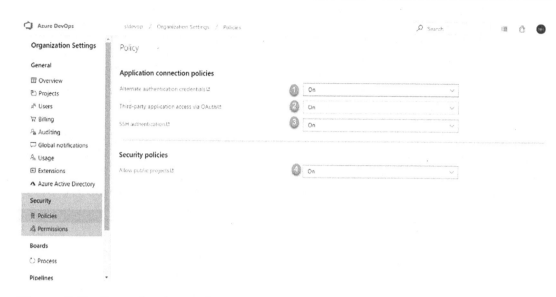

Figure 8-5. *Organization policies*

Azure DevOps provides the capability to integrate other apps with its services
and resources. When building a connection with these types of tools, Azure DevOps
introduces three authentication mechanisms that allow you to access Azure DevOps
without providing user credentials multiple times. You can see there is a drop-down in
front of each policy with the values On and Off to enable or disable each policy.

1. **Alternate authenticate credentials**: We will explain this in
   Lesson 8-8.

2. **Third-party application access via OAuth**: Authorize the app
   using the OAuth 2.0 protocol and generate the token for the
   access, which allows you to call a REST API from the app.

3. **SSH authentication**: You can setup SSH access for Azure DevOps
   by enabling this option.

4. **Allow public projects**: As discussed in Chapter 1, you can control
   the project authentication by creating public and private projects
   in Azure DevOps. You get the capability to create public projects
   only after enabling this policy.

   Let's move to the Permissions section now. Two tabs are available
   on this page: Groups and Users. Several groups are listed in this
   page. See Figure 8-6. Let's identify each group.

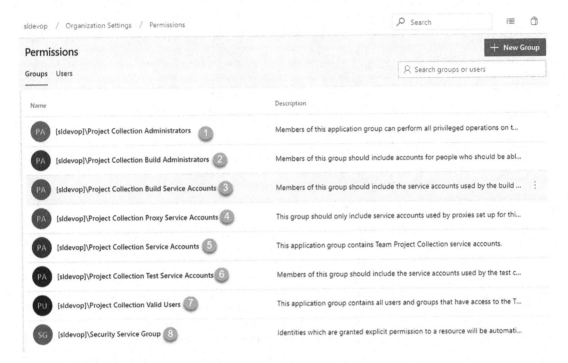

Figure 8-6. *Permission groups*

1. **Project Collection Administrators**: This group's members have permission to perform all the actions available in Azure DevOps.

2. **Project Collection Build Administrators:** This group's members have permission to view instance-level information, create workspaces, administer build resource permission, manage build resource, and view build resources.

3. **Project Collection Build Service Accounts**: This group's members have almost all the permissions that the Project Collection Build Administrators group has. They have permissions to view instance-level information, create workspaces, administer shelved changes, manage build resources, use build resources, and view build resources.

4. **Project Collection Proxy Service Accounts**: This group's members have permission to view instance-level information, create workspaces, and view build resources.

5. **Project Collection Service Accounts**: This group's members have almost all the permissions except permission to delete a team project.

6. **Project Collection Test Service Accounts**: This group's members have permission to view instance-level information, create workspaces, and view build resources.

7. **Project Collection Valid Users**: This group's members have permission to view instance-level information, create workspaces, and view build resources.

8. **Security Service Group**: This group's members have the same permissions that the Project Collective Valid Users group has.

Double-click any of the groups to see the permissions of the group. Also, on the Members tab, you will see the existing members of a group and can add new users to a group. Using the "Member of" tab, you can add the selected group as a member of another group. See Figure 8-7.

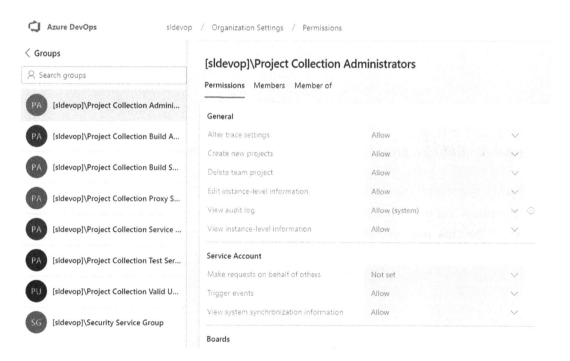

Figure 8-7. *Group permissions*

Let's see how you can add a group to the "Member of" tab. Go to the "Member of" tab and click the "Add members of" button. On the left side of the page, you can search for and add an existing group as a member of the selected group. See Figure 8-8.

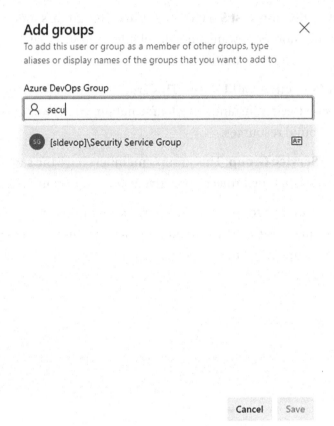

Figure 8-8. Adding a group as a member of another group

If you want to add a new member to the group, go to the Members tab and click the "Add members" button. The left side of the pane will open where you can search for and add Azure DevOps users as members to the selected group. See Figure 8-9.

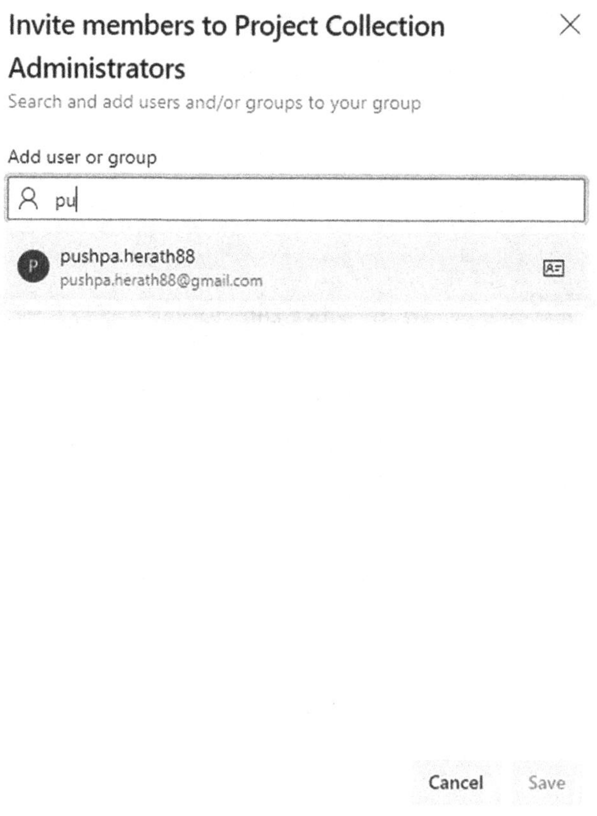

Figure 8-9. *Adding a new group member*

In this lesson, we discussed the security features available in the Azure DevOps organization settings. You learned how to set Azure DevOps control policies and permissions at the organization level in this lesson.

Lesson 8-3. Enabling Access to External Users in Organization-Backed Azure DevOps Accounts

If you have created an Azure DevOps organization and connected it to the Azure Active Directory (AAD) of the organization, you may want external stakeholders to be able to access your Azure DevOps organization without having an AAD account. In this lesson, let's look at how to grant external users access to AAD-backed Azure DevOps organizations.

You can identify whether the Azure DevOps organization is backed by Azure Active Directory by selecting Azure Active Directory under Organization Settings. Go to the General section. See Figure 8-10.

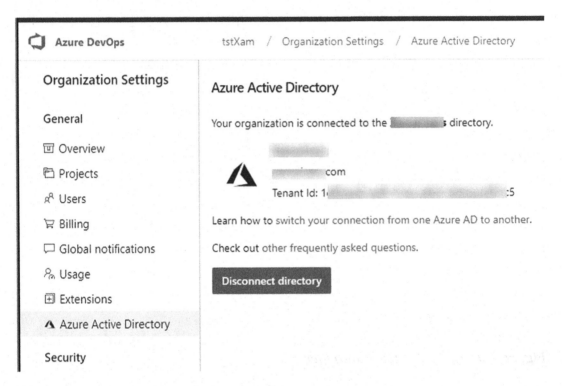

Figure 8-10. *Azure DevOps backed by an organization AAD*

In the Azure DevOps organization security policies, which can be found in the Security section of the organization settings, you have to set "External guest access" to On. See Figure 8-11. Note that you need to have project collection administrator permissions to make this policy change.

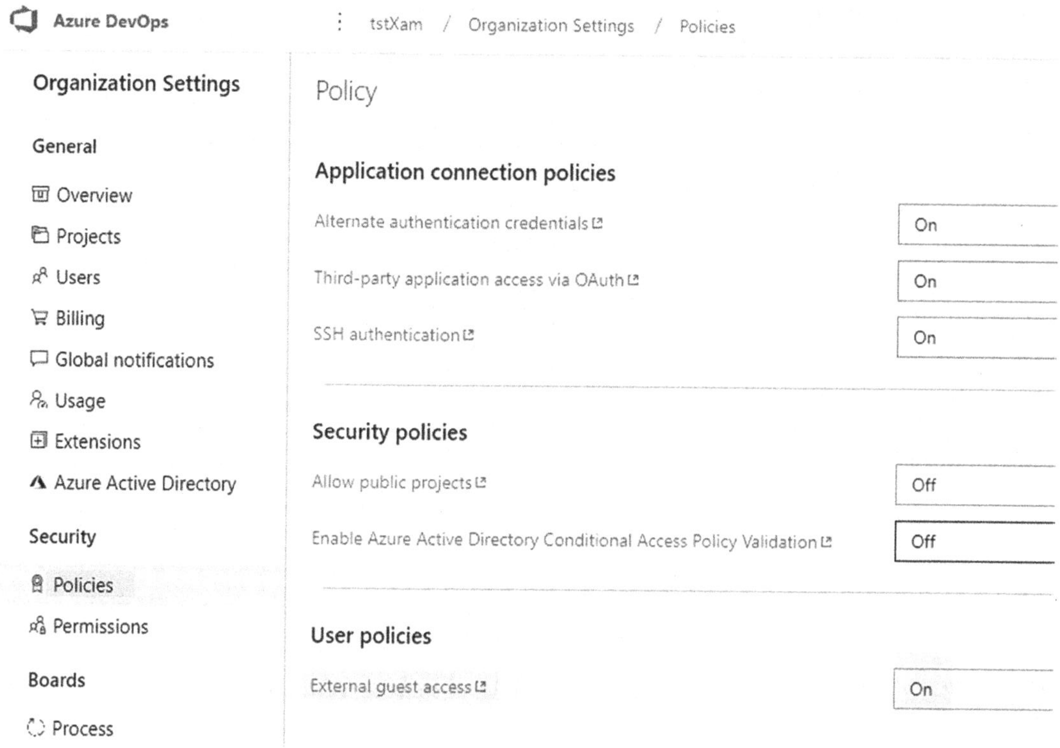

Azure DevOps   ⋮   tstXam / Organization Settings / Policies

Organization Settings

Policy

General

Application connection policies

🗔 Overview

🗂 Projects

Alternate authentication credentials ↗ | On

🗄 Users

Third-party application access via OAuth ↗ | On

🛒 Billing

SSH authentication ↗ | On

🗩 Global notifications

🗠 Usage

Security policies

⊞ Extensions

Allow public projects ↗ | Off

⋀ Azure Active Directory

Enable Azure Active Directory Conditional Access Policy Validation ↗ | Off

Security

🔒 Policies

User policies

🗝 Permissions

External guest access ↗ | On

Boards

🗘 Process

Figure 8-11. *External guest access enabled*

On the Users tab of the General section of the organization settings, click "Add new users." When you type in the username, the organization users will be listed, and you can quickly add the organization users to Azure DevOps. However, when you type in an e-mail address of one organization user, there will be a warning message saying that you are inviting an external user. The warning further says that the external user has to click the link in the e-mail sent by Azure DevOps to start using the Azure DevOps organization. Make sure to check the option to send an e-mail invitation and click "Add users." You can set the access level to Basic, Stakeholder, or Visual Studio Subscriber according to the user's licensing. See Figure 8-12.

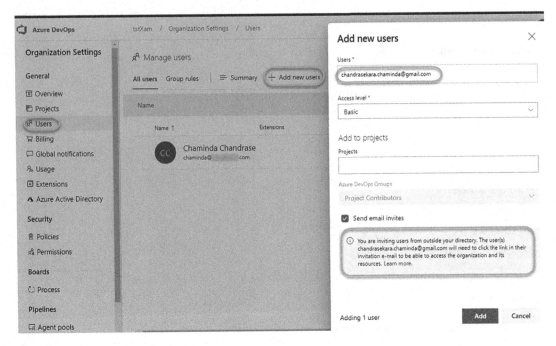

Figure 8-12. *Adding an external user to AAD-backed Azure DevOps*

An invitation e-mail will be sent to the external user. The external user can then click the Join button to access the organization. See Figure 8-13.

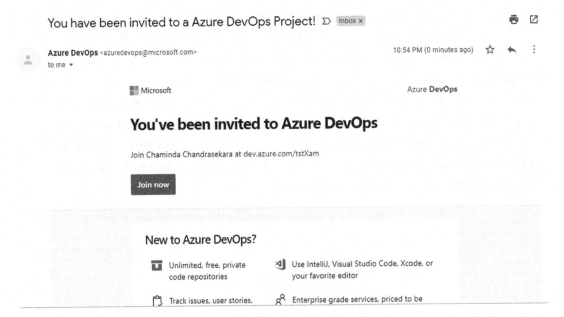

Figure 8-13. *Invitation to join AAD-backed Azure DevOps*

When prompted, the external user has to provide the credentials and login information using their Microsoft account. Then a review permission dialog will appear, granting access to the organization to capture activities such as logging in to the Azure DevOps organization. See Figure 8-14.

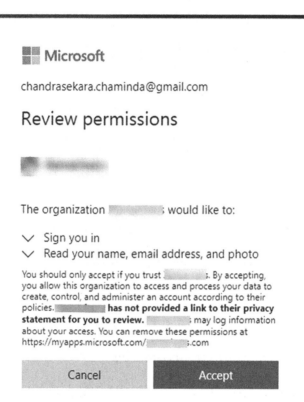

Figure 8-14. *Accepting permissions*

Once they've been accepted, the external user needs to provide some additional information, as shown in Figure 8-15.

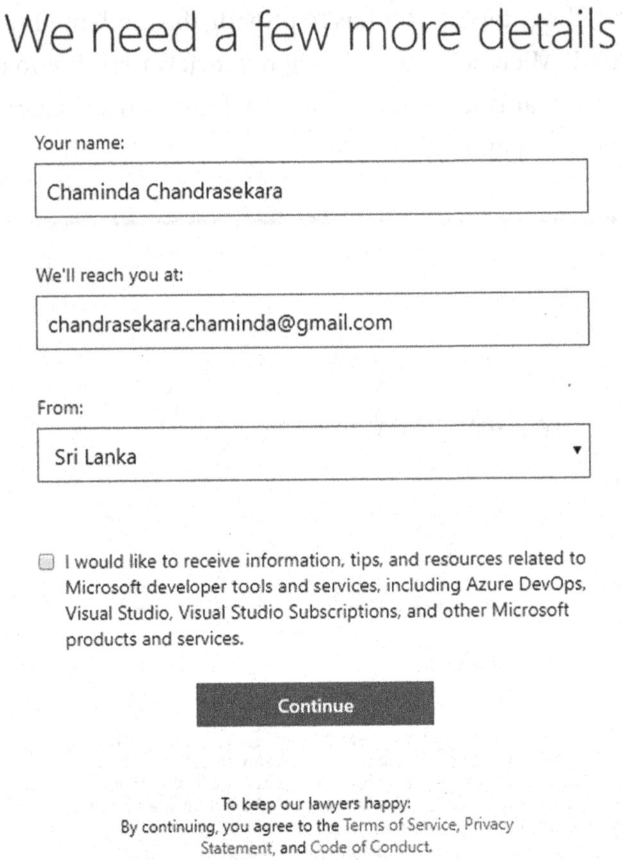

We need a few more details

Your name:

Chaminda Chandrasekara

We'll reach you at:

chandrasekara.chaminda@gmail.com

From:

Sri Lanka ▼

☐ I would like to receive information, tips, and resources related to
Microsoft developer tools and services, including Azure DevOps,
Visual Studio, Visual Studio Subscriptions, and other Microsoft
products and services.

Continue

To keep our lawyers happy:
By continuing, you agree to the Terms of Service, Privacy
Statement, and Code of Conduct.

Figure 8-15. *Additional information captured*

With that, the external user will be able to log on to the AAD-backed Azure DevOps
organization.

In this lesson, you explored the steps required to add external users to the
organization's AAD-backed Azure DevOps. This will be especially useful when you
want to add external stakeholders such as product owners or your software project
clients.

Lesson 8-4. Granting a License for Extended Paid Features

Many extensions are available in the Visual Studio Marketplace for Azure DevOps. (In fact, we will discuss setting up extensions in Chapter 10.) Many of them are free, but some of them come with a paid user license. For such extensions, users need to be granted the available licenses. Let's look at the steps required to grant access for paid extensions in Azure DevOps.

On the Users tab in the General section of the organization settings, all the users of the organization are listed. Select a user and click the three dots to get the user's context menu. See Figure 8-16.

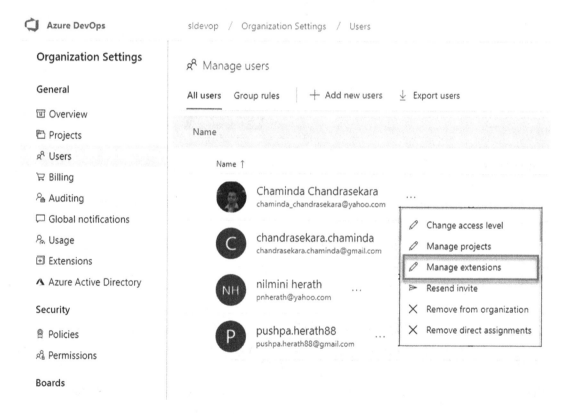

Figure 8-16. *Managing extensions for the user*

In the user extension management pop-up, you can see that the paid extensions are listed on the Extensions tab. If you have available licenses, you can select a check box for the required extension to grant the user access to the extension. See Figure 8-17.

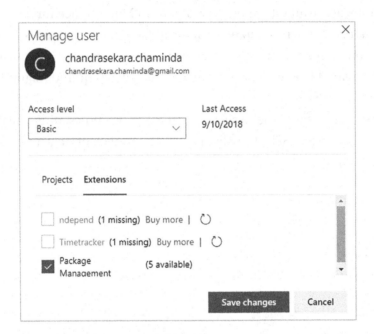

Figure 8-17. *Granting access to extensions*

The user will be able to use the additional features of the extension after you click "Save changes."

In this lesson, we discussed the steps required to grant access to users for the paid extensions in Azure DevOps.

Lesson 8-5. Setting Up Organization-Level Security Options for a Process Template

As you know, Azure DevOps provides four out-of-the-box process templates: Basic, Scrum, Agile, and CMMI. In addition to using these templates, you can create customized process templates based on the existing templates. Azure DevOps has a feature to control the access permission of each of these process templates so that users can customize them. Let's learn the process template security options available in this lesson.

Go to the organization settings, and select Process in the Boards section. You will be able to see the process templates. Click the three dots in front of the process template name and select Security.

The permission window will open where you can grant permission for the users. See Figure 8-18.

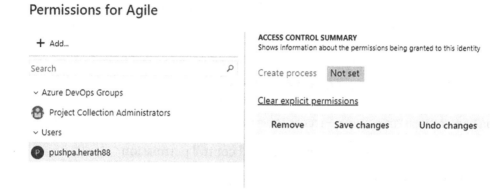

Figure 8-18. *Security of the process template*

By default, you can't edit the permission of Project Collection Administrators. Add a new user and change the "Create process" permission for this user by clicking the "Not set" value. By clicking this value, you can change the permission value to Allow or Deny. Also, you can use three buttons to update the permission.

- **Remove**: Removes the selected user from the permission grid

- **Save changes**: Saves the permission changes

- **Undo changes**: Undoes changes to the permission

You have learned what type of permissions you can set up for process template users. But when it comes to customizing process templates, you have more permission options. Let's see how to control the permission of a customized process template. Go to the process template area. Click the three dots in front of the customized process template name and select Security. You can add a new user to control the process permissions using this window. See Figure 8-19.

Figure 8-19. *Custom process template permission*

You can control three type of access for custom templates using this window.

- **Administer process permission**: Full control permission

- **Delete process**: Permission to delete the process template

- **Edit process**: Permission to edit the process template

This lesson walked you through the security options available in the process template settings so you can control the permissions of Azure DevOps users.

Lesson 8-6. Setting Up Project-Level Security Options

Team projects are mostly used to scope client software projects or products in Azure DevOps. Some organizations use a single team project to manage all their software projects. In either case, identifying the security options available on the team project level is vital to setting up the access permissions and to controlling who can access which functionality. Let's look at each of the project-level security options available in Azure DevOps.

Project security can mainly be set up on the Security tab of the project settings. See Figure 8-20.

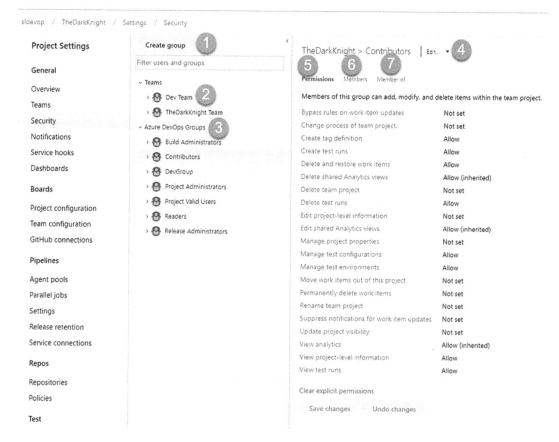

Figure 8-20. *Project security*

1. This allows you to create a security group. A group can be made a member of other groups and can contain other groups or members.

2. For each team there will be a group created. Generally, a new team is added as a member of the Contributors Azure DevOps group so that permission to contribute work to the project is granted to the team.

3. Built-in Azure DevOps groups and custom groups are available here.

4. You can edit the selected group's name, description, and image using the dialog that opens when you click the Edit link. See Figure 8-21.

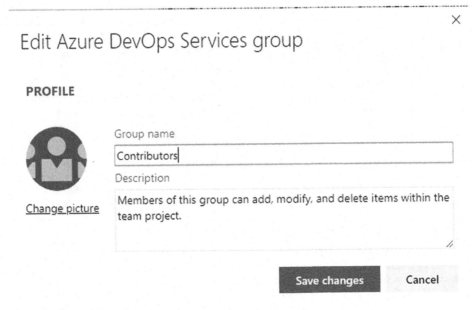

Figure 8-21. *Editing a group*

5. A team's project-level permission specification is available here. You can change the permissions for groups other than the Project Administrators group.

6. On the Members tab, you can add individuals or groups or teams as members of the selected group. See Figure 8-22.

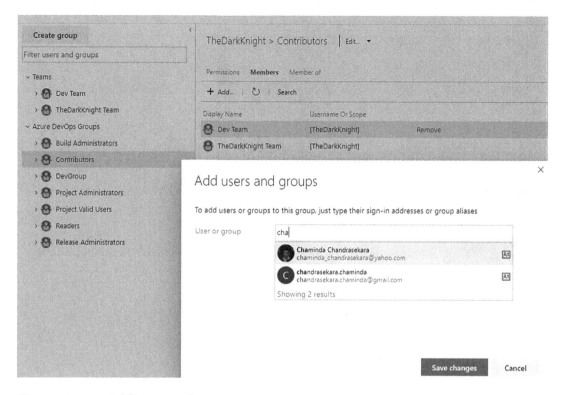

Figure 8-22. *Adding members to a group*

7. You can view the groups the currently selected group or team is a
    member of. You can make the current group or team a member of
    another group or team if required. See Figure 8-23.

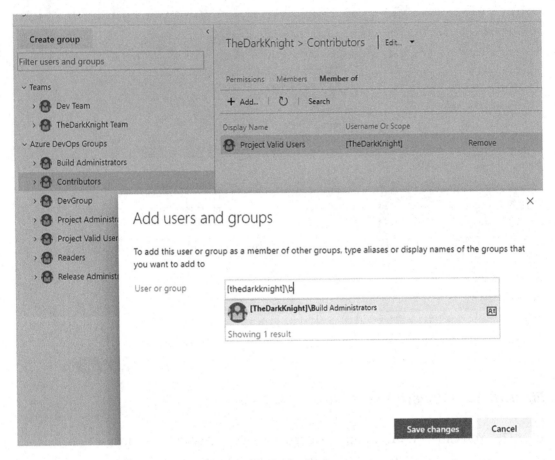

Figure 8-23. *Making a group a member of another*

The Project Administrators group in a team project is granted all the permissions for the team project, and those permissions cannot be altered.

In Azure DevOps, permissions are inherited from groups that users are a member of. When a permission is inherited, it will be shown as Allow (Inherited). Clicking Why? next to the permission shows which group the permission was inherited from. See Figure 8-24.

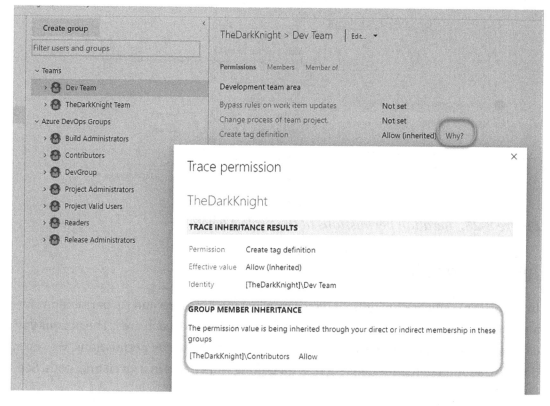

Figure 8-24. *Inherited permissions*

You can click individual permissions, and they will rotate from Not set to Allow to Deny. If the given permission is inherited from a group, the inherited Allow gets applied when the permission isn't explicitly set to Allow or Deny. Deny permission overrides any Allow inherited from a group to an individual or a group.

Iteration Permissions

On the project's configuration tab, you can click Iterations. Then in each iteration you can set the security options by clicking Security in the context menu of the iteration. You can set permissions to create child nodes, delete the current node, edit the current node, and view the permissions of the node. You can save the permission changes to available users, add a new user or group and set their permissions, or even remove the groups or users who already have permissions. Clicking "Clear explicit permissions" will remove the Allow permissions of the selected user or group and make them as "Not set." The Save button gets enabled when you do this action, and you can save or you're your changes. See Figure 8-25.

Figure 8-25. *Iteration permissions at the project level*

Area Permissions

In a project's configuration options, you can select the Areas tab and set permissions for an individual area by clicking Security in the context menu of each area. The actions you can perform with the area permissions are similar to the iteration permissions. However, there are additional permissions such as for editing work items in a given area path. See Figure 8-26.

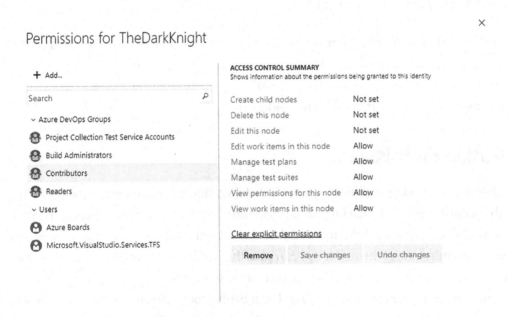

Figure 8-26. *Area permissions at the project level*

Shared Queries Permissions

The shared queries permissions can be set at the team project level. You can click Security in the context menu of an individual shared query or in the shared queries folder, which you can reach via the Queries page's All tab. The users/groups can be allowed to contribute, read, delete, and manage permissions for the shared queries folder or for individual shared queries. See Figure 8-27.

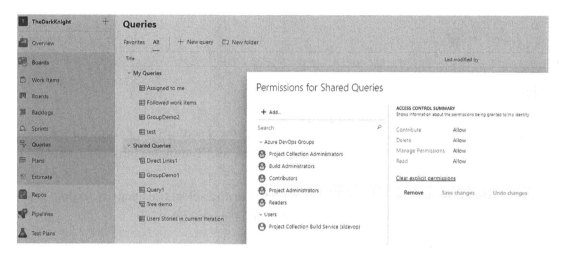

Figure 8-27. *Shared queries permissions*

In this lesson, you explored the permissions at the team project level including the permissions applicable to iterations and areas at the project level. Additionally, we discussed the shared queries permissions at the project level.

Lesson 8-7. Setting Up Team-Level Security

Azure DevOps has the capability to create multiple teams, and when you have multiple teams, it is important to control the access permission of each team. You can group users with the same permission on different teams.

Go to the project settings and select Teams in the General section. Click a team. You will be able to see the team profile, where you can add the team administrators. See Figure 8-28.

Figure 8-28. *Team profile*

Go to the Team Configurations section on the project settings page. You will see the boards section with the General, Iteration, Areas, and Templates tabs. Go to the Iterations tab.

Click the three dots in front of the iteration value and select the Security setting. The iteration permission control window will open. See Figure 8-29.

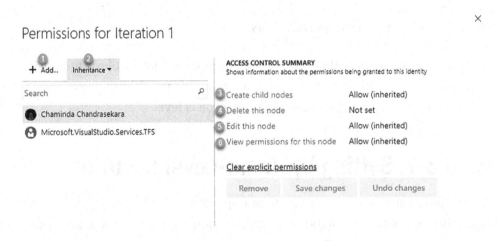

Figure 8-29. *Iteration permission*

1. You can add new users and groups to the permission.

2. You can enable or disable the inheritance.

    You can control the following permissions to each of the users or groups added to the iteration permission window.

3. The "Create child nodes" permission allows or denies the capability to add a child note.

4. The "Delete this node" permission allows you to delete the selected node.

5. The "Edit this node" permission allows you to edit the selected node.

6. You can view permissions for this node.

Close this permission window and go back to the Boards section; then go to Areas. You will see area values at the bottom of the page. Click the three dots in front of the area value and select Security. The area permission window will open. See Figure 8-30.

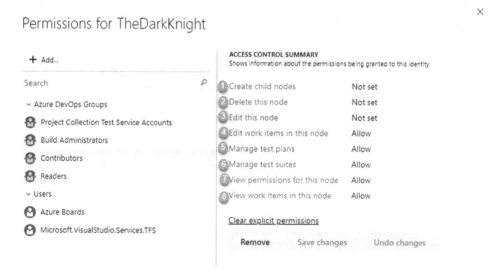

Figure 8-30. *Area permission*

1. Permission to add new nodes

2. Permission to delete the selected node

3. Permission to edit the selected node

4. Permission to edit the work items in the selected node

5. Permission to manage test plans

6. Permission to manage test suites

7. Permission to view the permission of the selected node

8. Permission to view the work items of the selected node

Lesson 8-8. Setting Up User-Level Security Options

You have a few ways to provide alternative access credentials in Azure DevOps. You can use personal access tokens, alternate credentials, and SSH public keys. In this lesson, let's look at these available options.

Log on to Azure DevOps, click the user avatar in the top-right corner, and click the Security menu option. See Figure 8-31.

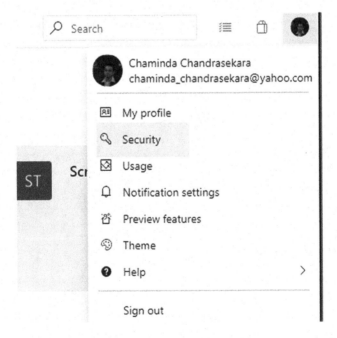

Figure 8-31. *User security*

In the "User settings" menu, select Security, and you will see three alternative credential options. See Figure 8-32.

Figure 8-32. *Alternative credential options for a user*

Personal Access Token

The *personal access token* (PAT) in Azure DevOps is an alternate password that you can use to authenticate with Azure DevOps. When a PAT is created for a user, it can be set to have the same access level of the user. You can also narrow the scope of access if required. Let's take a look at the steps involved in creating a PAT in Azure DevOps.

On the Personal Access Tokens tab, you can click "+ New Token" to create a new token. Existing tokens can be filtered by view so that you can see the active, all, revoked, and expired tokes as well. See Figure 8-33.

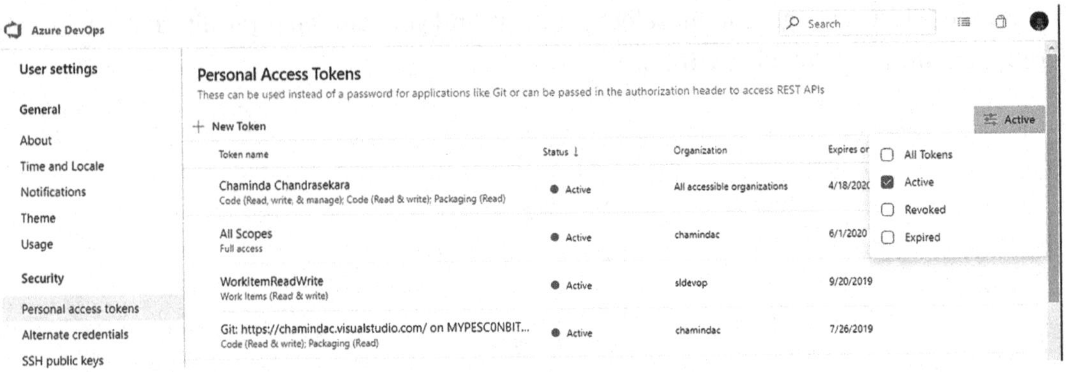

Figure 8-33. *Personal Access Tokens tab*

Once you click "+ New Token" to create a new PAT, a pane will open allowing you to create the token. You can provide a name and set an expiry date for the token. The scope of the token can be set to "Full access," which allows the user to access all the features that they normally have access to. Or you can narrow the scope to a specific access level for a given token. See Figure 8-34.

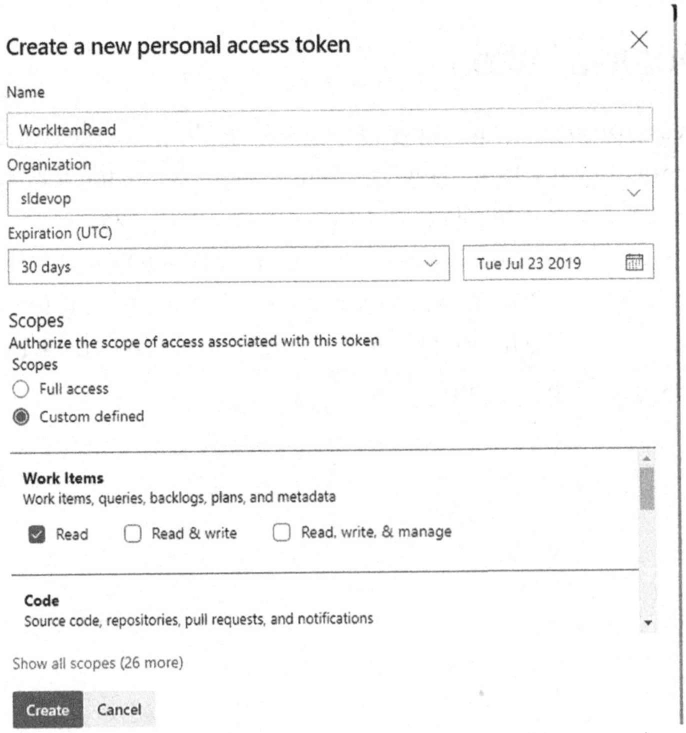

Figure 8-34. *Creating a PAT*

Once you click the Create button, a PAT is created for the defined scope, and you must copy the PAT value and save it in a secure location, as it will be shown only once. See Figure 8-35.

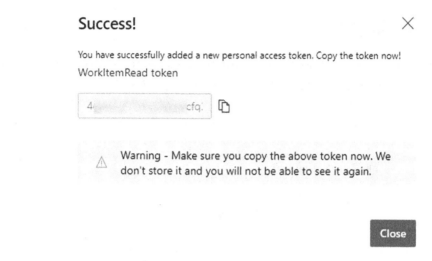

Figure 8-35. *PAT created*

After creating the PAT, you can select it on the Personal Access Tokens tab. Once a PAT is selected, you can regenerate the token for it. However, if you are already using the previously generated token value, you have to replace it with the newly generated value in each place it is used after regenerating a token. You can revoke a token as well by selecting a PAT on the Personal Access Tokens tab. To edit the scope, name, and expiry date of a given token, click Edit button. See Figure 8-36.

Personal Access Tokens

These can be used instead of a password for applications like Git or can be passed in the authorization header to access REST APIs

+ New Token   ⟲ Revoke   ✎ Edit   ◯ Regenerate

Token name	Status ↓	Organization	Expires on
Chaminda Chandrasekara Code (Read, write, & manage); Code (Read & write); Packaging (Read)	● Active	All accessible organizations	4/18/2020
All Scopes Full access	● Active	chamindac	6/1/2020
✓ WorkItemReadWrite Work Items (Read & write)	● Active	sldevop	9/20/2019

Figure 8-36. *Editing, revoking, and regenerating PAT*

Personal access tokens are really useful when using an Azure DevOps REST API and when performing various integrations with third-party applications. Chapter 9 will cover how to use PATs with a REST API.

Alternate Credentials

You can set up alternate credentials to work with Azure Git Repos. Unlike with PATs, the alternate credentials do not have expiry dates. See Figure 8-37.

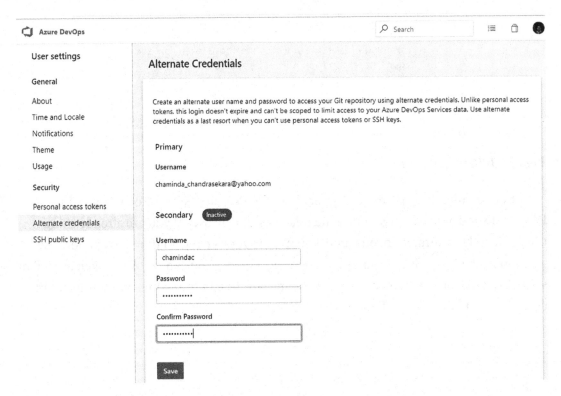

Figure 8-37. *Alternate credentials*

SSH Public Keys

You can use the SSH keys generated in Linux, macOS, and Windows running Git for Windows to authenticate Azure DevOps. For further details on SSH key usage with Azure DevOps, refer to `https://docs.microsoft.com/en-us/azure/devops/repos/git/use-ssh-keys-to-authenticate?view=azure-devops`.

In this lesson, we discussed alternative credential options available for users in Azure DevOps. Out of the options, the personal access tokens are commonly used, and you will learn more about them along with the REST APIs in Chapter 9.

Summary

We discussed the security options available in Azure DevOps specifically related to Azure Boards in this chapter. Organization-level permissions and team project and team permissions were described in detail so that you will be able to set up users with access levels based on your team requirements. Further, we explored how to add external users to AAD-backed Azure DevOps organizations and how to grant licenses to individual users for paid extensions. We also describes process template permissions so that you can control who is allowed to extend and customize the process of your Azure DevOps organization. In addition, you explored the project level, team level, and individual user-level permissions including how to create personal access tokens to use with the REST APIs and other third-party application integrations.

In the next chapter, we will discuss the REST APIs and Azure DevOps command-line interface, which allows you to develop extensions, integrate Azure DevOps with other tools, and manage Azure DevOps services and resources in a flexible and faster way.

CHAPTER 9

Working with REST APIs and the CLI

Azure DevOps comes with some Representational State Transfer (REST) APIs, which are service endpoints that support HTTP operations. These HTTP methods in Azure DevOps allow you to create, retrieve, update, and delete resources in Azure DevOps. The REST APIs can be used to develop extensions for Azure DevOps or to integrate various third-party applications with Azure DevOps. You may be using an application such as ServiceNow to manage tickets, and if you want ServiceNow and Azure DevOps to be integrated, you can leverage the capabilities in a REST API. The Azure Pipeline application (`https://store.servicenow.com/sn_appstore_store.do#!/store/application/fa788cb5dbb5630040669c27db961940`) for ServiceNow is a good example of using REST APIs for integration. Many extensions available to Azure DevOps in the Visual Studio Marketplace also use the REST API capabilities to extend and enhance the features of Azure DevOps.

For example, an Azure command-line interface (CLI) extension is available that provides command-line access to Azure DevOps. You can use an Azure DevOps command-line form of Windows, macOS, and Linux. The Azure DevOps CLI allows you to work with commands to perform various tasks on Azure DevOps without worrying about GUI flows. A CLI can be a faster and more flexible way to interact with Azure DevOps.

In this chapter, let's further understand the Azure DevOps REST APIs and CLI and explore how you can use them with practical lessons.

© Chaminda Chandrasekara and Pushpa Herath 2019
C. Chandrasekara and P. Herath, *Hands-on Azure Boards*, https://doi.org/10.1007/978-1-4842-5046-4_9

Lesson 9-1. Understanding the REST API Components

There are a few components in a REST API request/response pair. Let's look at each of these components in this lesson.

The Request URI

The request URI of an Azure DevOps REST API can be identified as follows:

```
VERB https://{instance}[/{team-project}]/_apis[/{area}]/{resource}?api-version={version}
```

Verb: This is an HTTP GET, POST, HEAD, PUT, or PATCH, and it is a required HTTP method.

Instance: This is the Azure DevOps Services organization or the TFS/Azure DevOps Server collection.

- For Azure DevOps Services, this would be dev.azure.com/{OrganizationName}.

- For Azure DevOps Server/TFS, this would be {server:port}/tfs/{CollectionName}.

Resource path: This is the path to the Azure DevOps resource in the format _apis/{area}/{resource}, as in _apis/wit/workitems.

API version: This is the version of the REST API to be used. Depending on the Azure DevOps Services or Azure DevOps Server version you are using, the REST API version should be specified with a call to the REST API. The following are examples:

- api-version=5.0

- api-version=5.1-preview.3

HTTP Request Message Header Fields

The header fields will be the HTTP verb (which is required) and the authorization header details for the HTTP method.

HTTP Request Message Body

This optional component is required in order for the HTTP POST and PUT methods to support the HTTP operation. For example, to create a work item, you have to pass the details of the work item in the request body to the work item. In addition, some of the services require you to define the Multipurpose Internet Mail Extensions (MIME) type such as `application/json`.

HTTP Response Message Header Fields

HTTP response status codes will be returned after a REST API call. The response code 2xx gives the success state, where 4xx and 5xx give error responses. Instead of generic response codes, a service-specific response code can be returned, as specified in the API documentation. Additional response header fields can be included to support the response such as `content-type`.

HTTP Reponses Message Body Fields

Response objects can be returned in the HTTP response body in situations such as when a GET request is returning data. Typically, returning objects will be JSON or XML data, and the type will be indicated in the response header field's `content-type` field.

In this lesson, you looked at the components in a REST API call to gain an understanding of a REST API call. This information will be useful in the following lessons in this chapter.

Lesson 9-2. Using a REST API from a Browser

The simplest way to invoke a REST API GET request is via a browser instance. In this lesson, let's explore how you can retrieve information from an Azure DevOps REST API using the Chrome browser.

Prerequisites: You need to have an Azure DevOps organization with projects and work items.

Use the following URI to call the Azure DevOps REST API to get a list of the available work items. Replace {`organization`} with your Azure DevOps organization name.

Replace {project} with your team project's name. Replace {ids} with the comma-separated work item IDs of your team project that you want to retrieve.

```
https://dev.azure.com/{organization}/{project}/_apis/wit/
workitems?ids={ids}&api-version=5.0
```

Here's an example:

```
https://dev.azure.com/sldevop/TheDarkKnight/_apis/wit/
workitems?ids=52,56,57&api-version=5.0 Open a chrome browser instance.
```

Launch a Chrome browser, copy the REST API URI to the address bar, and press Enter to invoke the REST API GET request. Once prompted, log in with your credentials to the Azure DevOps organization. You should be able to see that the work item data of the specified work items is retrieved to the browser as JSON content. See Figure 9-1.

Figure 9-1. *List work items using the REST API in a browser*

To enhance the view of the returned JSON content in the Chrome browser, you can add an extension such as a JSON formatter or JSON viewer. Once the extension is added to the browser, you will see a formatted view of the returned JSON from the Azure DevOps REST API. See Figure 9-2.

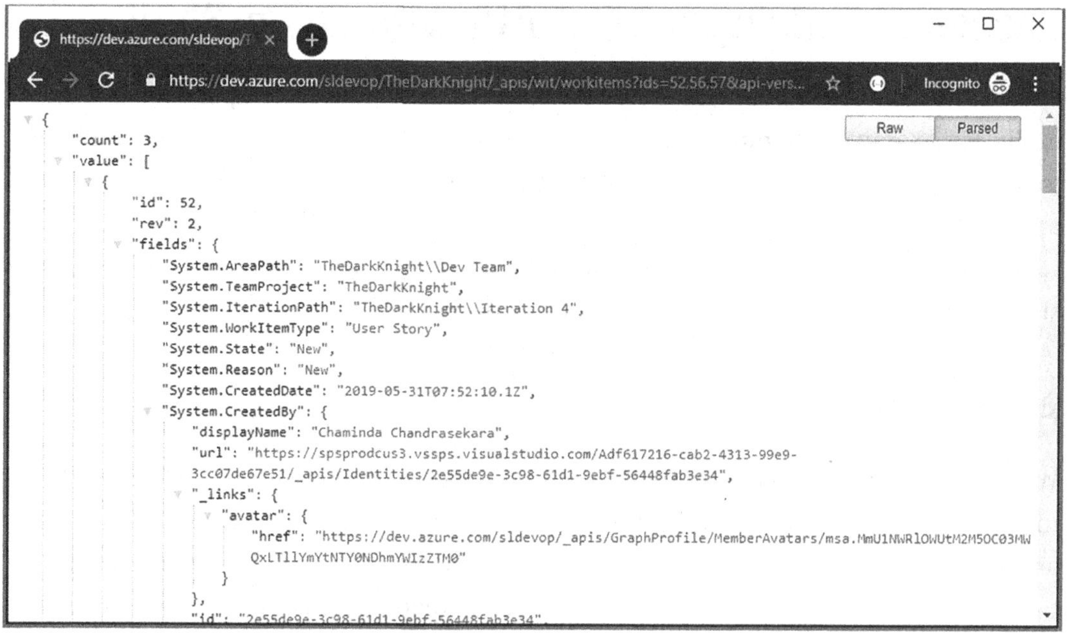

Figure 9-2. *Formatted JSON after REST API call*

You can pass several additional parameters to a REST API call in Azure DevOps. Let's look at a few useful parameters you can use with a REST API call to get a list of work items.

- **fields**: This allows you to specify the fields of the work item to retrieve as a comma-separated list.

  Here's an example: `https://dev.azure.com/sldevop/ TheDarkKnight/_apis/wit/workitems/6?fields=system. title,system.id&api-version=5.0.`

- **asof**: You can define the date and time that the work item should be retrieved by. This would be useful to retrieve work item details as of a given date instead of retrieving the latest state of the given work items.

- **$expand**: This lets you define the scope of the retrieved work item details.

In this lesson, you explored how you can invoke an Azure DevOps REST API call from a browser to execute GET requests. Using REST API calls in a browser is useful to understanding the content of the retrieved data quickly and for testing the REST API calls before you use them in the application, extension, or program you are implementing.

Lesson 9-3. Using a REST API with PowerShell

You can use PowerShell in many ways to interact with an Azure DevOps REST API easily. For example, you may want to perform certain activities during CI/CD pipelines to retrieve and update data from Azure DevOps. (CI/CD pipelines will be discussed in another book of this series.) You can even create extensions and additional tasks for CI/CD pipelines with PowerShell while using a REST API. Let's take a look at how to get started using PowerShell to call an Azure DevOps REST API.

Authorization

When a REST API is called from PowerShell, you need to provide header information to authorize the request. For this purpose, you can create a personal access token as described in Lesson 8-8. The scope of the PAT can be set to work item read/write because you are going to use the REST API calls for reading and updating work items in this lesson and in the next one. See Figure 9-3. Keep the PAT saved in a file in a secure location for use in the lesson.

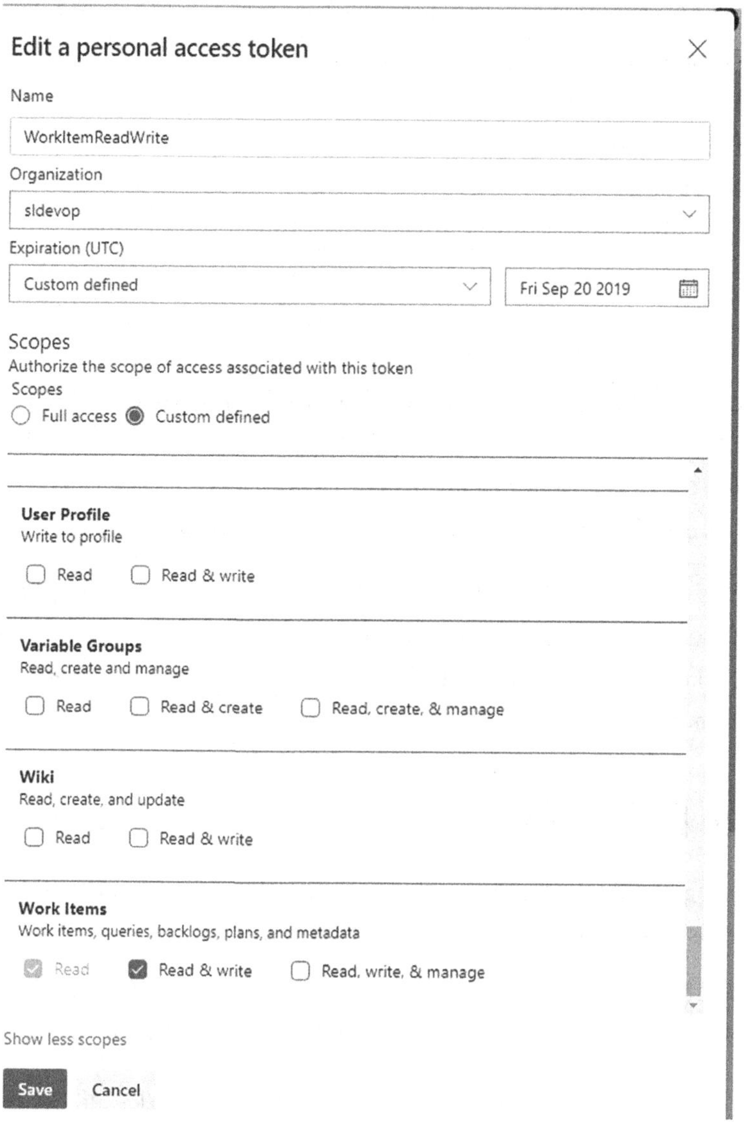

Figure 9-3. *Work item read/write PAT*

Open a PowerShell ISE window and add a new script file. In the script file, add the following code segment to prepare a header for authorization with the Azure DevOps REST API:

```
param(
  [Parameter(Mandatory=$true)]
  [string] $token,
  [Parameter(Mandatory=$true)]
```

```
    [string] $collectionUri,
    [Parameter(Mandatory=$true)]
    [string] $teamProjectName,
    [Parameter(Mandatory=$true)]
    [string] $workitemIDs,
    [string] $restAPIversion = '5.0'
)

$User=""

# Base64-encodes the Personal Access Token (PAT) appropriately
$base64AuthInfo = [Convert]::ToBase64String([Text.Encoding]::ASCII.
GetBytes(("{0}:{1}" -f $User,$token)));
$header = @{Authorization=("Basic {0}" -f $base64AuthInfo)};
```

We'll discuss the parameters other than the $token later in the chapter. The token is used with the username (which can be an empty string) to generate the Base64-encoded authorization token. Then it is added to a variable named $header in order to pass it as the header of the REST API call.

Calling the REST API

Add the following two lines of code to prepare the URI and invoke the REST API. Notice that the header is passed to the Invoke REST method.

```
$Uri = $collectionUri + '/' + $teamProjectName + '/_apis/wit/
workitems?ids='+ $workitemIDs + '&api-version=' + $restAPIversion

$workItems = Invoke-RestMethod -Method Get -ContentType application/json
-Uri $Uri -Headers $header
```

The content type to get is defined as application/json. Let's add a few more code lines to loop through the retrieved work items, as shown here:

```
foreach($workitem in $workItems.value)
{
  Write-Host ("Work item - Id:{0} Title: {1}" -f $workitem.id, $workitem.
  fields.'System.Title')
}
```

The code will loop through each of the work items and print the ID and title of each work item.

The complete code of the previous sample is as follows:

```
param(
  [Parameter(Mandatory=$true)]
  [string] $token,
  [Parameter(Mandatory=$true)]
  [string] $collectionUri,
  [Parameter(Mandatory=$true)]
  [string] $teamProjectName,
  [Parameter(Mandatory=$true)]
  [string] $workitemIDs,
  [string] $restAPIversion = '5.0'
)

$User=""

# Base64-encodes the Personal Access Token (PAT) appropriately
$base64AuthInfo = [Convert]::ToBase64String([Text.Encoding]::ASCII.
GetBytes(("{0}:{1}" -f $User,$token)));
$header = @{Authorization=("Basic {0}" -f $base64AuthInfo)};

$Uri = $collectionUri + '/' + $teamProjectName + '/_apis/wit/
workitems?ids='+ $workitemIDs + '&api-version=' + $restAPIversion
$workItems = Invoke-RestMethod -Method Get -ContentType application/json
-Uri $Uri -Headers $header

foreach($workitem in $workItems.value)
{
  Write-Host ("Work item - Id:{0} Title: {1}" -f $workitem.id, $workitem.
  fields.'System.Title')
}
```

Executing the Script

Save the script file; you can change the directory of the PowerShell ISE to the script's saved folder. Then to execute the script, use the following syntax:

```
.\GetWorkItems.ps1 -token 'patvalue' -collectionUri 'collectionuri'
-teamProjectName 'teamprojectname' -workitemIDs 'workitemids'
```

Here's an example:

```
.\GetWorkItems.ps1 -token 'h6gayknpatvalueml7qi74luna' -collectionUri
'https://dev.azure.com/sldevop' -teamProjectName 'TheDarkKnight'
-workitemIDs '52,56,57'
```

When you execute the script, you will see that the work items are retrieved and the ID and title are printed. See Figure 9-4.

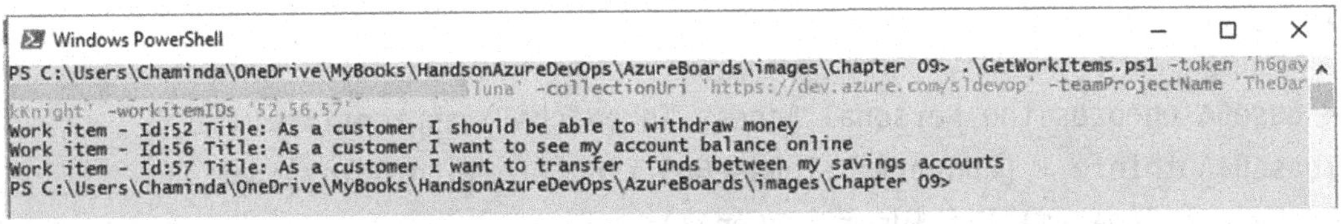

Figure 9-4. *Retrieving work items using a REST API in PowerShell*

WIQL

The sample used earlier is a simple one that retrieves work items by ID. It is also possible to implement REST API calls to retrieve work items using the Work Item Query Language (WIQL). For example, the following code passes some WIQL and retrieves and prints work item IDs and the REST API URI of each work item matching the query criteria:

```
param(
    [Parameter(Mandatory=$true)]
    [string] $token,
    [Parameter(Mandatory=$true)]
    [string] $collectionUri,
    [Parameter(Mandatory=$true)]
    [string] $teamProjectName,
```

```powershell
    [Parameter(Mandatory=$true)]
    [string] $wiql,
    [string] $restAPIversion = '5.0'
)

$User=""

# Base64-encodes the Personal Access Token (PAT) appropriately
$base64AuthInfo = [Convert]::ToBase64String([Text.Encoding]::ASCII.
GetBytes(("{0}:{1}" -f $User,$token)));
$header = @{Authorization=("Basic {0}" -f $base64AuthInfo)};

$Uri = $collectionUri + '/' + $teamProjectName + '/_apis/wit/wiql?api-
version=' + $restAPIversion

$requestBody = '{"query":"' + $wiql + '"}'

$workItems = Invoke-RestMethod -Method Post -ContentType application/json
-Uri $Uri -Body $requestBody -Headers $header

foreach($workitem in $workItems.WorkItems)
{
  Write-Host ("Work item - Id:{0} url: {1}" -f $workitem.id, $workitem.url)
}
```

You can pass WIQL to the script and execute it as follows:

```powershell
.\GetWorkItemswithWIQL.ps1 -token 'h6gayknpatvaluexbml7qi74luna'
-collectionUri 'https://dev.azure.com/sldevop' -teamProjectName
'TheDarkKnight' -wiql 'Select [System.Id], [System.Title], [System.
State] From WorkItems Where ([System.WorkItemType] = "Task" AND [State] <>
"Closed")'
```

Once executed, the script prints the ID and URI of each work item. See Figure 9-5.

Figure 9-5. *Executing WIQL with the REST API*

We went through the steps required to authorize and invoke an Azure DevOps REST API GET request using PowerShell in this lesson. You can use this knowledge to create custom scripts to generate reports by querying the work items with a REST API of Azure DevOps. You can learn about other options for REST APIs via the REST API documentation at `https://docs.microsoft.com/en-us/rest/api/azure/devops/?view=azure-devops-rest-5.0`.

Lesson 9-4. Creating a Work Item with a REST API

We discussed how to retrieve work items using a REST API in the previous lessons of this chapter, so let's now look at how you can use a REST API to create a new work item.

Prerequisites: You need to have performed the previous lessons of this chapter and have a good understanding of calling REST APIs with PowerShell.

Open a PowerShell ISE and create a new script. Use the following code as sample code to create a work item with the REST API:

```
param(
  [Parameter(Mandatory=$true)]
  [string] $token,
  [Parameter(Mandatory=$true)]
```

```
  [string] $collectionUri,
  [Parameter(Mandatory=$true)]
  [string] $teamProjectName,
  [Parameter(Mandatory=$true)]
  [string] $workitemType,
  [Parameter(Mandatory=$true)]
  [string] $workitemTitle,
  [string] $restAPIversion = '5.0'
)

$User=""

# Base64-encodes the Personal Access Token (PAT) appropriately
$base64AuthInfo = [Convert]::ToBase64String([Text.Encoding]::ASCII.
GetBytes(("{0}:{1}" -f $User,$token)));
$header = @{Authorization=("Basic {0}" -f $base64AuthInfo)};

$Uri = $collectionUri + '/' + $teamProjectName + '/_apis/wit/workitems/$' +
$workitemType + '?api-version=' + $restAPIversion

$requestBody = '[{
  "op": "add",
  "path": "/fields/System.Title",
  "from": null,
  "value": "' + $workitemTitle + '"
}]'

$workItemCreated = Invoke-RestMethod -Method Post -ContentType application/
json-patch+json -Uri $Uri -Body $requestBody -Headers $header

Write-Host $workItemCreated
```

Notice the REST API URI is set to use a parameter value of a given work item type name. The parameter $workitemType should be supplied with the exact work item type name. For example, User Story, Bug, Product Backlog Item, and Task are a few valid work item types. The request body in the previous code is defined with the work item title as the supplied parameter. Another change that the REST method invokes is that the content type is set to application/json-patch+json.

You can call the previous script with the following syntax to create a new work item:

```
.\CreateWorkItem.ps1 -token 'h6gayknpatvalueluna' -collectionUri 'https://
dev.azure.com/sldevop' -teamProjectName 'TheDarkKnight' -workitemType 'User
Story' -workitemTitle 'created with api 01'
```

Once the script executed, a new work item (a user story in this example) gets created in the team project. See Figure 9-6.

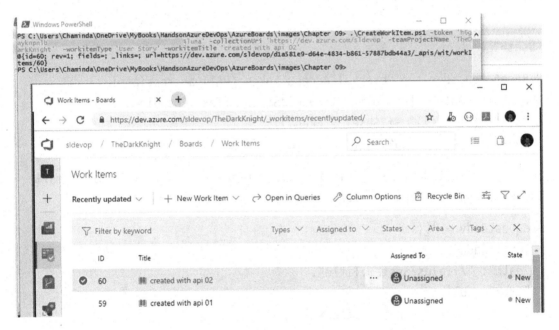

Figure 9-6. *Creating a work item using a REST API*

In this lesson, you used a REST API to create new work items in Azure DevOps. You can further implement the ability to update or delete work items with a REST API by following the documentation available at `https://docs.microsoft.com/en-us/rest/api/azure/devops/?view=azure-devops-rest-5.0`.

Lesson 9-5. Getting Started with the Azure DevOps CLI

The command-line interface for Azure DevOps allows you to perform various tasks in Azure DevOps without worrying about GUI flows. With the Azure DevOps CLI, you can execute commands against Azure DevOps in a flexible and fast manner. The Azure DevOps CLI is an extension to the Azure CLI. In this lesson, let's look at the steps required to get your machine ready to use the Azure DevOps CLI.

As the first step, you have to make sure that your system is set up with Azure CLI 2.0.49 or later. You can open a PowerShell window and execute `az --version` to check the Azure CLI version. See Figure 9-7.

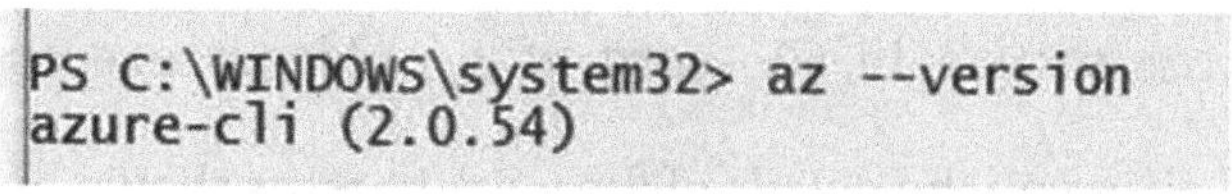

Figure 9-7. *Checking the Azure CLI version*

If Azure CLI is not installed in your machine, install it by following the instructions at `https://docs.microsoft.com/en-us/cli/azure/install-azure-cli?view=azure-cli-latest`.

To add the Azure DevOps CLI extension, execute the following command in PowerShell:

`az extension add --name azure-devops`

Executing `az --version` now will show the extension is added to your machine. See Figure 9-8.

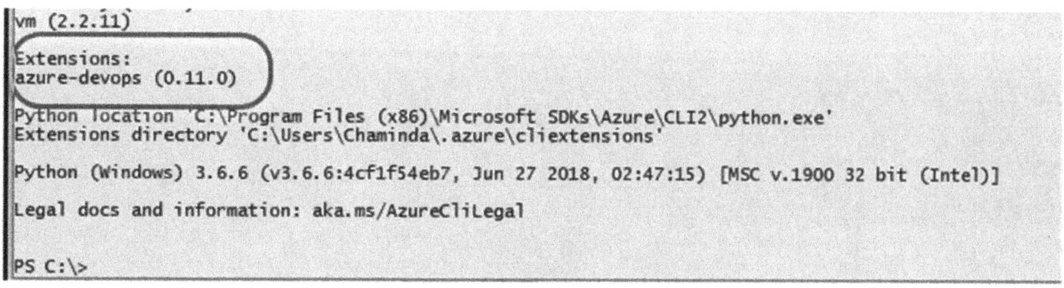

Figure 9-8. *Azure DevOps CLI extension added*

Showing a Work Item

Now that you have set up the Azure DevOps CLI, let's execute a simple command to see how it works. You need to log into your Microsoft/organization account, which is connected to the Azure DevOps organization in order to use the CLI. You can do this by using the `az login` command. Provide your credentials when prompted and complete the login. Then in the PowerShell window, you can execute the following command to show a given work item data:

```
az boards work-item show --id workitemid --org azuredevopsorganization
```

Here's an example:

```
az boards work-item show --id 60 --org https://dev.azure.com/sldevop
```

This command gives you the details of the work item, as shown in Figure 9-9.

> Windows PowerShell

```
]
PS C:\> az boards work-item show --id 60 --org https://dev.azure.com/sldevop
{
  "fields": {
    "Microsoft.VSTS.Common.Priority": 2,
    "Microsoft.VSTS.Common.StateChangeDate": "2019-06-22T10:39:45.46Z",
    "Microsoft.VSTS.Common.ValueArea": "Business",
    "System.AreaId": 6,
    "System.AreaLevel1": "TheDarkKnight",
    "System.AreaPath": "TheDarkKnight",
    "System.AuthorizedAs": {
      "_links": {
        "avatar": {
          "href": "https://dev.azure.com/sldevop/_apis/GraphProfile/MemberAvatars/msa.MmU1NWRlOWUtM2M5OC03MWQxLTllYmYtNT
YONDhmYWIzZTM0"
        }
      },
      "descriptor": "msa.MmU1NWRlOWUtM2M5OC03MWQxLTllYmYtNTYONDhmYWIzZTM0",
      "displayName": "Chaminda Chandrasekara",
      "id": "2e55de9e-3c98-61d1-9ebf-56448fab3e34",
      "imageUrl": "https://dev.azure.com/sldevop/_apis/GraphProfile/MemberAvatars/msa.MmU1NWRlOWUtM2M5OC03MWQxLTllYmYtNT
YONDhmYWIzZTM0",
      "uniqueName": "chaminda_chandrasekara@yahoo.com",
      "url": "https://spsprodcus3.vssps.visualstudio.com/Adf617216-cab2-4313-99e9-3cc07de67e51/_apis/Identities/2e55de9e
-3c98-61d1-9ebf-56448fab3e34"
    },
    "System.AuthorizedDate": "2019-06-22T10:39:45.46Z",
    "System.BoardColumn": "New Work",
    "System.BoardColumnDone": false,
    "System.ChangedBy": {
      "_links": {
        "avatar": {
          "href": "https://dev.azure.com/sldevop/_apis/GraphProfile/MemberAvatars/msa.MmU1NWRlOWUtM2M5OC03MWQxLTllYmYtNT
YONDhmYWIzZTM0"
        }
      },
      "descriptor": "msa.MmU1NWRlOWUtM2M5OC03MWQxLTllYmYtNTYONDhmYWIzZTM0",
      "displayName": "Chaminda Chandrasekara",
      "id": "2e55de9e-3c98-61d1-9ebf-56448fab3e34",
      "imageUrl": "https://dev.azure.com/sldevop/_apis/GraphProfile/MemberAvatars/msa.MmU1NWRlOWUtM2M5OC03MWQxLTllYmYtNT
YONDhmYWIzZTM0",
      "uniqueName": "chaminda_chandrasekara@yahoo.com",
      "url": "https://spsprodcus3.vssps.visualstudio.com/Adf617216-cab2-4313-99e9-3cc07de67e51/_apis/Identities/2e55de9e
-3c98-61d1-9ebf-56448fab3e34"
    },
    "System.ChangedDate": "2019-06-22T10:39:45.46Z",
    "System.CommentCount": 0,
    "System.CreatedBy": {
      "_links": {
        "avatar": {
          "href": "https://dev.azure.com/sldevop/_apis/GraphProfile/MemberAvatars/msa.MmU1NWRlOWUtM2M5OC03MWQxLTllYmYtNT
YONDhmYWIzZTM0"
        }
      },
      "descriptor": "msa.MmU1NWRlOWUtM2M5OC03MWQxLTllYmYtNTYONDhmYWIzZTM0",
      "displayName": "Chaminda Chandrasekara",
      "id": "2e55de9e-3c98-61d1-9ebf-56448fab3e34",
      "imageUrl": "https://dev.azure.com/sldevop/_apis/GraphProfile/MemberAvatars/msa.MmU1NWRlOWUtM2M5OC03MWQxLTllYmYtNT
YONDhmYWIzZTM0",
      "uniqueName": "chaminda_chandrasekara@yahoo.com",
      "url": "https://spsprodcus3.vssps.visualstudio.com/Adf617216-cab2-4313-99e9-3cc07de67e51/_apis/Identities/2e55de9e
-3c98-61d1-9ebf-56448fab3e34"
    },
    "System.CreatedDate": "2019-06-22T10:39:45.46Z",
    "System.Id": 60,
    "System.IterationId": 1,
    "System.IterationLevel1": "TheDarkKnight",
    "System.IterationPath": "TheDarkKnight",
    "System.NodeName": "TheDarkKnight",
    "System.PersonId": 118629497,
    "System.Reason": "New",
    "System.Rev": 1,
    "System.RevisedDate": "9999-01-01T00:00:00Z",
    "System.State": "New",
    "System.TeamProject": "TheDarkKnight",
    "System.Title": "created with api 02",
    "System.Watermark": 281,
    "System.WorkItemType": "User Story",
    "WEF_C975A0860A5E4A8CAA34BA57894495D0_Kanban.Column": "New Work",
    "WEF_C975A0860A5E4A8CAA34BA57894495D0_Kanban.Column.Done": false,
    "WEF_C975A0860A5E4A8CAA34BA57894495D0_System.ExtensionMarker": true
  },
  "id": 60,
  "relations": null,
```

Figure 9-9. *Showing the work item with the Azure CLI*

Updating a Work item

You can easily update a work item in the Azure CLI. Let's try to edit the title of a work item with the following command syntax:

```
az boards work-item update --id workitemid --title "updated title" --org
azuredevopsorganization
```

For example, you can update the title of a user story as shown here. See Figure 9-10.

```
az boards work-item update --id 60 --title "title updated with CLI" --org
https://dev.azure.com/sldevop
```

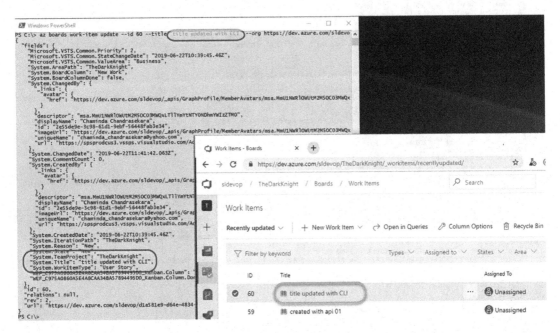

Figure 9-10.   *Updating the work item title with the Azure DevOps CLI*

In this lesson, we discussed how to get started using the Azure DevOps CLI. You can use the Azure Boards documentation available at `https://docs.microsoft.com/en-us/cli/azure/ext/azure-devops/boards?view=azure-cli-latest` to identify the various commands available and use them to view and update work items, boards, areas, iterations, and so on.

Summary

In this chapter, we discussed how to use a REST API with a browser and with PowerShell. Further, you learned how to use the REST API to retrieve and create work items. Additionally, we introduced the Azure DevOps CLI and showed how to get started with the CLI. We showed how to use the CLI for displaying and updating work items, and you know where to find the documentation for both REST APIs and the Azure DevOps CLI to do further exploring. Both the REST APIs and the CLI in Azure DevOps can be useful when integrating with other tools, developing extensions, or performing quick tasks on work items or boards.

In the next chapter, you'll look at using extensions from the Visual Studio Marketplace for Azure DevOps. You will explore a couple of useful extensions as well as see how to get the GitHub and Azure Boards integration to work.

CHAPTER 10

Using Extensions with Azure Boards and Linking with GitHub

You can add simple add-ons to Azure DevOps to customize and extend the capabilities of Azure DevOps. The extensions are written in HTML, JavaScript, CSS, and PowerShell, and they use REST APIs to interact with Azure DevOps Services as well as other applications and services. The Azure DevOps extensions are published in the Visual Studio Marketplace (`https://marketplace.visualstudio.com/azuredevops`). Specifically, Azure DevOps extensions can be used to provide custom views in dashboards as widgets; add tasks to CI/CD pipelines; extend the functionality of work item forms; develop new actions to run on hubs in Overview, Boards, Repos, Pipelines, or Test experiences; and create new hubs to perform new actions.

In this chapter, we'll show how you can add extensions from the marketplace to your Azure DevOps organizations and how to use some specific extensions to enhance the functionality of Azure Boards.

GitHub is a subsidiary of Microsoft, and it is a popular place to discover, share, and build software. It is a web-hosted source control platform based on Git and has been widely embraced by the open source developer community. Azure DevOps has close integrations with GitHub, and now you can use Azure Boards within GitHub.

In this chapter, we'll discuss how you can use Azure Boards with GitHub and use the integrations to provide a great project execution experience within GitHub.

© Chaminda Chandrasekara and Pushpa Herath 2019
C. Chandrasekara and P. Herath, *Hands-on Azure Boards*, https://doi.org/10.1007/978-1-4842-5046-4_10

Lesson 10-1. Using Extensions in Azure DevOps

Extensions for Azure DevOps are published and made available in the Visual Studio Marketplace (`https://marketplace.visualstudio.com/azuredevops`). Microsoft, other vendors, and the community develop these extensions. Many of these extensions are free to use; others are created as commercial extensions that you need to buy to use in your Azure DevOps organization. In this lesson, let's take a look at how you can install and manage extensions for your Azure DevOps organization.

In Azure DevOps, near your profile picture, click the shopping bag icon to access the Browse Marketplace and "Manage extensions" menu items. See Figure 10-1.

Figure 10-1. *Options to browse and manage extensions*

If you click Browse Marketplace, you will be redirected to `https://marketplace.visualstudio.com/azuredevops` where you can search for and install extensions. Clicking "Manage extensions" will open the Extensions tab of the Organization Settings page.

For now, click Browse Marketplace so you can find your first extension to install to your Azure Boards. In the marketplace, search for *estimate*; you will see a few related extensions in the results. See Figure 10-2.

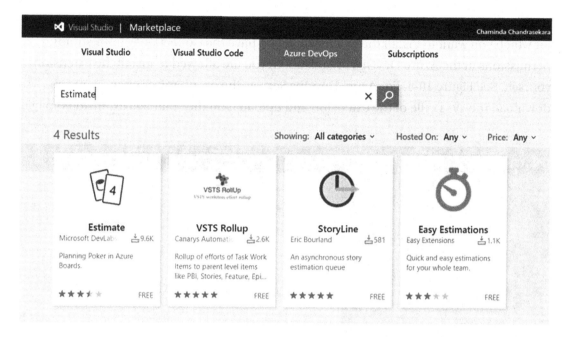

Figure 10-2. *Searching for extensions*

In this lesson, let's install the Estimate extension by Microsoft DevLabs; we will explain how to use this extension in Lesson 10-4.

Clicking the extension's card in the search results will take you to the extension's page in the marketplace. If it is a free extension, you can click the "Get it free" button. See Figure 10-3.

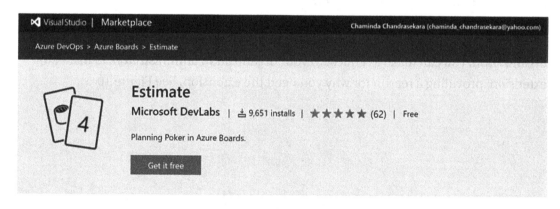

Figure 10-3. *Getting an extension for free*

A new window will open where you can select the Azure DevOps organization for which you want to install the extension. If you have the Collection Administrator permissions in the Azure DevOps organization, you are allowed to install the extension yourself. See Figure 10-4. For Azure DevOps Server (the on-premise server), you can download the .vsix file of the extension and upload it on the "Manage extensions" page.

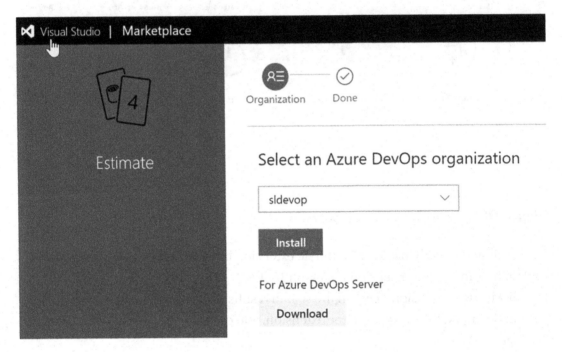

Figure 10-4. *Installing the extension*

If you do not have sufficient permissions to install an extension in the Azure DevOps organization, you can make a request to your organization administrators to install the extension, providing a reason for why you need the extension. See Figure 10-5.

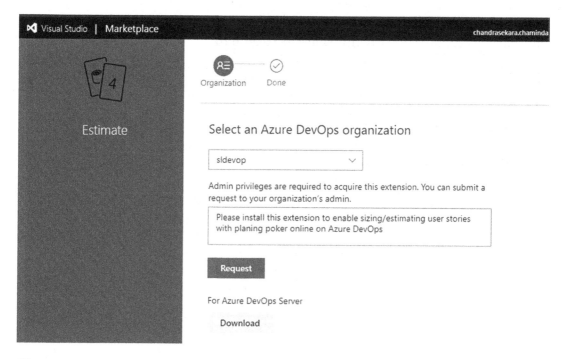

Figure 10-5. *Requesting an extension install*

Once the request is made, the collection administrators will be notified via e-mail. The collection administrators can view the request to install an extension on the Extensions page's Requested tab of the organization settings. Administrators can filter by Pending, Approved, and Rejected extensions on the Requested tab. See Figure 10-6.

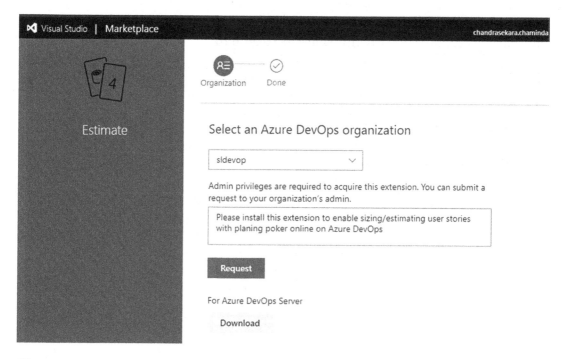

Figure 10-6. *List of requested extensions*

Click the pending extension request, and you can approve it or reject it if you have the Collection Administrator permissions. See Figure 10-7.

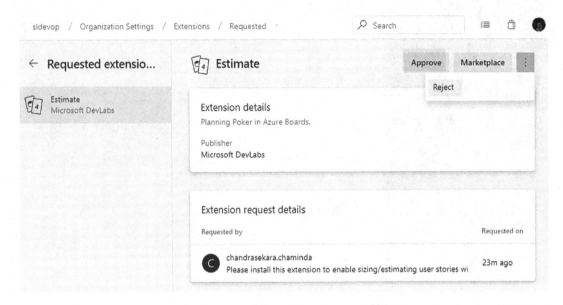

Figure 10-7. *Approving or rejecting the extension*

Clicking the Approve button will take you back to the Visual Studio Marketplace page of the extension. You can click the "Get it free" button (or Get for paid extensions) and install the extension for the Azure DevOps organization. Once installed, it will be listed on the Installed tab of the Extensions page in the organization settings. You can click an installed extension and uninstall or disable it if required. See Figure 10-8.

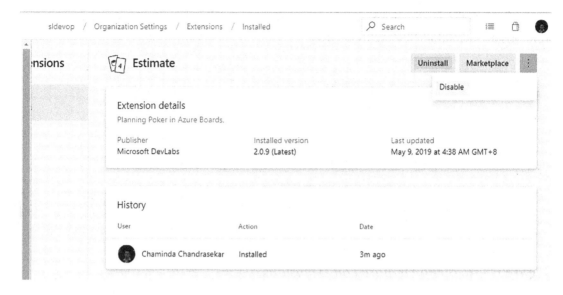

Figure 10-8. *Uninstalling or disabling an extension*

In addition, an extension publisher may publish an extension in the Visual Studio Marketplace privately and share it with your Azure DevOps organization. These shared extensions appear on the Shared tab of the Extensions page. See Figure 10-9. You can click a shared extension to open it and then click Install, which will take you to extension's page in the Visual Studio Marketplace where you can install the extension for the Azure DevOps organization.

Figure 10-9. *Shared extensions*

In the installed extensions, an "Action required" notification appears when new versions are available. See Figure 10-10.

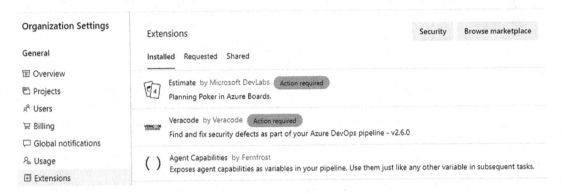

Figure 10-10. *Action required on extensions*

Clicking the extension will show you that a new version is available, and you can click the Authorize button to update the extension to the latest version. See Figure 10-11.

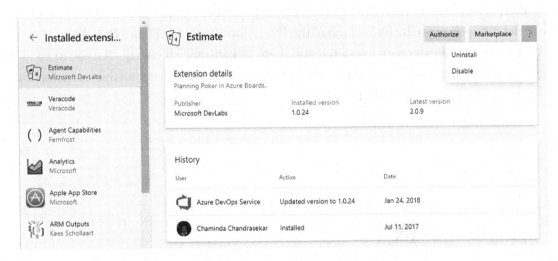

Figure 10-11. *Authorizing an update to an extension*

In this lesson, you explored how to install extensions for an Azure DevOps organization and how to disable, update, and uninstall options for an existing extension. Further, we discussed how to request an extension if you are not the collection administrator of the Azure DevOps organization and how an administrator can approve or reject an extension installation request.

Lesson 10-2. Using Work Item Layout Extensions

Certain extensions can help you customize the process templates. We discussed the customization process in Chapter 5, and you can add even more features to the customizations, especially to work item forms and fields using work item layout extensions in the Visual Studio Marketplace.

To search for work item layout extensions, first open an inherited process template's work item layout (explained in Chapter 5) and click "Get extensions." See Figure 10-12.

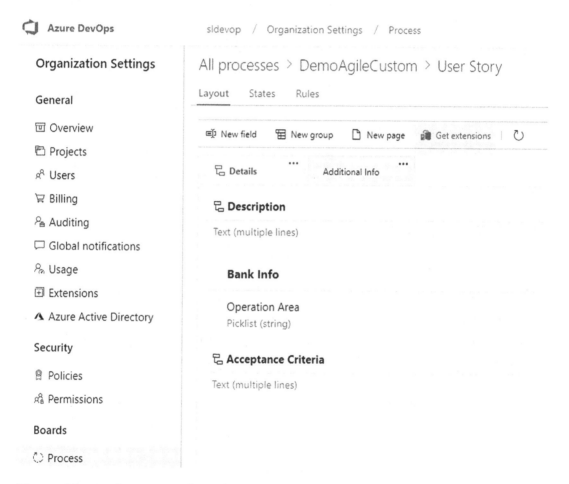

Figure 10-12. *Getting work item layout extensions*

You will be redirected to the Visual Studio Marketplace with a special search criterion of *control group tab page*, with the filters Azure Boards and Cloud. See Figure 10-13.

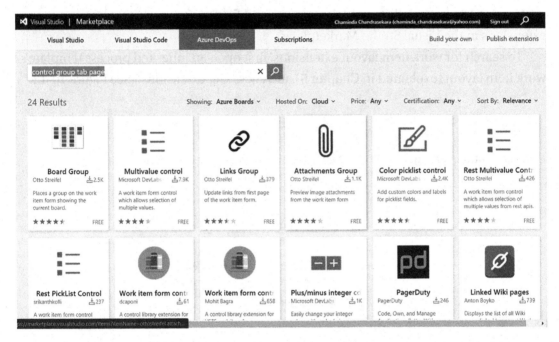

Figure 10-13. *Searching for work item layout extensions*

There are several extensions by Microsoft and community members available for work item layouts. Let's add the "Color picklist control" extension and see how it works as an example. To install the extension, click the extension card and click "Get it free" in the extension page that opens. Then install the extension as we discussed in Lesson 10-1. Once the extension is installed, you can see that the additional menu item "Add custom control" appears on the Layout tab of the Process page. See Figure 10-14.

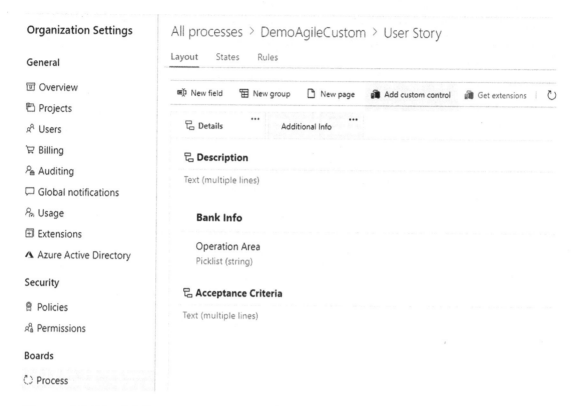

Figure 10-14. *Adding a custom control*

When you click "Add custom control," a dialog will open, and you can select the installed "Color picklist control" extension. See Figure 10-15.

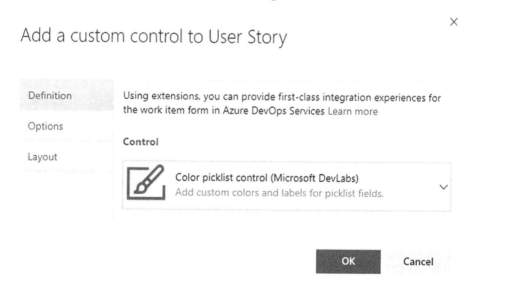

Figure 10-15. *Adding the "Color picklist control" extension*

On the Options tab of the dialog, you can select the field to which to apply the "Color picklist control" extension. Let's select the Priority field and specify the labels and colors. See Figure 10-16.

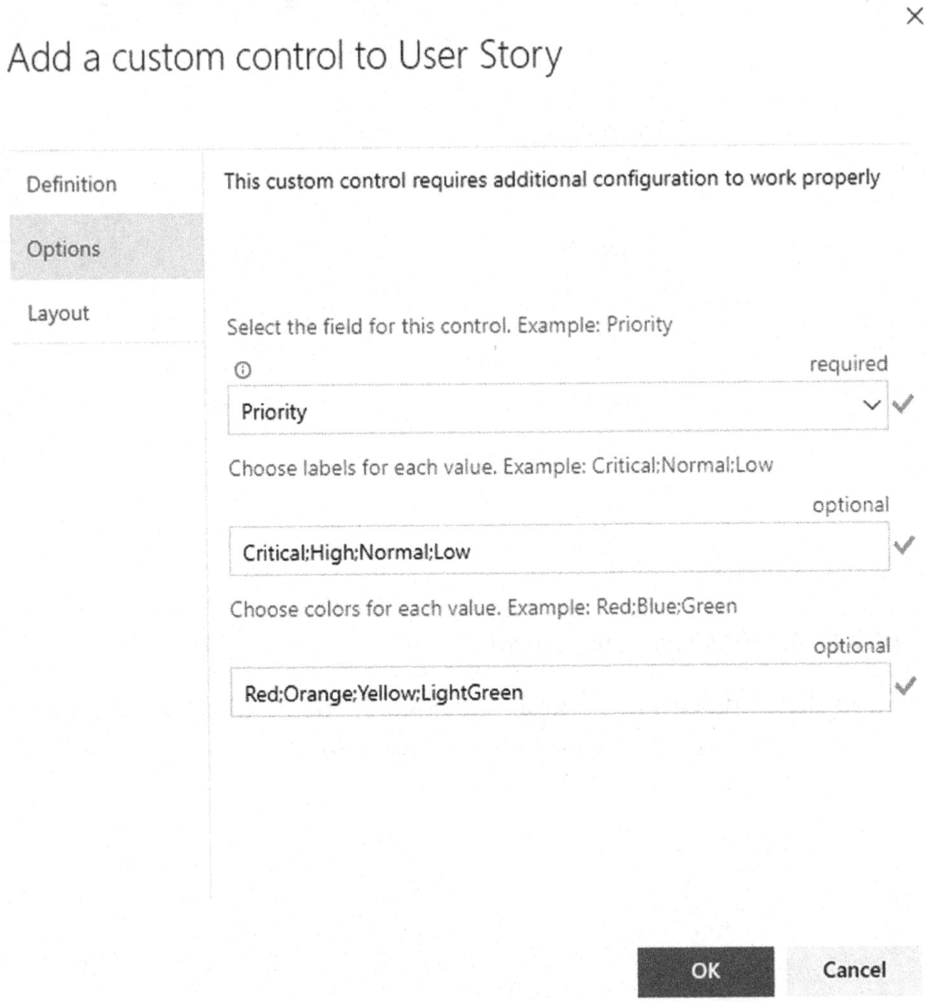

✕

Add a custom control to User Story

Definition	This custom control requires additional configuration to work properly
Options	
Layout	Select the field for this control. Example: Priority
	ⓘ required
	Priority ⌄ ✓
	Choose labels for each value. Example: Critical;Normal;Low
	optional
	Critical;High;Normal;Low ✓
	Choose colors for each value. Example: Red;Blue;Green
	optional
	Red;Orange;Yellow;LightGreen ✓

OK   Cancel

Figure 10-16. *Options of the color picklist field*

On the Layout tab of the dialog, let's set the Priority field to appear in the Planning section of the Details page. See Figure 10-17.

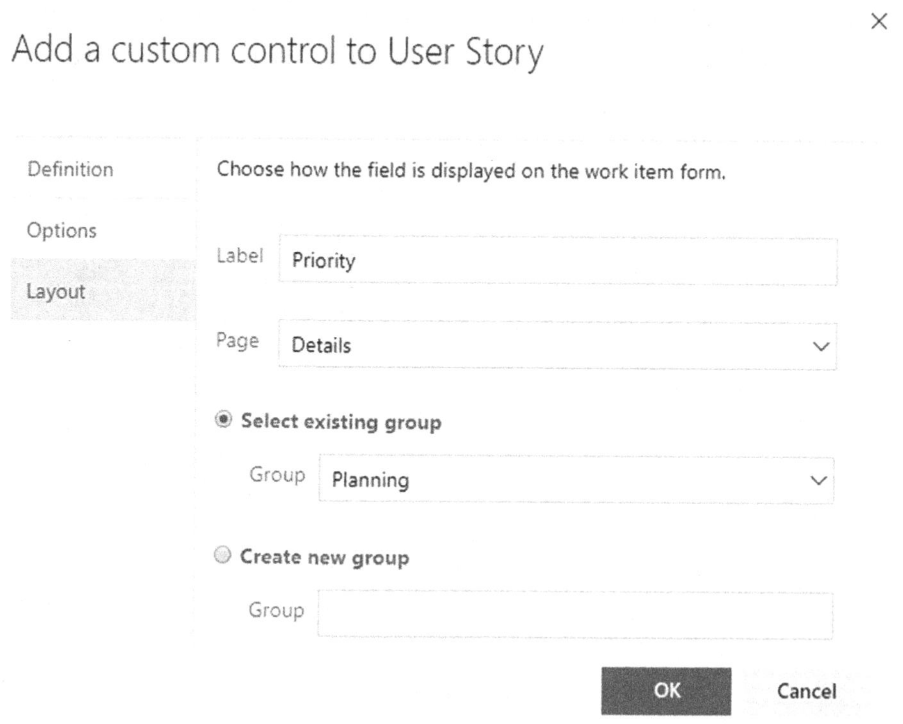

Add a custom control to User Story   ✕

Definition   Choose how the field is displayed on the work item form.

Options
                    Label   Priority

Layout

                    Page   Details   ∨

                    ◉ Select existing group

                        Group   Planning   ∨

                    ○ Create new group

                        Group

                                                    OK   Cancel

Figure 10-17. *Layout of the color picklist*

As you have added the custom extended control for the Priority field, the default
available Priority field can be hidden in the layout of the work item. See Figure 10-18.

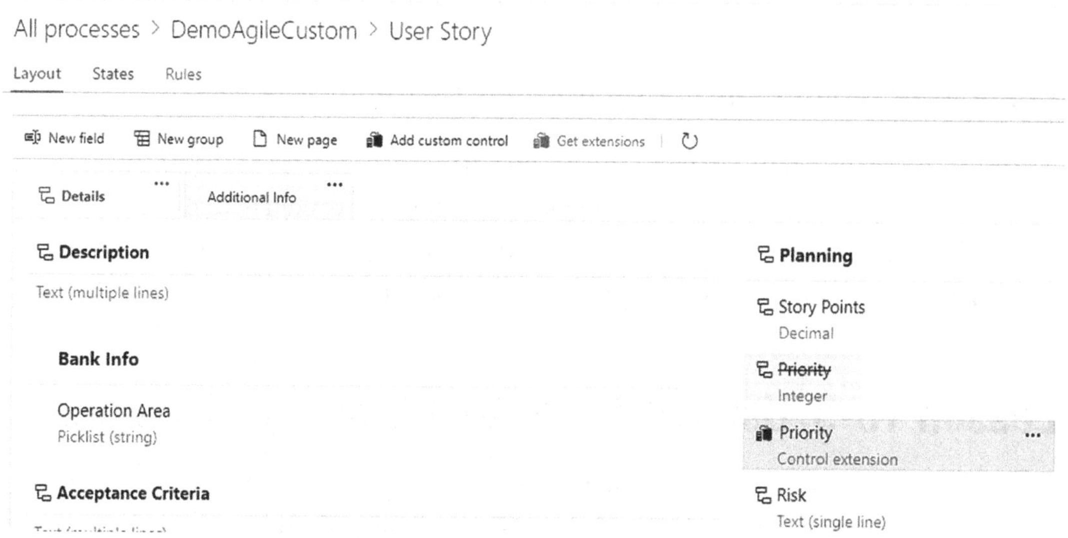

All processes > DemoAgileCustom > User Story

Layout   States   Rules

⊞ New field   ⊞ New group   ▯ New page   ▣ Add custom control   ▣ Get extensions   ↻

⊟ Details   ⋯   Additional Info   ⋯

⊟ **Description**   ⊟ **Planning**

Text (multiple lines)   ⊟ Story Points
                                                  Decimal

Bank Info   ⊟ ~~Priority~~
                                                  Integer
Operation Area
Picklist (string)   ▣ Priority   ⋯
                                                  Control extension

⊟ **Acceptance Criteria**   ⊟ **Risk**

Text (multiple lines)   Text (single line)

Figure 10-18. *Hiding the default field*

317

With this change, the User Story work item will have a colored picklist for the Priority field. The default Priority field is used and extended to introduce color by using this extension. See Figure 10-19.

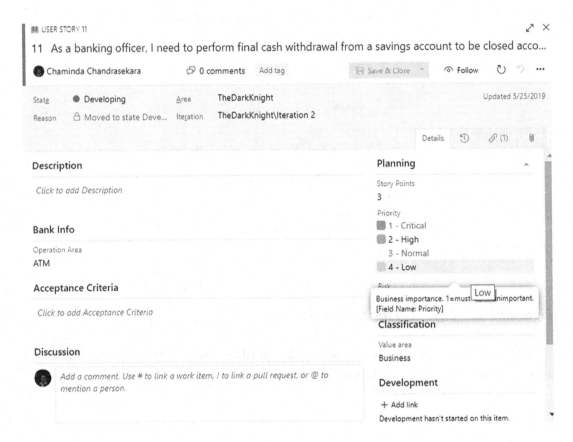

Figure 10-19. *Priority field as color picklist in User Story work item*

In this lesson, we discussed how to add custom layout controls as extensions to Azure Boards to enhance the work item layouts, and you worked with one of the extensions to see how it works. You can add more extensions and further enhance the customization experience of the process in Azure Boards.

Lesson 10-3. Using a Few Other Useful Extensions

There are many useful extensions available in the Visual Studio Marketplace for Azure Boards. For this lesson, you will take a brief look at a couple of popular extensions to understand the value they add to Azure Boards.

318

Delivery Plans

Once you install the Delivery Plans add-on (extension) available at `https://marketplace.visualstudio.com/items?itemName=ms.vss-plans`, you will see that a Plans tab is added to the Boards section. See Figure 10-20.

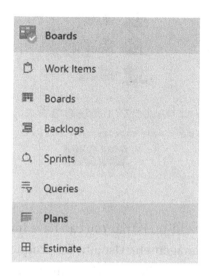

Figure 10-20. *Plans tab*

So, where exactly could you use this tool, and what level of information does it give you? Sometimes two or more teams will be working together on the same project, probably because of the complexity or maybe to speed up the delivery. Your program manager/product owner wants to see this whole picture.

You can easily create a delivery plan. No queries are required, and you can use the existing information from the backlog. For the tool to work, you must first set up the teams and your release cadence. Also, you have to assign your work items to the teams. Once all these are in place, it is pretty easy to build the delivery plan. Just click the "New plan" button to create a new plan. See Figure 10-21.

Plans

Favorites   **All** | + New plan   ▽ Filter plans

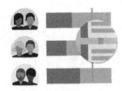

You haven't created a Plan yet!

Once you create a plan you will be able to visualize and track work across all your teams.

New plan

Figure 10-21. *New plan*

The nice thing about this add-on is that you can have multiple plans, which makes it an ideal tool for product management. Usually, for product management, you need to have a current plan and a future plan, where the future plan provides information to answer end-user queries. So, let's go back to the scenario where multiple teams are working on the same project. When you try to create a plan, you can specify the team projects, teams, and backlog levels you want to include in the plan. Additionally, you can specify the filter criteria. See Figure 10-22.

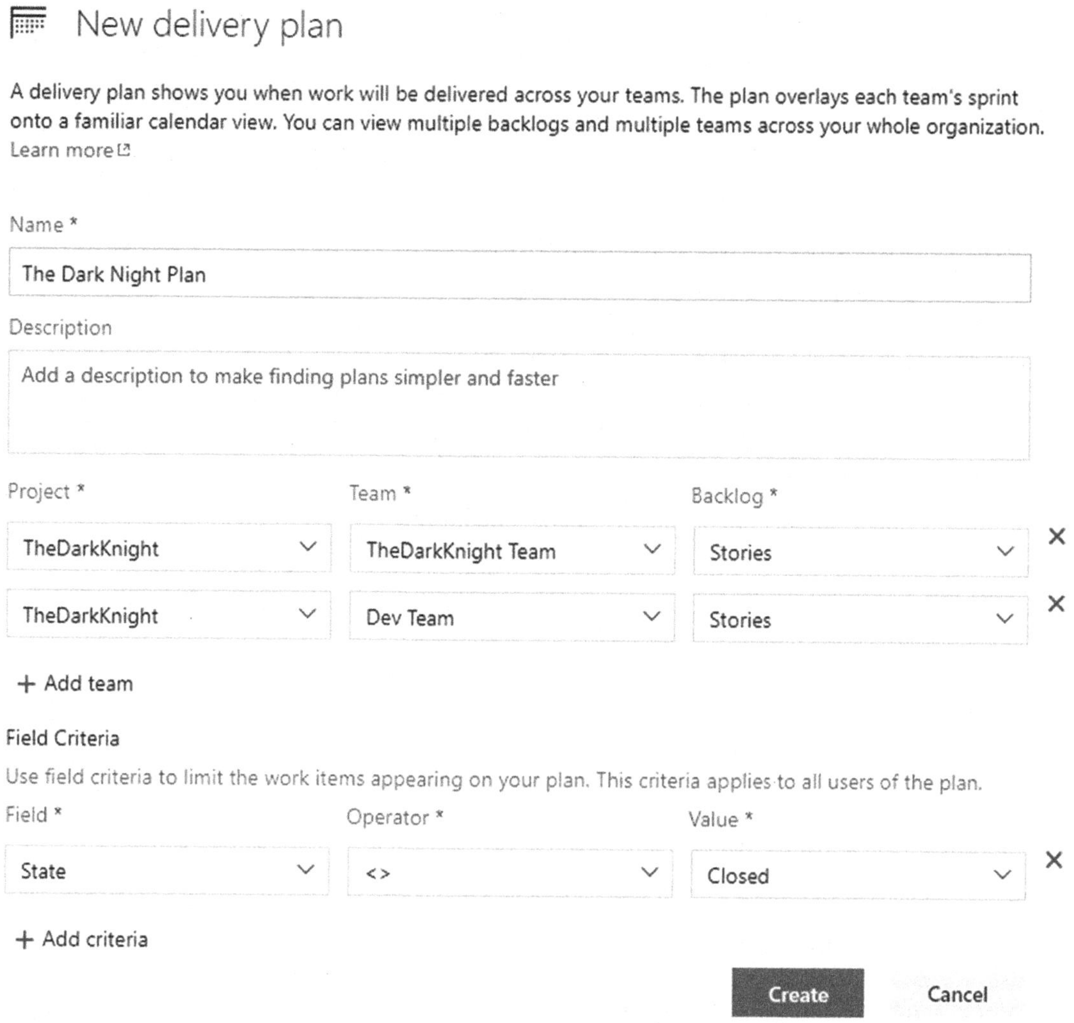

New delivery plan

A delivery plan shows you when work will be delivered across your teams. The plan overlays each team's sprint onto a familiar calendar view. You can view multiple backlogs and multiple teams across your whole organization. Learn more

Name *

> The Dark Night Plan

Description

> Add a description to make finding plans simpler and faster

Project *	Team *	Backlog *	
TheDarkKnight ⌄	TheDarkKnight Team ⌄	Stories ⌄	✕
TheDarkKnight ⌄	Dev Team ⌄	Stories ⌄	✕

+ Add team

Field Criteria

Use field criteria to limit the work items appearing on your plan. This criteria applies to all users of the plan.

Field *	Operator *	Value *	
State ⌄	< > ⌄	Closed ⌄	✕

+ Add criteria

                                        [Create]   [Cancel]

Figure 10-22. *Creating a delivery plan*

Once you create the plan, you will see that the plan includes the backlog items from each team (even from multiple team projects if you have selected to include them). There is some other functionality available on the plan's page. See Figure 10-23.

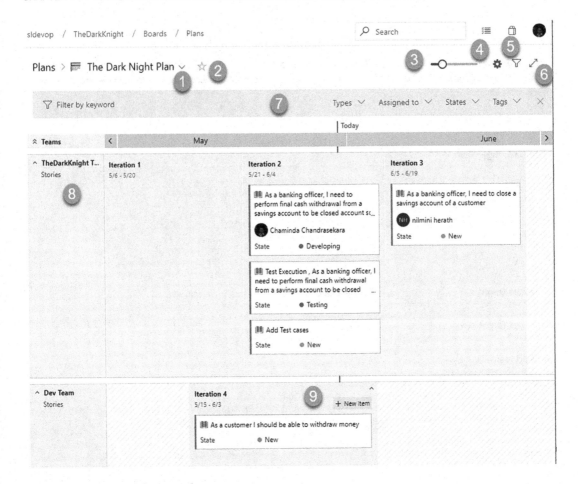

Figure 10-23. *Delivery plan*

1.   You can select a delivery plan.

2.   You can add a plan to the favorites list.

3.   You can scale the plan view.

4.   You can open the settings of the plan.

5.   You can enable additional filters in the plan to visualize the plan
     with diffrent set of work items.

6.   You can make the plan full-screen.

7.   You can filter the criteria pane.

8. This lists the teams in a team project.

9. You can add new work items from the plan.

When you set up your plan, it will look something similar to Figure 10-24.

In the delivery plan settings, in addition to modifying the team projects, teams, backlogs, and filter criteria for the plan, you can add markers to specify milestones such as a release deadline.

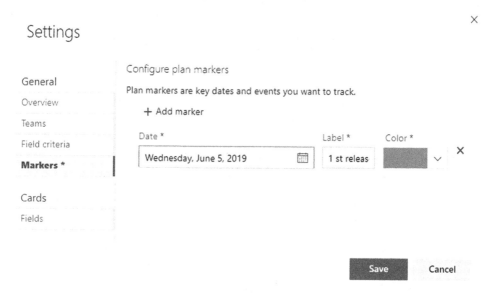

Figure 10-24. *Markers*

Additionally, you can customize how the card appears in the delivery plans using the settings. See Figure 10-25.

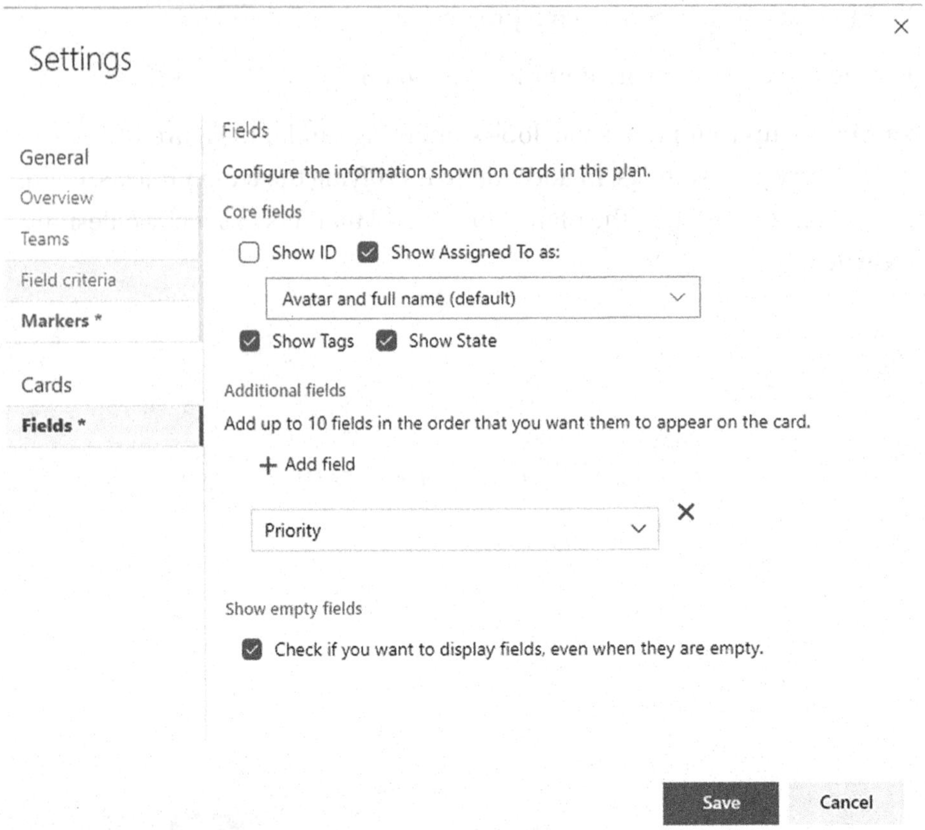

Figure 10-25. *Card fields in delivery plans*

Once saved, markers and card customizations get applied to the delivery plans. See Figure 10-26.

Plans > ▦ The Dark Night Plan ∨   ☆

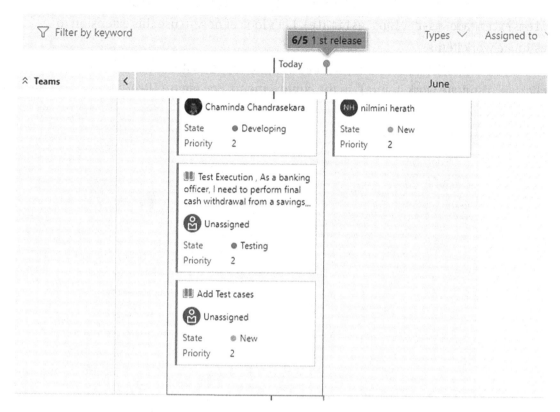

Figure 10-26. *Delivery plan markers*

You can use a delivery plan to move work items to required iterations by dragging and dropping them from the plan itself. When created with multiple teams to obtain a holistic view of a project, delivery plans provide useful and valuable information to project managers, making the Delivery Plans add-on an invaluable extension for Azure Boards.

Estimate

Estimating work is an important part of project delivery. In Agile development, empowering your team and identifying their velocity (how much they can deliver in an iteration) is especially vital. For backlog items in general Agile/Scrum practices, you are familiar with estimating using relative sizes. The work item field Story Points/Effort/Size is used to capture the relative sizing of a backlog item. The Estimate extension developed by Microsoft DevLabs is effective and integrates well with the backlog items to play planning poker on backlogs (`https://marketplace.visualstudio.com/items?itemName=ms-devlabs.estimate`). Let's look at how to use this extension to estimate work items.

You can launch an estimation session by selecting work items in the backlog and clicking "Estimate work item(s)" in the context menu. See Figure 10-27.

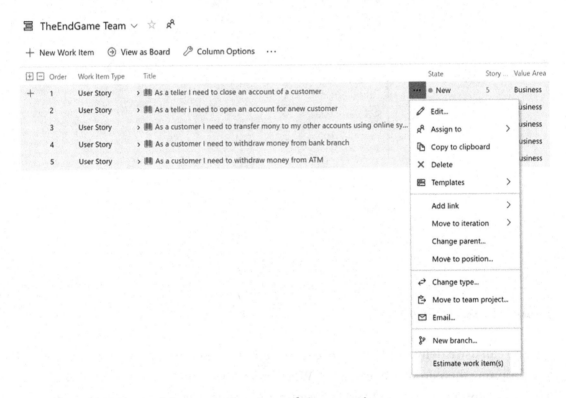

Figure 10-27. *Launching an estimate work item session*

You can provide a name for the estimation session and select the size cards as a size or by the default number of cards. Then create the session in online or offline mode. See Figure 10-28.

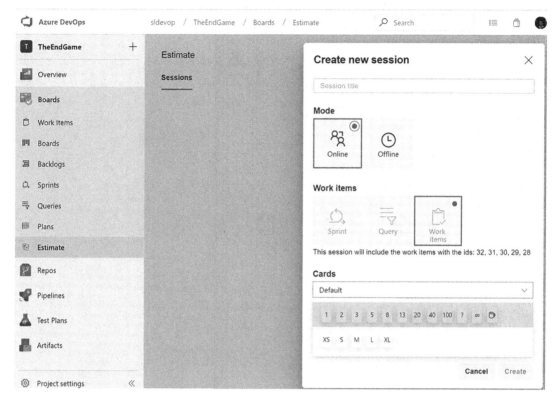

Figure 10-28. *New estimate session*

Or you can go to the Estimate tab and create a new session. In the new session, you can select a query to get work items to estimate or use an iteration to select work items. See Figure 10-29. If you want to go for the work items option, you have to select work items from the backlog and use the context menu as explained earlier.

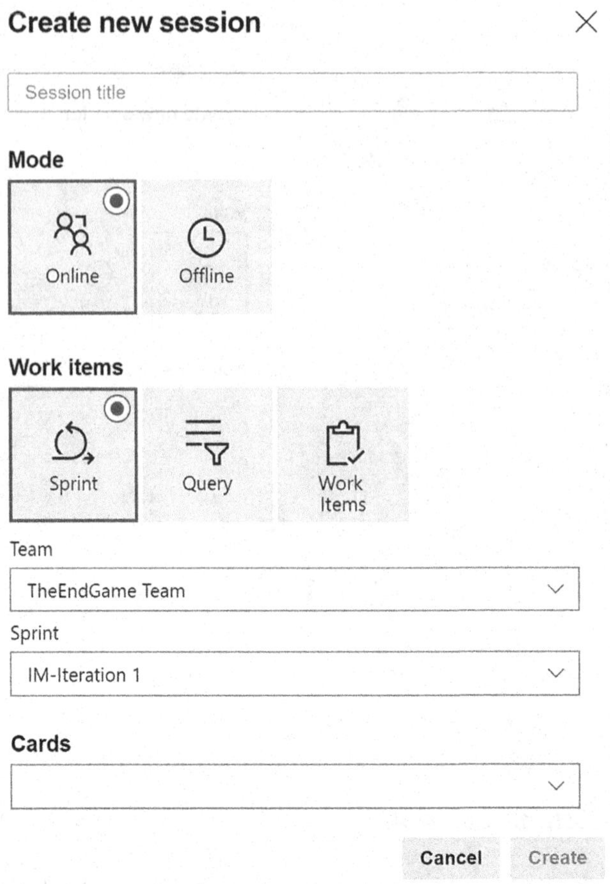

Figure 10-29. *Starting a new estimation session from the Estimate page*

Either way, once a session starts, other team members can join an existing estimation session via the Estimate page. Once the team joins, you can start discussing the story, and each member can vote. Other members' vote value will be hidden until everyone votes or session initiator reveals the votes. See Figure 10-30. In offline mode, individuals can vote as they want after analyzing the work items.

Figure 10-30. *Voting for a story*

Once the votes are revealed, you can select a card from the voted-on values to apply it to the work item as the estimate, or you provide a custom value and save it to the work item as an estimate. See Figure 10-31. You can click on a story to start a new vote for it if required.

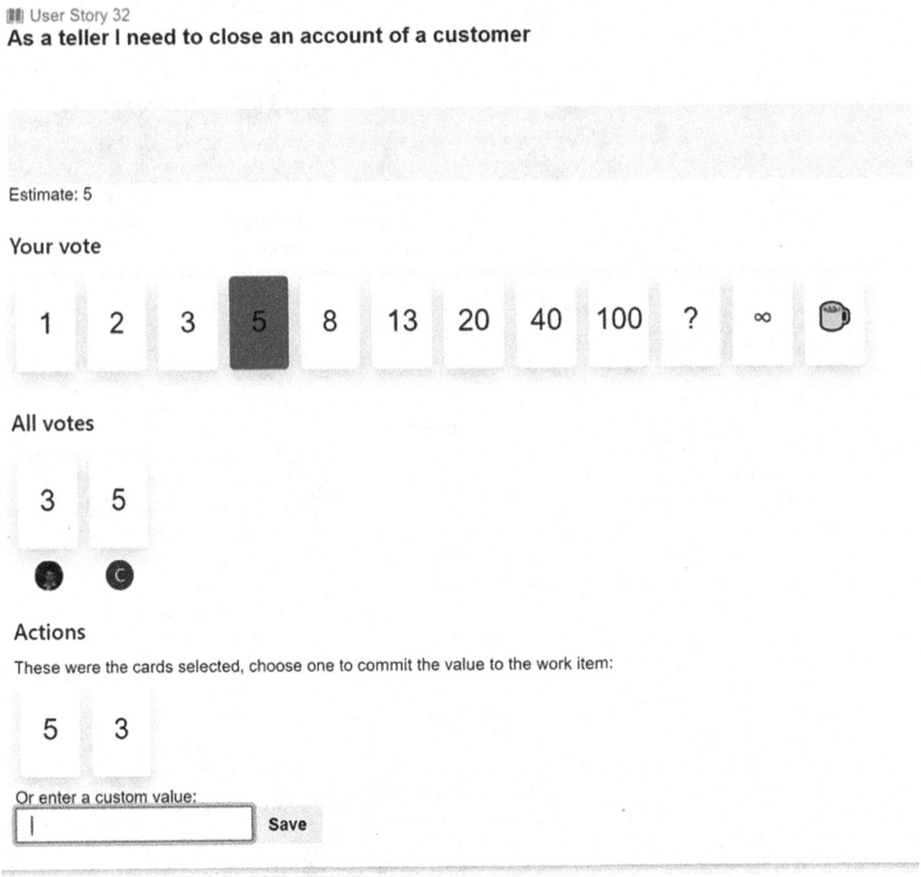

▐▐ User Story 32

As a teller I need to close an account of a customer

Estimate: 5

Your vote

| 1 | 2 | 3 | **5** | 8 | 13 | 20 | 40 | 100 | ? | ∞ | ☕ |

All votes

| 3 | 5 |

Actions

These were the cards selected, choose one to commit the value to the work item:

| 5 | 3 |

Or enter a custom value:

| | Save

Figure 10-31. Saving an estimate to a story

The estimate extension is really useful because it can help Agile/Scrum teams to size their backlogs with ease, especially with the offline mode support.

Feature Timeline and Epic Road Map

Portfolio backlog level features and epics can be visualized in a sprint calendar using the extension available at `https://marketplace.visualstudio.com/items?itemName=ms-devlabs.workitem-feature-timeline-extension`. This extension is useful for tracking the progress of features; it gives you a facility to plan your features and gives you a road map of an epic. Install the extension to your Azure DevOps organization and let's take a look at how it works.

Once the extension is installed, you can click the Feature Timeline tab of the Backlogs page in the Boards section. See Figure 10-32.

Figure 10-32. *Feature timeline*

1. This is an epic card. Clicking the title will open the epic work item.

2. You can add features available to the timeline by dragging them from the side pane, which opens when the Plan Features box is selected.

3. You can show the story details in the feature cards, as shown in #8.

4. You can show the progress of stories as a completed stories count or a completed estimate value against the total estimation. You can select the option from this drop-down.

5. You can select a range to show closed features in the timeline.

6. This is the iteration calendar.

7. This is a feature card. You can drag the right edge of the card to expand the feature to the next iteration. Clicking the title will open the feature work item.

8. This is the progress of stories within the feature. Clicking the progress will open the feature panning card dialog. In this dialog, you can drag and drop stories from a backlog to an iteration, drag stories to different iterations or back to the backlog, and set the starting and ending iterations for the feature. See Figure 10-33. Clicking the title of a story or bug will open the relevant work item form.

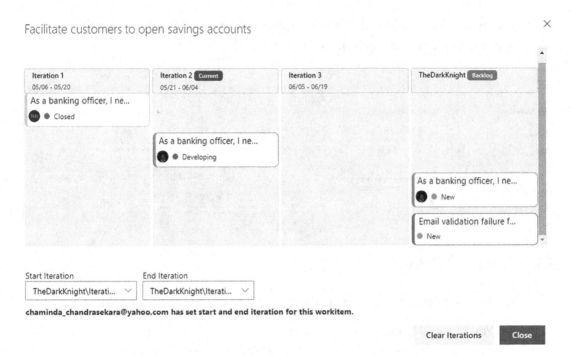

Figure 10-33. *Feature plan in timeline*

The extension adds another tab named Epic Roadmap to Azure Boards, which lets you track the progress of an epic across multiple features worked on by multiple teams. See Figure 10-34.

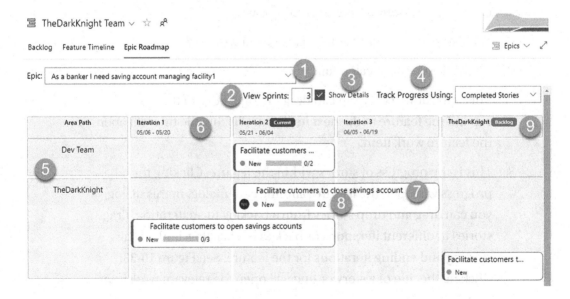

Figure 10-34. *Epic Roadmap tab*

1. You can select the epic to see a road map across several teams.

2. You can set how many sprints to show on the road map.

3. The feature card details will show the progress, as shown in #8.

4. You can track the progress using story counts or using the estimated size values.

5. You can set up the area paths of different teams.

6. This is the iterations calendar.

7. This is a feature card. It can be dragged from the right side to expand to the next iterations. Clicking the title will open the feature.

8. This is the progress of the feature showing story counts or estimated value progress. Clicking the progress will open a feature timeline plan dialog, which allows you to drag and drop stories to different iterations of the feature and to set the start and ending iterations for the feature, as shown in Figure 10-33.

The feature timeline and epic road map are useful for visualizing and planning the progress of teams, especially the epic road map, which will give you an opportunity to track an epic being worked on across multiple teams.

In this lesson, we discussed a few extensions that are really useful and that enhance the Azure Boards functionality. Many more extensions are available in the Visual Studio Marketplace for Azure Boards, and you may try them out and add capabilities to Azure Boards as per your team needs.

Note   In addition to using the available extensions, you can build your own extensions for Azure DevOps. You can find more information about building your own extensions at `https://docs.microsoft.com/en-us/azure/devops/extend/get-started/node?view=azure-devops`.

Lesson 10-4. Linking GitHub to Azure Boards

GitHub is a Microsoft subsidiary providing cloud-hosted services to handle source control for free, with unlimited public and private repositories. A three-contributor limitation applies for any private repository if you are using it for free, but you can add more contributors if you pay. You can integrate Azure Boards into GitHub to track your project work with Azure Boards while working on your repos in GitHub. Let's look at how this integration works.

Prerequisites: You need to be familiar with working with GitHub and have a GitHub repo with code that you want to integrate with Azure Boards.

Go to the GitHub Marketplace and search for *Azure*. You should see Azure Boards in the search results. Click Azure Boards. See Figure 10-35.

Figure 10-35. *Azure Boards in the GitHub Marketplace*

On the page that opens, click the "Set up a plan" button. Then click the "Install it for free" button. See Figure 10-36.

Pricing and setup

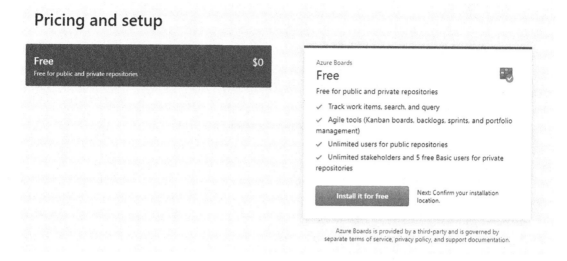

Figure 10-36. *Installing for free*

Then click the "Complete order and begin installation" button that appears on the next page. See Figure 10-37.

Review your order

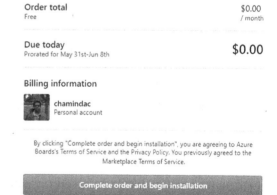

Figure 10-37. *Beginning the install*

On the next page, select the repository you want to integrate with Azure Boards and click the Install & Authorize button. See Figure 10-38.

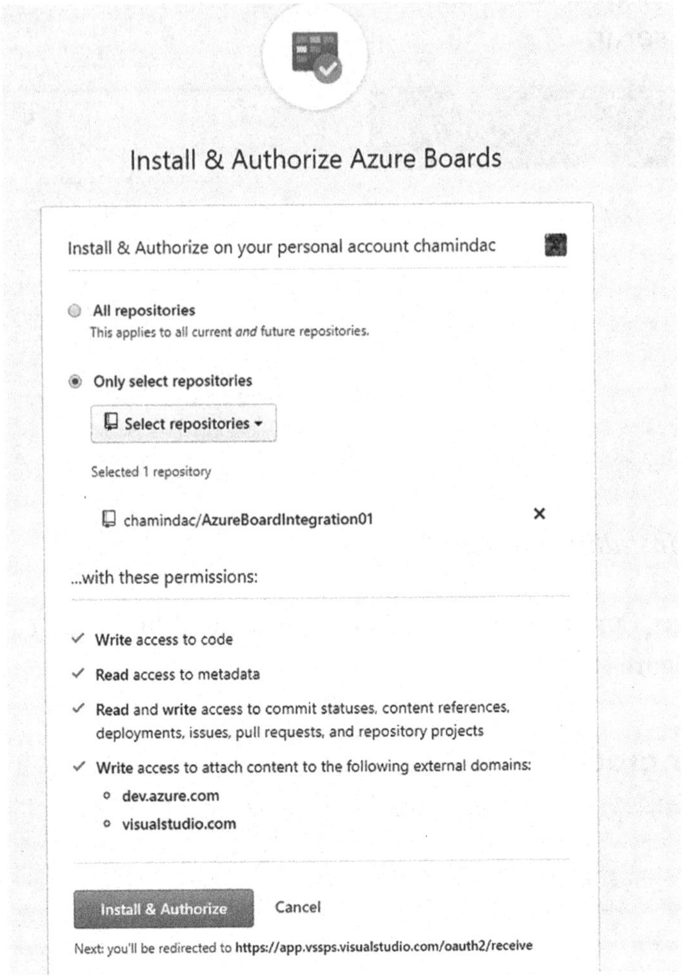

Figure 10-38. *Installing and authorizing*

The next page will request that you confirm your GitHub password to continue. Provide the password and click the "Confirm password" button. You will be prompted to sign in to Azure DevOps with your credentials. Sign in and proceed. Then in the next page that loads, you are allowed to create or select a new Azure DevOps organization and a team project. Click Continue after selecting an existing project or providing a name to create a new one. See Figure 10-39.

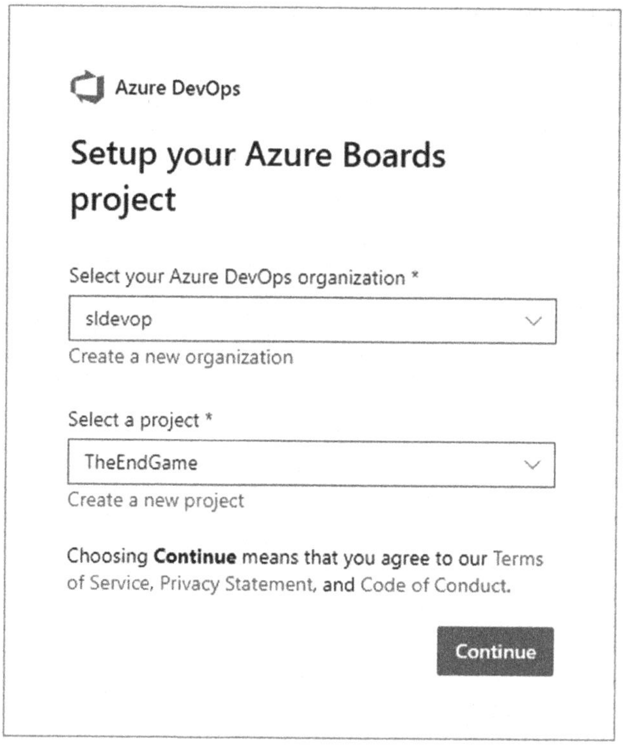

Figure 10-39. *Setting up Azure Boards*

Then you will be navigated to Azure Boards and be able to create a new story, create a new pull request, and add an Azure Boards badge in GitHub. Let's proceed with these steps. See Figure 10-40.

Success!

Your GitHub repository is connected to Azure Boards.

Get started

We'll help you create a sample User Story, link it to a GitHub pull request with mentions, and add a badge to your README.

1 First, let's create a User Story in the New column on your board.

Create

2 Second, let's create a pull request to add an Azure Boards badge in GitHub and link it to your new User Story.

Skip

Figure 10-40. *Creating a work item and pull request to add a Boards badge*

Once these two steps are done, you can view the work item by clicking "View work item." See Figure 10-41.

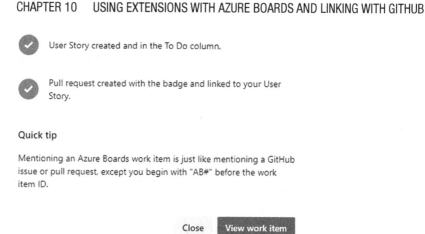

Figure 10-41. *Viewing the work item*

As mentioned in Figure 10-41, from GitHub you can refer to any work item in Azure Boards using the AB# prefix before the work item ID. This will link up the commits and pull requests with the work item in Azure Boards. Once you open the work item that was created in the previous step, you can see a commit and a pull request are linked to the work item. See Figure 10-42.

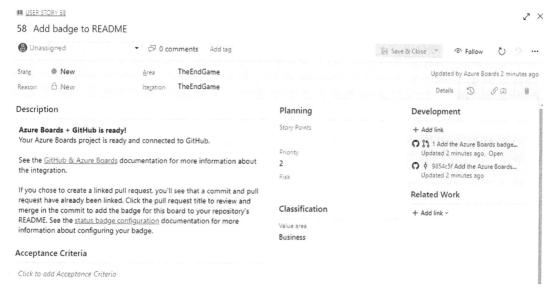

Figure 10-42. *Work item linked to GitHub*

You can click any of the links to navigate to the commit or pull request. Click the "Pull request" link. You can see that it mentions Fixes AB#*workitemID*. Complete the pull request by merging it. See Figure 10-43.

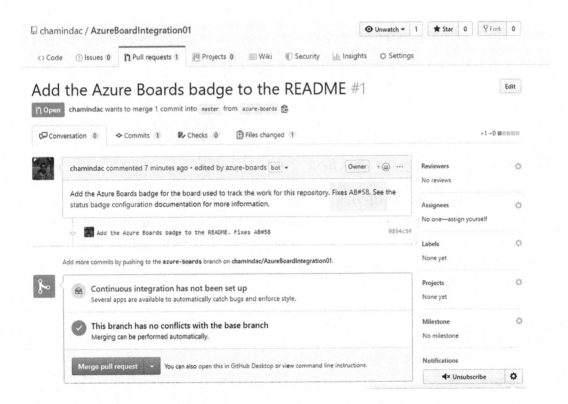

Figure 10-43. *Merging the pull request*

The words *fix*, *fixes*, and *fixed* can be used in the pull request or commit to make merging the pull request automatically close the work item in Azure Boards. Click "Merge pull request" and confirm the merge to complete the pull request. When the Azure Boards work item is refreshed, you can see it automatically gets closed. See Figure 10-44.

Figure 10-44. *Work item closed by merging the pull request*

In GitHub you can see that the readme is added with an Azure Boards status badge. See Figure 10-45.

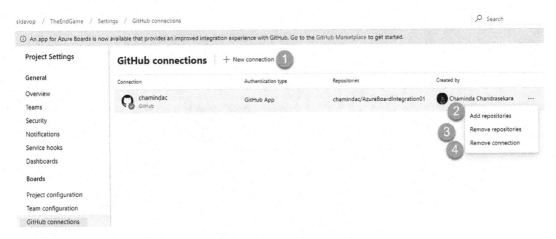

⊙ 3 commits	⅌ 2 branches	◇ 0 releases	👥 1 contributor

| Branch: master ▾ | New pull request | | Create new file | Upload files | Find File | Clone or download ▾ |

chamindac Merge pull request #1 from chamindac/azure-boards ⋯   Latest commit 6216abd 4 minutes ago

📁 Pages	Add a web app	1 hour ago
📁 Properties	Add a web app	1 hour ago
📁 wwwroot	Add a web app	1 hour ago
📄 .gitignore	Add a web app	1 hour ago
📄 AzureBoarIntegration01.csproj	Add a web app	1 hour ago
📄 Program.cs	Add a web app	1 hour ago
📄 README.md	Add the Azure Boards badge to the README. Fixes AB#58	25 minutes ago
📄 Startup.cs	Add a web app	1 hour ago
📄 appsettings.Development.json	Add a web app	1 hour ago
📄 appsettings.json	Add a web app	1 hour ago

📖 README.md ✏

🔲 Azure Boards Active 0 | Resolved 0

Figure 10-45. *Boards status badge in GitHub*

You can create a connection from Azure Boards to GitHub from the project settings of Azure Boards as well. Since you have linked Azure Boards with the GitHub repo, you will see an existing link in the current project. See Figure 10-46.

sidevop / TheEndGame / Settings / GitHub connections   🔍 Search

ⓘ An app for Azure Boards is now available that provides an improved integration experience with GitHub. Go to the GitHub Marketplace to get started.

Project Settings	**GitHub connections** + New connection ①			
General	Connection	Authentication type	Repositories	Created by
Overview				
Teams	🔘 chamindac	GitHub App	chamindac/AzureBoardIntegration01	👤 Chaminda Chandrasekara ⋯
Security	GitHub			
Notifications				② Add repositories
Service hooks				③ Remove repositories
Dashboards				④ Remove connection
Boards				
Project configuration				
Team configuration				
GitHub connections				

Figure 10-46. *Linking GitHub with Azure Boards*

1. This allows you to add a new connection to GitHub. You will be prompted for your GitHub credentials, and then you can create the connection and add repositories.

2. You can add more repositories. See Figure 10-47.

Add GitHub repositories

Add the GitHub repositories you want to use with your Azure Boards. Learn more

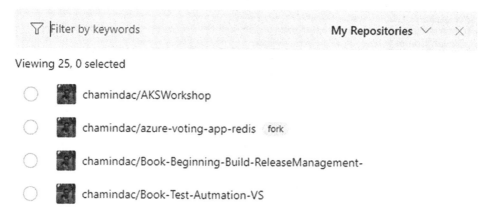

Figure 10-47. Adding repositories

3. You can remove any repositories connected.

4. You can remove the GitHub connection from Azure Boards.

After making the connection to GitHub from Azure Boards, you can open any work item and from the work item form's Development group link a GitHub commit or a pull request. See Figure 10-48.

Figure 10-48. Adding a GitHub link to a work item

You can add or select a GitHub commit or a GitHub pull request from the drop-down and use a URL to link it with the work item. See Figure 10-49.

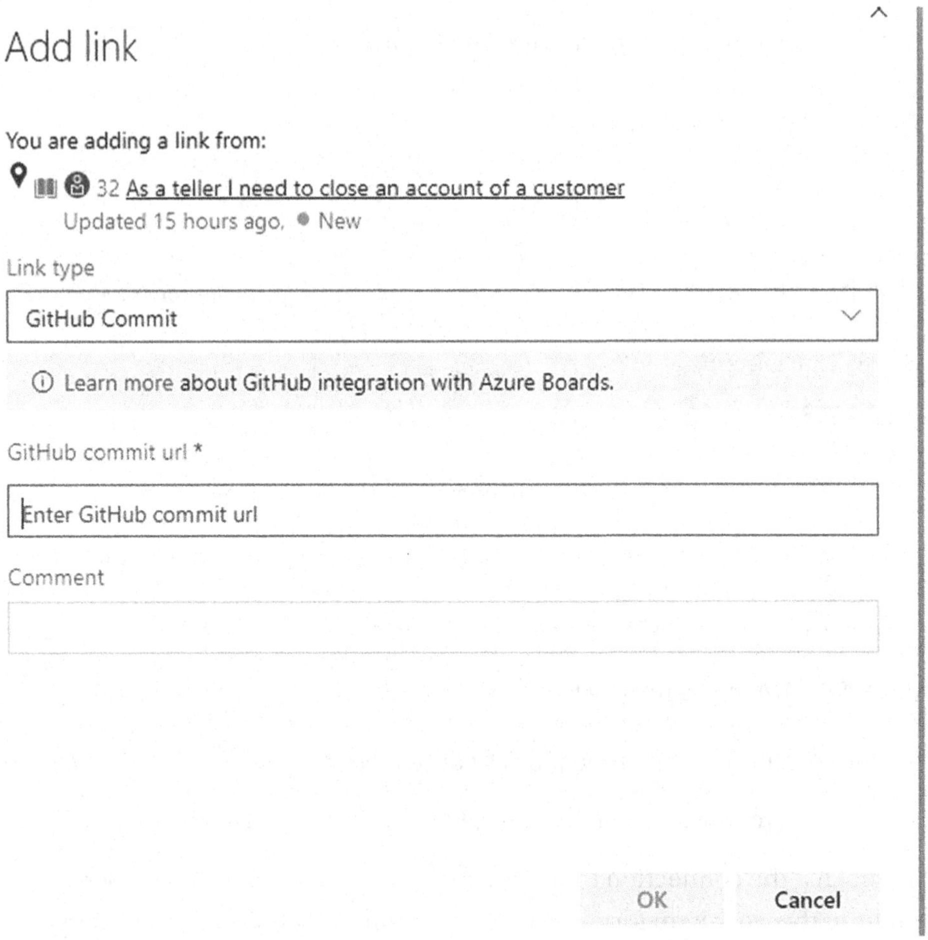

Add link

You are adding a link from:

📍 📖 ⚓ 32 As a teller I need to close an account of a customer
Updated 15 hours ago. ● New

Link type

GitHub Commit	⌄

ⓘ Learn more about GitHub integration with Azure Boards.

GitHub commit url *

Enter GitHub commit url

Comment

OK	Cancel

Figure 10-49. Linking a GitHub commit

From GitHub you can link a commit or pull request to a work item by mentioning the work item with AB#*workitemID*. Using *fix, fixes,* or *fixed* before AB#*workitemID* in a commit will make the work item be completed when it is merged via a pull request to the master.

In this lesson, we discussed how to integrate GitHub with Azure Boards. Using Azure Boards to track the work for your projects in GitHub greatly improves the way you work with GitHub.

Summary

In this chapter, we discussed how to use extensions to enhance the capabilities and features of Azure Boards. Further, we explored a couple of useful extensions in detail. In addition, we discussed how to integrate Azure Boards with GitHub to provide a rich experience in both GitHub and Azure Boards.

Throughout this book, we have discussed Azure Boards in detail, from getting started to configuring it for small and large teams to customizing it. We discussed the reporting and visualization capabilities of Azure Boards to give your teams the ability to track the progress of the projects. Additionally, we talked about security and administration as well as using a REST API and the command line. The book has provided you with comprehensive coverage of Azure Boards features and how to use them to effectively plan and track your teams' work.

In the next book of the series, we will explore the source control capabilities of Azure DevOps. *Hands-On Azure Repos* will cover both Team Foundation Version Control (TFVC) and Azure Git Repos in detail with practical examples.

Index

A

AAD-backed Azure DevOps
  accepting permissions, 263
  adding external user, 262
  additional information, 264
  grant external users access, 259
    policy, 261
  join button, 262
Alternate credentials, 282
Area permissions, 274
Azure active directory (AAD), 37, 253, 259,
    260, 262, 264, 283
Azure Boards customizations, 123
Azure DevOps
  adding users, 249
    AAD, 253
    group rule, access levels, 253, 254
    group rule menu items, 252, 253
    management, 250, 251
  auditing, 36
  billing for, 35
  global notifications, 36
  granting access to extensions, 266
  login page, 2
  navigation
    backlog, 24–26
    boards, 22, 23
    column options pane, 21
    dashboards, 14, 15
    edit page, 11

    Invite button, 14
    message section, 13
    pencil icon, 10
    queries, 29, 31, 32
    sprint backlog, 26–29
    Summary page, 9, 10
    team capacity, 27
    team settings, 15
    widgets, 16
    wiki, 17
    Work Items, 19, 20
  organization
    creation, 1
    naming, 3
    policies, 255
  paid user license, 265
  permission groups, 256, 257, 259
  previewing features and themes, 38
  usage, 37
  user extension management pop-up, 266
Azure DevOps CLI
  extension, 299
  show work item, 300, 301
  update work item, 302
  version, 299

B

Backlog
  adding task, user stories, 98, 99
  agile process, 89

347